Teach Yourself

VISUALLY™

MacBook Pro®
and MacBook Air®
5th Edition

by Guy Hart-Davis

Visual
A Wiley Brand

Teach Yourself VISUALLY™ MacBook Pro®
and MacBook Air®

5th Edition
Published by
John Wiley & Sons, Inc.
9200 Keystone Crossing, Suite 800
Indianapolis, IN 46240
www.wiley.com

Published simultaneously in Canada

Wiley publishes in a variety of print and electronic formats and by print on-demand. Some material included with standard print versions of this book may not be included in e-books or in print-on-demand. If this book refers to media such as a CD or DVD that is not included in the version you purchased, you may download this material at http://booksupport.wiley.com. For more information about Wiley products, visit www.wiley.com.

Library of Congress Control Number: 2020932950

ISBN: 978-1-119-68389-6; ISBN: 978-1-119-68391-9 (ebk); ISBN: 978-1-119-68394-0 (ebk)

Manufactured in the United States of America

Trademark Acknowledgments

Wiley, the Wiley logo, Visual, the Visual logo, Teach Yourself VISUALLY, Read Less - Learn More and related trade dress are trademarks or registered trademarks of John Wiley & Sons, Inc. and/or its affiliates. MacBook Pro and MacBook Air are registered trademarks of Apple, Inc. All other trademarks are the property of their respective owners. John Wiley & Sons, Inc. is not associated with any product or vendor mentioned in this book. *Teach Yourself VISUALLY™ MacBook Pro® and MacBook Air® 5th Edition* is an independent publication and has not been authorized, sponsored, or otherwise approved by Apple, Inc.

Contact Us

For general information on our other products and services please contact our Customer Care Department within the U.S. at 877-762-2974, outside the U.S. at 317-572-3993 or fax 317-572-4002.

For technical support please visit https://hub.wiley.com/community/support.

Sales | Contact Wiley at (877) 762-2974 or fax (317) 572-4002.

About the Author

Guy Hart-Davis is the author of more than 150 computer books, including *Teach Yourself VISUALLY iPhone 11, 11 Pro, and 11 Pro Max; Teach Yourself VISUALLY iPad;* and *Teach Yourself VISUALLY Android Phones and Tablets, 2nd Edition*.

Author's Acknowledgments

My thanks go to the many people who turned my manuscript into the highly graphical book you are holding. In particular, I thank Devon Lewis for asking me to write the book; Lynn Northrup for keeping me on track; Kim Cofer for skillfully editing the text; Doug Holland for reviewing the book for technical accuracy and contributing helpful suggestions; and SPi Global for laying out the book.

How to Use This Book

Who This Book Is For

This book is for the reader who has never used this particular technology or software application. It is also for readers who want to expand their knowledge.

The Conventions in This Book

① Steps

This book uses a step-by-step format to guide you easily through each task. **Numbered steps** are actions you must do; **bulleted steps** clarify a point, step, or optional feature; and **indented steps** give you the result.

② Notes

Notes give additional information — special conditions that may occur during an operation, a situation that you want to avoid, or a cross reference to a related area of the book.

③ Icons and Buttons

Icons and buttons show you exactly what you need to click to perform a step.

④ Tips

Tips offer additional information, including warnings and shortcuts.

⑤ Bold

Bold type shows command names, options, and text or numbers you must type.

⑥ Italics

Italic type introduces and defines a new term.

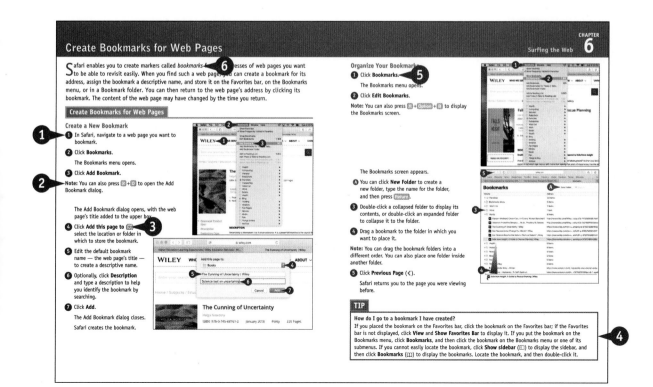

Table of Contents

Chapter 3   Sharing Your MacBook with Others

Chapter 4   Running Apps

Table of Contents

Chapter 6   Surfing the Web

Chapter 7   Sending and Receiving E-Mail

Table of Contents

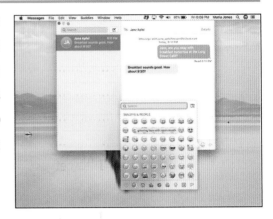

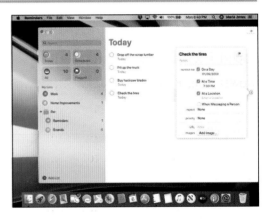

Chapter 10 — Enjoying Music, Video, and Books

Chapter 11 — Making the Most of Your Photos

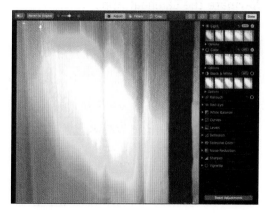

Table of Contents

Chapter 12 — Networking and Protecting Your MacBook

Chapter 13 — Troubleshooting Your MacBook

CHAPTER 1

Getting Started with Your MacBook

Apple's MacBook laptops are among the best portable computers you can get. The powerful MacBook Pro and the lightweight MacBook Air enable you to work — or play — anywhere that suits you.

Each MacBook comes with macOS, Apple's easy-to-use operating system. This chapter shows you how to set up your MacBook, navigate the macOS interface, and perform essential actions.

Understanding the MacBook Pro and MacBook Air

M acBook is the family name for Apple's laptop computers. As of this writing, the MacBook family includes only the MacBook Pro and the MacBook Air, since Apple in 2019 discontinued the MacBook usually called simply "MacBook" but also known as "12-inch MacBook" or "Retina MacBook" for clarity.

Each MacBook has similar core features, such as the display for viewing information and the keyboard and trackpad for entering data and controlling the computer. Beyond that, the MacBook models differ in various ways, from design, size, and weight to screen size, memory and storage capacity, and processor type and speed.

Identify Your MacBook's Main Features

A Display

The MacBook's display provides a sharp, bright, and colorful view into all that you do.

B Camera

The built-in camera enables you to videoconference, take photos, and more.

C Keyboard

Along with the standard letter and number keys, the keyboard provides modifier keys — such as ⌘, Option, and Control — to control your MacBook. The keyboard has a backlight that illuminates automatically when you are using the MacBook in dim light, enabling you to see what you are doing.

D Trackpad

The trackpad enables you to manipulate objects on the screen using finger gestures. The entire trackpad is also the button that you click or double-click to give commands. On some MacBook models, you can also use a pressing movement called force-touch or 3D touch to access commands quickly.

E USB-C Ports

The USB-C ports enable you to connect your MacBook to its power adapter and to other devices, such as external drives, external displays, iPhones and iPads, and so on. Current MacBook Air and MacBook Pro models have only USB-C ports. Older MacBook models have different ports.

F Microphones

The microphones enable you to use your MacBook for audio and video calls without needing to connect a headset.

G Speakers

The speakers enable you to listen to music or other audio.

Meet Your MacBook's Keyboard

The MacBook Air includes a row of hardware function keys above the top row of the keyboard, as shown in the illustration here. By contrast, the MacBook Pro models include the Touch Bar, a multitouch control strip whose contents change to suit the current app and selection. See the next section, "Understanding and Using the Touch Bar," for more information.

Ⓐ Brightness

Press F1 to decrease your screen's brightness or F2 to increase it.

Ⓑ Mission Control

Press F3 to open Mission Control so you can quickly move between working spaces.

Ⓒ Launchpad

Press F4 to open or close Launchpad.

Ⓓ Keyboard Backlight Brightness

Press F5 to decrease the brightness of the keyboard backlighting, or press F6 to increase it.

Ⓔ Previous/Rewind

Press F7 to move to the previous item or rewind in Music and other applications.

Ⓕ Play/Pause

Press F8 to play or pause Music and other applications.

Ⓖ Next/Fast-Forward

Press F9 to move to the next item or fast-forward in Music and other applications.

Ⓗ Volume

Press F10 to mute your MacBook, F11 to turn the volume down, and F12 to turn it up.

Ⓘ Power Button

Press the Power button to turn on your MacBook; press and hold the Power button to force your MacBook to turn off.

Ⓙ Alternate Function Key

Hold down the Alternate Function key while pressing a function key to perform the alternate task.

Ⓚ Modifier Keys

Macs and macOS use four modifier keys that you press to enter capital letters or symbols or to invoke keyboard shortcuts. As usual, you press Shift (Shift) to type capital letters or the symbols that appear on the upper part of the keys. You press Command (⌘), Option (Option), and Control (Control) to give keyboard shortcuts.

Ⓛ Arrow Keys

Press the arrow keys to move around the screen.

Understanding and Using the Touch Bar

Current MacBook Pro models include the Touch Bar, a flat sensor strip that replaces the row of physical function keys at the top of the keyboard with virtual keys that change depending on the app and the actions available to you. The current MacBook Air retains the row of physical functions keys, so it does not have the Touch Bar.

You can take a wide variety of actions from the Touch Bar, depending on the apps you use and what you do in them. This section illustrates some of the possibilities with the apps that come installed on the MacBook.

Work with the Standard Touch Bar

The Touch Bar automatically displays controls, such as buttons or sliders, for taking actions in the app or feature with which you are currently working.

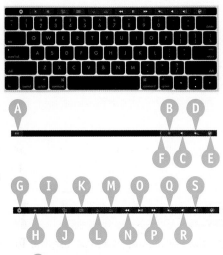

A Esc Button

Tap **esc** to issue a Cancel command — for example, to cancel an open dialog.

B Brightness Button

Tap **Brightness** (🔅) to display the Brightness controls on the Touch Bar.

C Volume Button

Tap **Volume** (🔊) to display the Volume controls on the Touch Bar.

D Mute Button

Tap **Mute** (🔇) to mute the audio output.

E Siri Button

Tap **Siri** (◉) to launch the Siri virtual assistant.

F Expand Button

Tap **Expand** (<) to display standard functions on the Touch Bar, as shown in the next illustration.

G Close Button

Tap **Close** (⊗) to collapse the Touch Bar controls to how they were before you tapped Expand.

H Decrease Brightness Button

Tap **Decrease Brightness** (🔅) to decrease the screen brightness.

I Increase Brightness Button

Tap **Increase Brightness** (🔆) to increase the screen brightness.

J Mission Control Button

Tap **Mission Control** (🗔) to invoke the Mission Control feature for managing windows and apps.

K Launchpad Button

Tap **Launchpad** (🎛) to display the Launchpad screen for launching an app.

L Decrease Keyboard Brightness Button

Tap **Decrease Keyboard Brightness** (🔅) to decrease the brightness of the keyboard lighting.

M Increase Keyboard Brightness Button

Tap **Increase Keyboard Brightness** (🔆) to increase the brightness of the keyboard lighting.

N Previous/Rewind Button

Tap **Previous/Rewind** (⏪) once to go back to the start of the current song or item; tap again to go back to the start of the previous song or item. Tap and hold **Previous/Rewind** (⏪) to rewind through the current song or item.

O Play/Pause Button

Tap **Play/Pause** (⏯) to start, pause, or resume playback.

P Next/Fast-Forward Button

Tap **Next/Fast-Forward** (⏩) to go to the start of the next song or item. Tap and hold **Next/Fast-Forward** (⏩) to fast-forward through the current song or item.

Q Mute Button

Tap **Mute** (🔇) to mute the audio output.

R Decrease Volume Button

Tap **Decrease Volume** (🔉) to decrease the volume.

S Increase Volume Button

Tap **Increase Volume** (🔊) to increase the volume.

Using the Touch Bar in Safari

In Safari, the Touch Bar displays buttons for taking actions such as opening web pages on the Top Sites list and navigating among open pages. For example, tap **Apple** to go to the Apple website.

Using the Touch Bar in Mail

In Mail, you can use the Touch Bar to take frequent actions quickly.

Ⓣ New Message Button

Tap **New Message** (🖊) to start a new message from your default e-mail account.

Ⓤ Reply All Button

Tap **Reply All** (↩) to begin a reply to the message.

Ⓥ Archive Button

Tap **Archive** (🗄) to archive the selected message.

Ⓦ Move To Button

Tap **Move To** (📁) to begin moving the selected message to another mailbox or folder.

Ⓧ Delete Button

Tap **Delete** (🗑) to delete the selected message.

Ⓨ Flag Button

Tap **Flag** (🚩) to toggle the flag on the selected message.

Using the Touch Bar in Photos

In the Photos app, you can use the Touch Bar extensively. The following list gives some examples:

- Slide your finger on the Thumbnails bar to move quickly through the photos in an album or other collection.

- To start editing a photo, tap **Adjust** (🔆), **Filters** (🔘), or **Crop** (🔲).

- When editing a photo, tap the button for the editing tool you want to use, such as **Color** (⚫) or **Light** (🔆).

- Drag the slider bar to adjust the selected tool, or tap **Reset** to reset the control to its original position. When you finish editing, tap **Done**.

- To set the aspect ratio, tap the appropriate button on the Touch Bar, such as **Square** or **8:10**.

Display Regular Function Keys on the Touch Bar

Press Fn to display the regular function keys on the Touch Bar. You can then tap these keys to get their regular actions.

Set Up Your MacBook

I f you have just bought your MacBook, you need to set up macOS and create your user account before you can use it. Your user account is where you store your files and settings on the MacBook.

This section shows you the key decisions you make when setting up your MacBook. The first user account you create is an administrator account, which can create other accounts later for other users. You may also choose to create a personal account for yourself, leaving the administrator account strictly for administration.

Begin Setup and Choose Your Country

To begin setup, position your MacBook on a desk or table, connect its power supply, and then press the power button. On most MacBook models, the power button is at the upper-right corner of the keyboard. On the MacBook models with Touch Bar, the power button is at the right end of the Touch Bar and doubles as the fingerprint reader.

When the Welcome screen appears, click your country, and then click **Continue** (⊕).

Choose Written and Spoken Languages Settings

On the Written and Spoken Languages screen, verify that Preferred Languages (⊕) shows the language you want the macOS user interface to use, that Input Sources (⊞) shows the keyboard layout you want to use, and that Dictation (🎤) shows the language you will use for dictating text to your MacBook. If you want to change any of these settings, click **Customize Settings**, and then choose your preferred language, keyboard layout, or dictation language.

When the Written and Spoken Languages screen shows the settings you want, click **Continue** (⊕) to proceed.

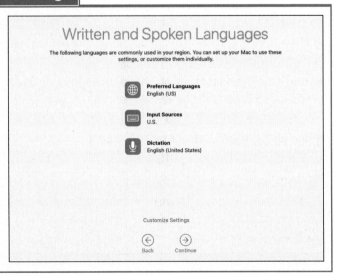

Choose Whether to Transfer Information to Your MacBook

On the Transfer Information to This Mac screen, you can choose whether to transfer information to your MacBook.

If you have information on another Mac, a Time Machine backup, or a Mac's startup disk, click **From a Mac, Time Machine backup, or startup disk** (○ changes to ●), click **Continue** (→), and follow the prompts.

If you have information on a Windows PC, click **From a Windows PC** (○ changes to ●), click **Continue** (→), and follow the prompts.

If you have no information to transfer, click **Don't transfer any information now** (○ changes to ●), and then click **Continue** (→) to proceed.

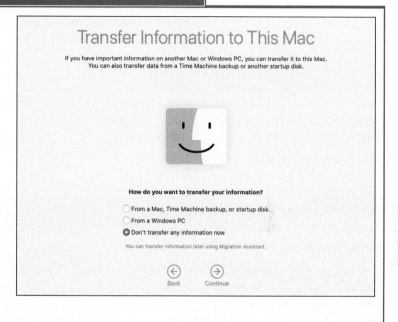

Sign In to Apple's Services with Your Apple ID

The Sign In with Your Apple ID screen enables you to sign in to Apple's services using your Apple ID, a credential consisting of an e-mail address and a password.

If you already have an Apple ID, type the e-mail address in the Apple ID box, type the password in the Password box, and then click **Continue** (→).

If you do not have an Apple ID, you can click **Create new Apple ID** and follow the prompts to create one.

If you prefer not to sign in with an Apple ID at this point, click **Set Up Later**.

continued ▶

When creating an account, you can use either your full name or a shortened version. You can edit the username that macOS suggests based on that name. You can choose whether to set a password hint to help yourself remember your password. You can also choose whether to let your Apple ID reset the password, enabling you to recover from a lost password by logging in using your Apple ID.

Set Up Your Computer Account

On the Create a Computer Account screen, type your name the way you want it to appear in the Full Name box. In the Account Name box, macOS automatically enters a default account name consisting of your Full Name entry changed to lowercase and stripped of spaces and punctuation — for example, if you type *Maria Jones* as the full name, macOS suggests *mariajones* as the account name. You can edit the account name as needed.

Type a new password twice, once in each Password box. Optionally, click **Hint** and type a password hint that will help you to recall your password.

Select (✅) **Allow my Apple ID to reset this password** if you want to be able to reset this

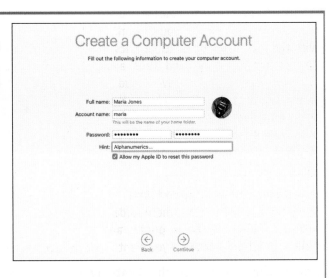

password by using your Apple ID. This feature helps you avoid getting locked out of your MacBook.

Click the account icon and choose the icon or image you want to use for your account. Then click **Continue** (→).

Choose Between Express Setup and Customizing Settings

On the Express Set Up screen, you can choose whether to speed up the setup process a little by allowing macOS to apply settings for Siri, Location Services, and the collection of analytics of usage and data on your MacBook.

If you want to let macOS apply these settings, click **Continue** (→). If you prefer to go through the settings yourself, click **Customize Settings** and follow the prompts.

Choose Settings on the All Your Files and Photos in iCloud Screen

The All your files and photos in iCloud screen lets you decide whether to store your key files in iCloud. Storing the files in the Documents folder and the Desktop folder, plus your photos and videos, in iCloud enables you to work with the files easily on multiple Macs, devices such as iPhones and iPads, and Windows computers that have iCloud integration installed. It also keeps the files backed up online, reducing the possibility of you losing the files if your MacBook gets damaged or goes missing.

Select (☑) **Store files from Documents and Desktop in iCloud Drive** if you want to store these folders in iCloud. Select (☑) **Store photos and videos in iCloud Photos** if you want to store your photos and videos in iCloud as well.

After making your choices, click **Continue** (⊙).

All your files and photos in iCloud

Keep the most important things on your Mac safely stored and available everywhere.

☑ **Store files from Documents and Desktop in iCloud Drive**
All your files from the Documents folder and the Desktop will automatically upload to iCloud Drive and stay up to date on all your devices.

☑ **Store photos and videos in iCloud Photos**
All your photos and videos from the Photos app will automatically upload to iCloud Photos and stay up to date on all your devices.

⊙ Back   ⊙ Continue

Choose Light, Dark, or Auto Appearance

On the Choose Your Look screen, specify the appearance you want by clicking **Light**, **Dark**, or **Auto**. The appearance controls a wide range of aspects of the macOS interface, including the Dock, the menus, the buttons, and the windows. The Auto setting causes macOS to switch appearances based on whether it is day or night in your current location.

After making your choice, click **Continue** (⊙). The Setting Up Your Mac screen appears while macOS sets up your MacBook. The macOS desktop then appears, and you can start using your MacBook as explained in the rest of this book.

Choose Your Look

Light   Dark   Auto

Select an appearance and see how the Dock, menus, buttons, and windows adjust depending on which one you choose.

You can change this later by going to System Preferences.

⊙ Back   ⊙ Continue

Start Your MacBook and Log In

Whesn you are ready to start a computing session, start your MacBook and log in to macOS with the credentials for the user account you have set up or an administrator has created for you. After you start your MacBook, macOS loads and automatically displays the login screen by default or logs you in automatically. From the login screen, you can select your username and type your password.

When you log in, macOS displays the desktop with your apps and settings.

Start Your MacBook and Log In

1 Press the power button on your MacBook.

A screen showing the list of users appears.

Note: Your MacBook may not display the list of users and login window. Instead, it may simply log you in automatically or show a different login screen. Chapter 12 shows you how to change this behavior.

Note: You may need to swipe right with two fingers on the trackpad to display your username. Alternatively, start typing the username to display it.

Note: On a Touch Bar–equipped MacBook, the message "Your password is required to log in" appears when Touch ID is not available, such as after restarting the MacBook.

2 Click your username.

The login window appears.

3 Type your password in the Enter Password box.

Ⓐ If you cannot remember your password, click **Hint** (?).

B macOS displays the password hint below the Enter Password box.

4 Type your password if you have not already done so.

5 Click **Log In** (⯈).

Note: Instead of clicking Log In (⯈), you can press **Return**.

The MacBook displays your desktop, the menu bar, and the Dock. You can now start using the MacBook.

TIPS

Why does my MacBook go straight to the desktop instead of displaying the list of usernames?
Your MacBook is set to log in automatically. Logging in automatically is convenient when you are the only one who uses your MacBook, but it means that anyone who can start your MacBook can use it without providing credentials. Chapter 12 shows you how to turn off automatic login.

Why does my MacBook not show the list of usernames?
Hiding the list of usernames provides extra security and is widely used in companies, but it is usually not necessary for a MacBook used at home. Type your username in the Name field and your password in the Password field, and then click **Log In** (⯈).

Explore the macOS Desktop

Your MacBook runs the macOS operating system, which is currently in version 10.15, a version called Catalina. The Macintosh operating system has long been known for being intuitive and is also pleasing to look at. It was the first major system interface to focus on graphical elements, such as icons. The macOS desktop is the overall window through which you view all that happens on your MacBook, such as looking at the contents of folders, working on documents, and surfing the Web.

Explore the macOS Desktop

A Menu Bar

A menu bar usually appears at the top of the screen so that you can access the commands it contains. macOS hides the menu bar in certain situations. The menu bar shows the menus for the active application.

B Drives

The MacBook stores its data, including the software it needs to work, on an internal drive. This drive is a solid-state device, or SSD, rather than an external drive with moving platters, but it is often referred to as a hard drive. You can also connect external drives for extra storage.

C iPod, iPhone, or iPad

You can connect one or more iPods, iPhones, or iPads to your MacBook to transfer files.

D Folders

Folders are containers that you use to organize files and other folders stored on your MacBook.

E Files

Files include documents, applications, or other sources of data. There are various kinds of documents, such as text, graphics, songs, or movies.

F Finder Windows

You view the contents of drives, folders, and other objects in Finder windows.

G App and Document Windows

When you use apps, you use the windows that those apps display, for documents, web pages, games, and so on.

Finder Menu Bar and Menus

Ⓐ Apple Menu

This menu is always visible so that you can access special commands, such as Shut Down and Log Out.

Ⓑ Finder Menu

This menu enables you to control the Finder app itself. For example, you can display information about Finder or set preferences to control how it behaves.

Ⓒ File Menu

This menu contains commands you can use to work with files and Finder windows.

Ⓓ Edit Menu

This menu is not as useful in Finder as it is in other applications, but here you can undo what you have done or copy and paste information.

Ⓔ View Menu

This menu enables you to determine how you view the desktop; it is especially useful for choosing Finder window views.

Ⓕ Go Menu

This menu takes you to various places, such as specific folders.

Ⓖ Window Menu

This menu enables you to work with open Finder windows.

Ⓗ Help Menu

This menu provides help with macOS or the other applications.

Ⓘ Configurable Menus

You can configure the menu bar to include specific menus, such as Screen Mirroring, Volume, Wi-Fi, Battery, and many more.

Ⓙ Clock

Here you see the current day and time.

Ⓚ Spotlight Menu

This menu enables you to search for information on your MacBook.

Ⓛ Fast User Switching

This feature enables you to switch user accounts and open the Login window.

continued ▶

Explore the macOS Desktop (continued)

The Finder app controls the macOS desktop, and so you see its menu bar whenever you work with this application. When you view the contents of a folder, you do so through a Finder window. There are many ways to view the contents of a Finder window, such as Icon view and List view. The sidebar enables you to quickly navigate the file system and to open files and folders with a single click. The Dock on the desktop and the sidebar in Finder windows enable you to access items quickly and easily.

Finder Windows

A Close Button

Click to close a window.

B Minimize Button

Click to shrink a window and move it onto the Dock.

C Zoom Button

Click to expand a Finder window to the maximum size needed or possible; click it again to return to the previous size.

D Window Title

The name of the location whose contents you see in the window.

E Toolbar

Contains tools you use to work with files and folders.

F Search Box

Enables you to find files, folders, and other information.

G Sidebar

Enables you to quickly access devices, folders, files, and tags, as well as searches you have saved.

H Files and Folders

Shows the contents of a location within a window;

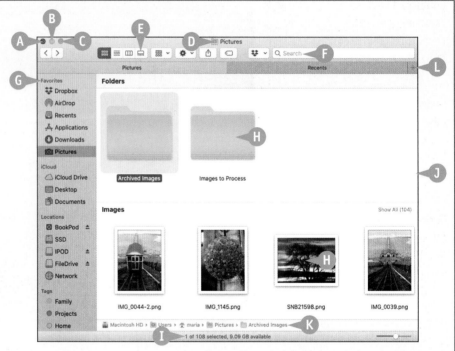

this example shows the Icon view.

I Status Bar

Shows information about the current location, such as the amount of free space when you are viewing the MacBook's drive.

J Window Border

Drag a border or a corner to change the size of a window.

K Path Bar

Shows the path to the location of the folder displayed in the window.

L Tab Bar

Enables you to open multiple tabs containing different Finder locations within the same Finder window and quickly switch among them.

Dock and Sidebar

Ⓐ Favorites

Contains files, folders, searches, and other items that you can open by clicking them.

Ⓑ iCloud

Shows the folders you have stored in your space on iCloud Drive, such as Desktop and Documents.

Ⓒ Locations

Contains your MacBook's internal drive or drives, any DVD or CD in an external optical drive, external drives, network drives, and other devices that your MacBook can access.

Ⓓ Tags

Shows the list of tags you can apply to files and folders to help you identify and sort them easily.

Ⓔ Dock

Shows apps, files, and folders you can access with a single click, along with apps currently running.

Ⓕ Dock Divider Line

Divides the left side of the Dock from the right side. You can

press Control +click the line to display the contextual menu for configuring the Dock.

Ⓖ Apps

Icons on the left side of the Dock are for apps; each open app has a dark dot under its icon unless you turn off this preference.

Ⓗ Files, Folders, and Minimized Windows

Icons on the right side of the Dock are for files, folders,

and minimized windows. The default Dock includes the Downloads folder for files you download from the Internet.

Ⓘ Trash/Eject

macOS puts items you delete in the Trash; to get rid of them, you empty the Trash. When you select an ejectable device, such as a DVD, the Trash icon changes to the Eject icon.

Point and Click with the Trackpad

To tell the MacBook what you want to do, slide your finger across the trackpad to move the on-screen pointer over the object with which you want to work. After you point to an object, you press the trackpad down to click, telling the computer what you want to do with the object. The number of times you click, and the manner in which you click, determine what happens to the object you point at.

Point and Click with the Trackpad

Point and Click

1 Slide your finger across the trackpad until the pointer points at the appropriate icon.

2 Press the trackpad once to click the trackpad. This is a single click.

A The object becomes highlighted, indicating that it is now selected.

Double-Click

1 Slide your finger across the trackpad until the pointer points at the appropriate icon.

2 Click the trackpad twice.

Your selection opens.

Point, Click, and Drag

1 Slide your finger across the trackpad until the pointer points at the appropriate icon.

2 Press down the trackpad and hold it.

The object at which you were pointing becomes attached to the arrow and remains so until you release the trackpad.

3 Drag your finger on the trackpad to move the object.

4 When you get to the object's new position, release the trackpad.

Note: Dragging an item to a different external drive, flash drive, or disk volume copies it there. Changing an item's location on the same drive moves the item instead.

Secondary Click (Control+Click)

1 Point to an object in a Finder window or on the desktop, or to the desktop itself.

Note: To select more than one item at the same time, press and hold ⌘ while you click each item you want to select.

2 Press `Control`+click the trackpad.

A contextual menu appears.

3 Point to the appropriate command on the menu and click the trackpad once to give the command.

TIP

Why do things I click stick to the arrow?
You can configure the trackpad so you can drag items without having to hold down the trackpad. When this setting is on and you click an item, it gets attached to the pointer. When you move the pointer, the item moves too. To configure this setting, see the section "Configure the Trackpad or Other Pointing Device" in Chapter 2.

Connect to a Wireless Network

If you have set up a wireless network, you can connect your MacBook to it. Wireless networks are convenient for both homes and businesses because they require no cables and are fast and easy to set up.

Your MacBook includes a wireless network feature that uses some of the wireless network standards called Wi-Fi. You can control wireless networks directly from the Wi-Fi menu at the right end of the menu bar. To connect to a Wi-Fi network, you need to know its name and password.

Connect to a Wireless Network

Note: If you connected your MacBook to a wireless network during setup, you do not need to set up the connection to the same network again.

1 Click **Wi-Fi status** (◇) on the menu bar.

The menu opens.

Note: If the list of wireless networks appears on the menu, go to step **4**.

2 Click **Turn Wi-Fi On**.

macOS turns Wi-Fi on.

3 Click **Wi-Fi status** (🛜) on the menu bar.

The menu opens and displays a list of the wireless networks your MacBook can detect.

Ⓐ A lock icon (🔒) indicates that the network is secured with a password or other security mechanism.

Ⓑ The signal strength icon (🛜) indicates the relative strength of the network's signal.

4 Click the network to which you want to connect your MacBook.

If the wireless network uses a password, your MacBook prompts you to enter it.

5 Type the password in the Password box.

C If you want to see the characters of the password to help you type it, click **Show password** (☐ changes to ☑).

D If you do not want your MacBook to remember this wireless network for future use, deselect (☐) **Remember this network**.

6 Click **Join**.

Your MacBook connects to the wireless network, and you can start using network resources.

E The number of arcs on the Wi-Fi status icon (🛜) indicates the strength of the connection, and ranges from one arc to four arcs.

7 To see more details about the wireless network, press `Option`+click **Wi-Fi status** (🛜) on the menu bar.

F The network's details appear, including the physical mode, the wireless channel, and the security type.

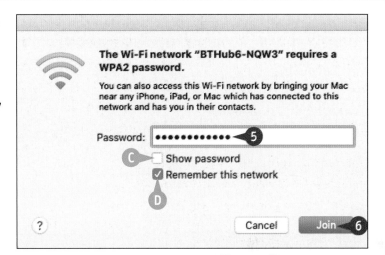

TIPS

How do I disconnect from a wireless network?

When you have finished using a wireless network, you can disconnect from it by turning Wi-Fi off. Click **Wi-Fi status** (🛜) on the menu bar and then click **Turn Wi-Fi Off**.

What kind of Wi-Fi network do I need for my MacBook?

Wi-Fi networks use several different standards. As of this writing, the latest standard that MacBook models support is 802.11ac, which provides very fast data rates. Your MacBook can also use older Wi-Fi standards, such as 802.11a, 802.11b, 802.11g, and 802.11n, so you can use most Wi-Fi networks.

Give Commands

The easiest ways to give commands in macOS are by using the menus and the toolbar. You can also give commands by pressing keyboard shortcuts.

The menu bar at the top of the window shows the Apple menu (🍎) on the left followed by the menus for the active app. Any open window can have a toolbar, usually across its top but sometimes elsewhere in the window.

Give Commands

Give a Command from a Menu

1 On the Dock, click the app you want to activate — **Finder** (🙂) in this example.

Note: You can also click the app's window if you can see it.

2 On the menu bar, click the menu you want to open.

The menu opens.

3 Click the command you want to give.

The app performs the action associated with the command.

Choose Among Groups of Features on a Menu

1 On the Dock, click the app you want to activate — **Finder** (🙂) in this example.

2 On the menu bar, click the menu you want to open.

The app opens the menu.

3 Click the option you want to use.

The app activates the feature you selected.

Give a Command from a Toolbar

1 On the Dock, click the app you want to activate — **Finder** (🙂) in this example.

2 Click the button for the command on the toolbar, or click a pop-up menu, and then click the menu item for the command.

The app performs the action associated with the toolbar button or menu item.

Choose Among Groups of Features on a Toolbar

1 On the Dock, click the app you want to activate — **Finder** (🙂) in this example.

2 In the group of buttons, click the button you want to choose.

A The app highlights the button you clicked to indicate that the feature is turned on.

B The app removes highlighting from the button that was previously selected.

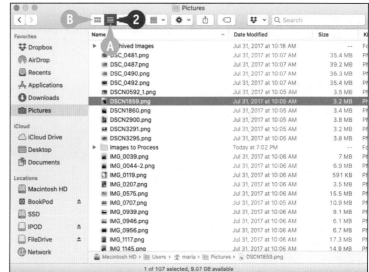

TIP

Is it better to use the menus or the toolbar?

If the toolbar contains the command you need, using the toolbar is usually faster and easier than using the menus. You can customize the toolbar in many apps by opening the **View** menu, choosing **Customize Toolbar**, working in the dialog that opens, and then clicking **Done**. Use this command, or other similar commands, to place the buttons for your most-used commands just a click away. If your MacBook has the Touch Bar, you can customize the Touch Bar in some apps by opening the **View** menu, choosing **Customize Touch Bar**, working in the dialog that opens, and then clicking **Done**.

Open, Close, and Manage Windows

Most macOS apps use windows to display information so that you can see it and work with it. You can resize most windows to the size you need or expand a window so that it fills the screen. You can move windows and position them so that you can see those windows you require, minimize other windows to icons on the Dock, or hide an app's windows from view.

Open, Close, and Manage Windows

Open a Window

1. Click anywhere on the desktop.

    macOS activates Finder and displays the menu bar for it.

    Note: Clicking anywhere on the desktop activates Finder because the desktop is a special Finder window. You can also click **Finder** ( ) on the Dock.

2. Click **File**.

    The File menu opens.

3. Click **New Finder Window**.

    A Finder window opens, showing your files in your default view.

Move, Resize, and Zoom a Window

1. Click the window's title bar and drag the window to where you want it.

2. Click a border or corner of the window and drag until the window is the size and shape you want.

3. Click **Zoom** ( ).

    The window zooms to full screen.

4. Move the pointer to the upper-left corner of the screen.

    The macOS menu bar and the app's title bar appear.

5. Click **Zoom Back** ( ).

    The window zooms back to its previous size.

Close a Window

1 Click **Close** (●).

Note: When you move the pointer over the upper-left corner of a window, Close (●) changes to Close (✖), Minimize (●) changes to Minimize (➖), and Zoom (●) changes to Zoom (⊕).

The window closes.

Note: You can also close a window by pressing ⌘+W. To close all the windows of the app, press Option+click **Close** (●) or press ⌘+Option+W.

Minimize or Hide a Window

1 Click **Minimize** (●).

macOS minimizes the window to an icon on the right side of the Dock.

Note: You can also minimize a window by pressing ⌘+M.

2 Click the icon for the minimized window.

macOS expands the window to its original size and position.

TIP

How can I find out where a document in a window is located?
To quickly see what folder contains a file or folder, press ⌘+click the window's name in the title bar. The window displays a pop-up menu showing the path of folders to this folder. Click a folder in the path to display that folder in Finder, or click the title bar to hide the pop-up menu again.

Using Notifications

macOS's Notification Center feature keeps you up to date with what is happening in your apps. Notification Center puts all your alerts, from incoming e-mail messages and instant messages to calendar requests and software updates, in a single place where you can easily access and manage them.

You open Notification Center by clicking the icon at the right end of the menu bar. Notification Center opens as a pane on the right side of the screen, and it contains sections you can expand or collapse as needed.

Using Notifications

View a Notification

Ⓐ When you receive a notification, a notification banner appears in the upper-right corner of the screen for a few seconds.

Note: Notification Center can display either banners or alerts. A banner appears for a few seconds, and then disappears. An alert remains on screen until you dismiss it.

① If you want to see the item that produced the notification, click the banner.

Display Notification Center When Your Desktop Is Visible

① Click **Notification Center** (:≡).

Notification Center opens.

② Click **Notifications**.

The Notifications pane appears.

③ Optionally, click a notification to display the related item in its app.

Ⓑ You can click **Today** to display the Today pane, which shows your calendar events, stock information, weather forecasts, and other data.

④ When you are ready to close Notification Center, click **Notification Center** (:≡).

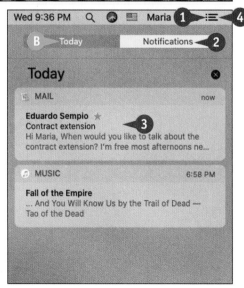

Choose What Types of Notifications to Display and Set Your Do Not Disturb Hours

1 Press **Control**+click **System Preferences** (⚙) on the Dock.

The contextual menu opens.

2 Click **Notifications**.

System Preferences opens and displays the Notifications pane.

3 Click **Do Not Disturb**.

The Do Not Disturb settings appear.

4 Click **From** (☐ changes to ☑) and then set the hours.

5 Choose which calls to accept during Do Not Disturb times.

6 Click an app or feature.

The controls for the app or feature appear.

7 Set the **Allow Notifications from** switch to On (⬤) to allow notifications.

8 Click **None**, **Banners**, or **Alerts** to set the alert style.

9 Choose other options for the app or feature.

10 Repeat steps **6** to **9** for other apps and features.

11 Click **Notification Center sort order** (⬥) and click **Recents**, **Recents by App**, or **Manually by App**, as needed.

12 Click **Close** (⬤).

System Preferences closes.

TIP

How do I display Notification Center in a full-screen app?
Move the pointer up to the top of the screen to display the menu bar. You can then click **Notification Center** (☰) toward the right end of the menu bar to display Notification Center.

Put Your MacBook to Sleep and Wake It Up

macOS enables you to put your MacBook to sleep easily and wake it up quickly. So when you are ready for a break but you do not want to end your computing session, put the MacBook to sleep instead of shutting it down.

Sleep keeps all your apps open and lets you start computing again quickly. When you wake your MacBook up, your apps and windows are where you left them, so you can swiftly resume what you were doing.

Put Your MacBook to Sleep and Wake It Up

Put Your MacBook to Sleep

 Click **Apple** (🍎).

The Apple menu opens.

Note: You can also put your MacBook to sleep by closing its lid.

② Click **Sleep**.

The MacBook turns its screen off and puts itself to sleep.

Note: You can also put your MacBook to sleep by pressing its power button for a moment.

Wake Your MacBook

1 Click the trackpad or press any key on the keyboard.

Note: If you put the MacBook to sleep by closing its lid, lift the lid instead.

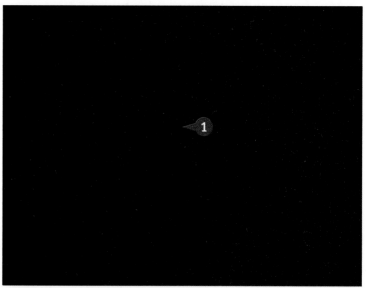

The MacBook wakes up and turns on the screen. All the apps and windows that you were using are open where you left them.

The MacBook reestablishes any network connections that it normally uses and performs regular tasks, such as checking for new e-mail.

TIP

When should I use sleep and when should I shut down my MacBook?
Put your MacBook to sleep when you want to be able to resume using it quickly. Sleep uses only a minimal amount of power. Shut down your MacBook when you plan not to use it for several days or when your MacBook has almost run out of battery power.

Log Out, Shut Down, and Resume

When you have finished using your MacBook for now, end your computing session by logging out. From the login screen, you can log back in when you are ready to use your MacBook again. When you have finished using your MacBook and plan to leave it several days, shut it down.

Whether you log out or shut down your MacBook, you can choose whether to have macOS reopen your apps and documents when you log back on. This helpful feature can help you get back to work — or play — quickly and easily.

Log Out, Shut Down, and Resume

Log Out from Your MacBook

1 Click **Apple** (🍎).

The Apple menu opens.

2 Click **Log Out**.

The MacBook shows a dialog asking if you are sure you want to log out.

3 Click **Reopen windows when logging back in** (☐ changes to ☑) if you want to resume your apps and documents.

4 Click **Log Out**.

Note: Instead of clicking Log Out, you can wait for 1 minute. After this, the MacBook closes your apps and logs you out automatically. To log out quickly, bypassing the dialog, click **Apple** (🍎), press and hold Option, and then click **Log Out**.

The MacBook displays the window showing the list of users. You or another user can click your name to start logging in.

Shut Down Your MacBook

1 Click **Apple** (🍎).

The Apple menu opens.

2 Click **Shut Down**.

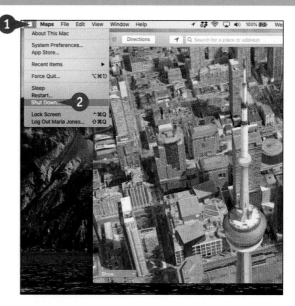

A dialog opens asking if you are sure you want to shut down.

3 Click **Reopen windows when logging back in** (☐ changes to ☑) if you want to resume your apps and documents.

4 Click **Shut Down**.

Note: Instead of clicking Shut Down, you can wait for 1 minute. After this, the MacBook shuts down automatically. To shut down quickly, bypassing the dialog, click **Apple** (🍎), press and hold Option, and then click **Shut Down**.

The screen goes blank, and the MacBook switches itself off.

TIP

Do I need to save my documents before logging out?
If the apps you are using are designed to use macOS's automatic-saving features, your MacBook automatically saves any unsaved changes to your documents before logging you out. But because not all apps use these features, it is better to save all your documents yourself before you log out. Otherwise, an app may display a dialog prompting you to save unsaved changes, and this dialog may prevent logout or shutdown.

CHAPTER 2

Configuring Your MacBook

You can customize many aspects of macOS to make it work the way you prefer. You can change the desktop background, personalize the Dock icons, and adjust the keyboard and trackpad or other pointing device. You can also run apps or open specific documents each time you log in or set your MacBook to go to sleep automatically when you are not using it.

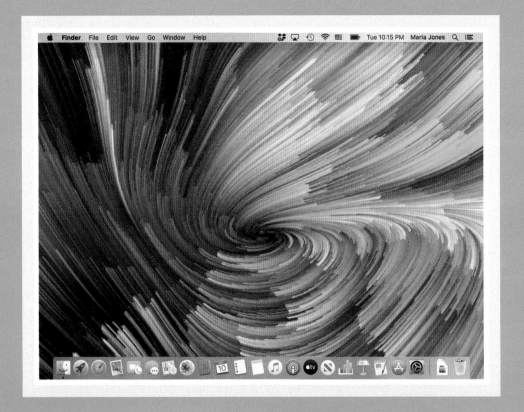

Change the Desktop Background

macOS enables you to change the desktop background to show the picture you prefer. macOS includes many varied desktop pictures and solid colors, but you can also set any of your own photos as the desktop background. You can tile, stretch, or crop the photo to fill the screen or center it on the screen.

You can also choose between displaying a single picture on the desktop and displaying a series of images that change automatically.

Change the Desktop Background

1 Press **Control** +click the desktop.

The contextual menu opens.

2 Click **Change Desktop Background**.

The Desktop pane in System Preferences appears.

3 Click the category of image you want to see.

A Apple contains the built-in desktop backgrounds and solid colors.

B Photos contains your Photos library.

C Folders contains your folders.

D Click **Add** (+) to add a folder.

The images appear in the right-hand pane.

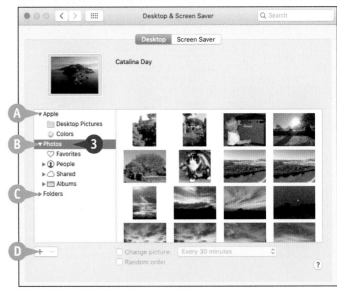

4 Click the image you want to use.

The image appears on the desktop.

5 If you chose a photo or picture of your own, click the pop-up menu (⬦), and then click the way to fit the image to the screen. See the tip for details.

6 If you want to set a series of background images, click the category.

7 Click **Change picture** (☐ changes to ☑) if you want macOS to change the desktop picture automatically for you.

8 Click **Change picture** (⬦) and click the interval — for example, **Every 30 minutes**.

9 Click **Random order** (☐ changes to ☑) if you want the images to appear in random order.

10 Click **Close** (●).

System Preferences closes.

Which option should I choose for fitting the image to the screen?
In the Desktop & Screen Saver preferences, choose **Fit to Screen** to match the image's height or width — whichever is nearest — to the screen. Choose **Fill Screen** to make an image fill the screen without distortion but cropping off parts that do not fit. Choose **Stretch to Fill Screen** to stretch the image to fit the screen exactly, distorting it as needed. Choose **Center** to display the image at full size in the middle of the desktop. Choose **Tile** to cover the desktop with multiple copies of the image.

Set Up a Screen Saver

macOS enables you to set a screen saver to hide what your screen is showing when you leave your MacBook idle. A *screen saver* is an image, a sequence of images, or a moving pattern that appears on the screen. You can choose what screen saver to use and the length of the period of inactivity before it starts.

macOS comes with a variety of attractive screen savers. You can download other screen savers from websites.

Set Up a Screen Saver

1 Press **Control** +click the desktop.

The contextual menu opens.

2 Click **Change Desktop Background**.

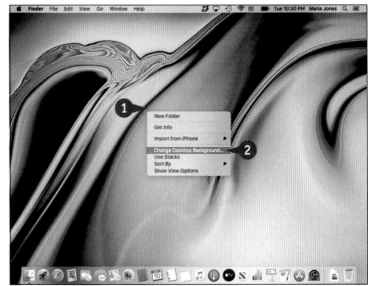

The Desktop pane of Desktop & Screen Saver preferences opens.

3 Click **Screen Saver**.

The Screen Saver pane appears.

4 Click a screen saver in the list on the left.

The screen saver you clicked starts playing in the Preview area.

A You can click **Show with clock** (☐ changes to ☑) to display a clock on the screen saver.

5 Click **Start after** (◉).

The pop-up menu opens.

6 Click the length of time to wait until the screen saver starts, such as **20 Minutes**.

Note: To turn off the screen saver, select **Never** in the Start After pop-up menu.

7 Position the pointer over the preview.

The Preview button appears.

8 Click **Preview**.

The screen saver preview appears full screen.

9 Click anywhere on the screen saver when you want to stop the preview.

The Screen Saver pane appears.

10 Press ⌘+Q.

System Preferences closes.

Must I use a screen saver to protect my MacBook's screen from damage?

No. Screen savers originally protected cathode ray tube (CRT) displays from having static images "burned in" to their screens. LCD and LED screens, such as that on your MacBook, do not suffer from this problem, so you need not use a screen saver; however, future screens based on technologies such as OLED — organic light-emitting diode — may suffer burn-in problems. Nowadays you can use a screen saver to protect the information on-screen or to provide visual entertainment — or you may prefer to simply put your MacBook to sleep, which has the additional benefit of saving battery power.

Configure Energy Saver and Sleep Settings

Energy Saver enables you to configure power settings separately for when your MacBook is running from the battery and from the power adapter. You can set your MacBook to turn off the display after a period of inactivity, put the drive to sleep when possible, dim the display on battery power, and enable the Power Nap feature. You can put your MacBook to sleep manually at any time by closing the lid or by clicking **Apple** (🍎) and **Sleep**.

Configure Energy Saver and Sleep Settings

1 Press `Control`+click **System Preferences** (⚙) on the Dock.

The System Preferences contextual menu opens.

2 Click **Energy Saver**.

The Energy Saver pane appears.

3 Click **Battery**.

The Battery tab appears.

Note: If your MacBook has a dedicated graphics card, click **Automatic graphics switching** (☐ changes to ☑) to have the MacBook switch automatically between the dedicated graphics card and the integrated graphics processor to save power when running from the battery.

4 Drag the **Turn display off after** slider to set the period of inactivity before turning off the display.

5 Click **Put hard disks to sleep when possible** (☐ changes to ☑) to reduce disk power usage.

6 Click **Slightly dim the display while on battery power** (☐ changes to ☑) to reduce power usage by dimming the display.

7 Click **Enable Power Nap while on battery power** (☐ changes to ☑) to use the Power Nap feature. See the first tip for details.

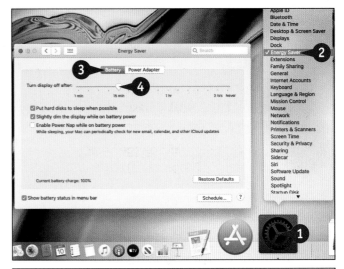

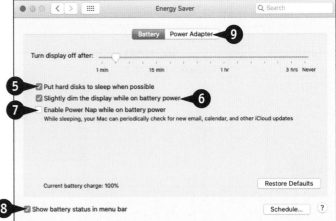

8 Click **Show battery status in menu bar** (☐ changes to ☑) to display a battery readout in the menu bar. This is usually helpful.

9 Click **Power Adapter**.

The Power Adapter tab appears.

10 Drag the **Turn display off after** slider to set the period of inactivity before turning off the display.

11 Click **Prevent computer from sleeping automatically when the display is off** (☐ changes to ☑) if you need to keep the MacBook awake.

12 Click **Put hard disks to sleep when possible** (☐ changes to ☑) to reduce disk power usage.

13 Click **Wake for Wi-Fi network access** (☐ changes to ☑) to enable waking the MacBook via Wi-Fi.

14 Click **Enable Power Nap while plugged into a power adapter** (☐ changes to ☑) to use the Power Nap feature.

15 Click **Schedule**.

The Schedule dialog opens.

16 On the top row, click **Start up or wake** (☐ changes to ☑) to start or wake your MacBook, set the frequency, and set the time.

17 On the second row, click **Sleep**, **Restart**, or **Shut Down** (☐ changes to ☑) and set the time.

18 Click **OK**.

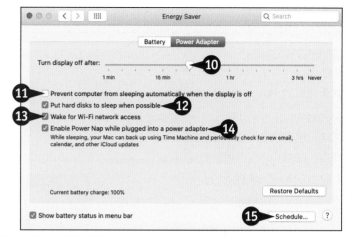

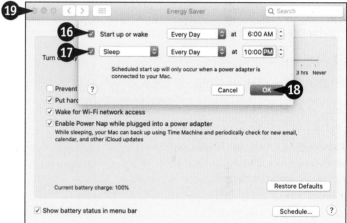

The Schedule dialog closes.

19 Click **Close** (⬤).

System Preferences closes.

TIPS

What is the Power Nap feature?
Power Nap enables your MacBook to wake periodically during sleep to check for new e-mail messages, calendar items, and other online updates. Power Nap uses a small amount of battery power but is usually very helpful.

Which button do I press to wake my MacBook from sleep?
You can press any key; if the MacBook has the Touch Bar, touch the Touch ID sensor. If you are not certain whether the MacBook is asleep or preparing to run a screen saver, press Shift, Control, Option, or ⌘. These keys do not type a character if the MacBook turns out to be awake instead of asleep. You can also move your finger on the trackpad to wake your MacBook.

Customize the Dock

macOS enables you to customize the Dock so that it contains the icons you find most useful and it appears in your preferred position on the screen. You can add apps, files, or folders to the Dock; reposition the Dock's icons; and remove most of the existing items if you do not need them.

To customize the Dock, you drag items to it, from it, or along it. You can also use the Dock's contextual menu to change the Dock's position, configuration, or behavior.

Customize the Dock

Add an App to the Dock

1 Click **Launchpad** (📌) on the Dock.

The Launchpad screen appears.

2 Drag the app to the left side of the divider line on the Dock.

The app's icon appears on the Dock.

Note: You can also add an app to the Dock by opening the app, pressing Control +clicking its Dock icon, highlighting or clicking **Options**, and then clicking **Keep in Dock**.

Add a File or Folder to the Dock

1 Click **Finder** (🙂) on the Dock.

2 In the Finder window, navigate to the file or folder you want to add to the Dock.

3 Drag the file or folder to the right side of the divider line on the Dock.

The item's icon appears on the Dock.

Note: When you drag a file or folder to the Dock, macOS creates a link to the file or folder rather than moving the original item.

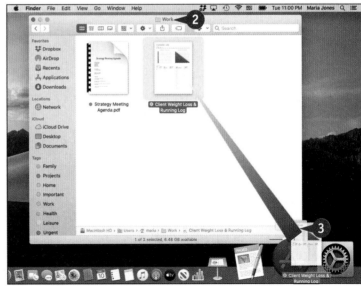

Remove an Item from the Dock

1 If the app is running, press `Control`+click its Dock icon, and then click **Quit** on the contextual menu.

2 Press `Control`+click the app's icon on the Dock.

The contextual menu opens.

3 Highlight or click **Options**.

The Options submenu opens.

4 Click **Keep in Dock**, removing the check mark.

macOS removes the icon from the Dock.

Note: You can also click an icon and drag it from the Dock toward the desktop. When a Remove pop-up message appears, release the icon.

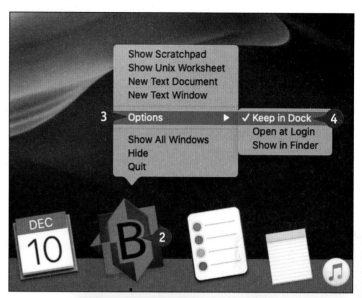

Configure the Dock

1 Press `Control`+click the Dock divider bar.

Ⓐ Click **Turn Hiding On** to hide the Dock when the pointer is not over it.

Ⓑ Click **Turn Magnification Off** to turn off magnification.

Ⓒ Click **Position on Screen** and then click **Left**, **Bottom**, or **Right** to reposition the Dock.

Ⓓ Click **Minimize Using** and then click **Genie Effect** or **Scale Effect**.

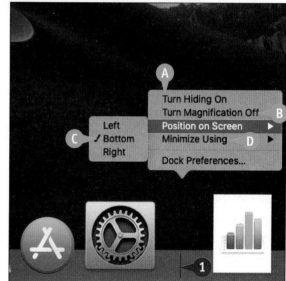

How else can I customize the Dock?

You can increase or decrease the size of the Dock by clicking the Dock divider bar and dragging it up or down. For more precise control of the Dock, press `Control`+click the Dock divider bar, and then click **Dock Preferences** to display the Dock pane in System Preferences. Here you can change the Dock size, turn on and adjust magnification, set the Dock's position, and choose the effect for minimizing windows. You can also choose other options for controlling the Dock's appearance and behavior.

Add or Remove Desktop Spaces

macOS enables you to create multiple desktop spaces on which to arrange your documents and apps. You can switch from space to space quickly to move from app to app. You can tie an app to a particular space so that it always appears in that space or allow it to appear in any space.

When you no longer need a desktop space, you can remove it in just moments. To configure desktop spaces, you use Mission Control.

Add or Remove Desktop Spaces

① Swipe up the trackpad with three fingers or press `Control`+`⬆`.

Note: On some keyboards, you press `F9` to invoke Mission Control. On other keyboards, you press `F3`. Depending on your MacBook's settings, you may need to press `F3` in combination with the function key.

Note: Another way to invoke Mission Control is to run the Mission Control app from Launchpad or from an icon you add to the Dock.

The Mission Control screen appears.

Ⓐ You can click a window to switch quickly to it.

② Move the pointer to the top of the screen.

The bar at the top of the screen grows deeper when the pointer is over it.

A panel showing a+sign appears.

Note: If you have positioned the Dock on the right, the+sign appears in the upper-left corner of the screen.

③ Click the+panel.

B Another desktop space appears at the top of the Mission Control screen.

C You can click a window and drag it to the desktop space in which you want it to appear.

4 Click a window you want to display full screen, and then drag it to the bar at the top of the screen.

The app appears as a full-screen item on the row of desktops.

D When you need to close a desktop, move the pointer over it, and then click **Close** (ⓧ).

5 Click the desktop space or full-screen app you want to display.

The desktop space or app appears.

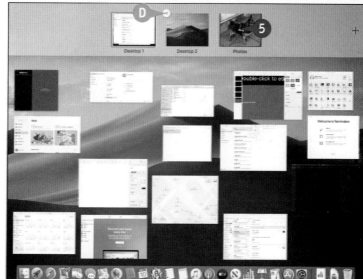

How can I assign an app to a particular desktop?

First, use Mission Control to activate the desktop to which you want to assign the app. Then press `Control`+click or right-click the app's Dock icon, click **Options**, and click **This Desktop**. If you want to use the app on all desktops, click **All Desktops** in the Assign To section of the Options submenu.

Create Hot Corners to Control Screen Display

The Hot Corners feature enables you to trigger actions by moving the pointer to the corners of the screen. You can set up hot corners for as many of the four corners of the screen as you want. Each hot corner can perform an action such as opening Mission Control, displaying your desktop, or starting the screen saver.

To set up hot corners, you use the Hot Corners dialog. You can open this dialog from the Mission Control pane or the Screen Saver pane in System Preferences.

Create Hot Corners to Control Screen Display

Set Up a Hot Corner

1. Press **Control**+click **System Preferences** (⚙) on the Dock.

   The contextual menu opens.

2. Click **Mission Control**.

   System Preferences opens and displays the Mission Control pane.

3. Click **Hot Corners**.

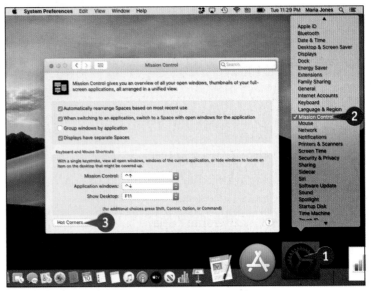

The Hot Corners dialog opens.

4. Click the pop-up menu (🔼) for the hot corner you want to set.

   The pop-up menu opens.

5. Click the action you want to assign to the corner.

6. Choose other hot corner actions as needed.

Note: You can set up multiple hot corners for the same feature if you want.

7. Click **OK**.

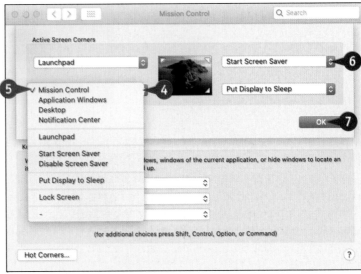

The Hot Corners dialog closes.

8 Press **Control**+click **System Preferences** (⚙) on the Dock.

The contextual menu opens.

9 Click **Quit**.

System Preferences closes.

Use a Hot Corner to Run Mission Control

1 Move the pointer to the hot corner you allocated to Mission Control.

The Mission Control screen appears.

2 Click the window you want to display.

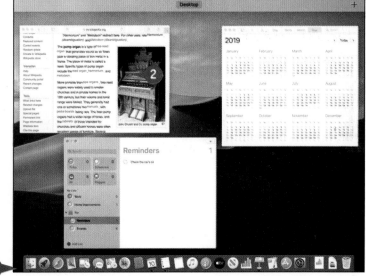

Are there other ways I can run Mission Control?

You can also run Mission Control by using a gesture, a trackpad click, or a button on a mouse you have connected to your MacBook. In the Keyboard and Mouse Shortcuts section in Mission Control preferences, click **Mission Control** (⬡) and select the gesture or mouse button. Press and hold **⌘**, **Option**, **Control**, **Shift**, or a combination of the four keys to add them to the keystroke. Use the same technique for the Application Windows pop-up menu, and the Show Desktop pop-up menu.

Make the Screen Easier to See

The Accessibility features in macOS include several options for making the contents of your MacBook's screen easier to see. You can invert the colors, use grayscale instead of colors, enhance the contrast, and increase the cursor size. You can also turn on the Zoom feature to enable yourself to zoom in quickly up to the limit you set. To configure these options, you open System Preferences and work in the Accessibility pane.

Make the Screen Easier to See

1 Press **Control** + click **System Preferences** (⚙) on the Dock.

The System Preferences contextual menu opens.

2 Click **Accessibility**.

The Accessibility pane appears.

3 Click **Zoom**.

The Zoom options appear.

4 Click **Use keyboard shortcuts to zoom** (☐ changes to ✓).

5 Click **Use scroll gesture with modifier keys to zoom** (☐ changes to ✓) if you want to zoom by holding a modifier key and scrolling on the trackpad.

6 Click the drop-down menu (⌄) and then click **Control**, **Option**, or **Command** to specify the modifier key.

7 Click **Zoom style** (◆) and then click **Full screen**, **Split screen**, or **Picture-in-picture**, as needed.

8 If your MacBook uses multiple displays, click **Choose Display**, and then click the display to use for zoom.

9 Click **Advanced**.

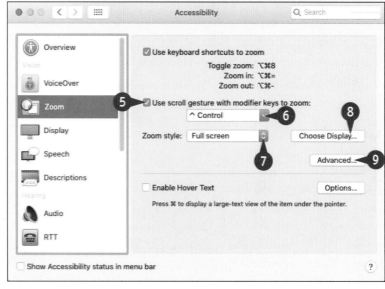

The Advanced dialog opens, with the Appearance tab displayed.

10 In the When Zoomed In, the Screen Image Moves list, click **Continuously with pointer**, **Only when the pointer reaches an edge**, or **So the pointer is at or near the center of the zoomed image**, as needed.

11 Click **Smooth images** (☐ changes to ☑) to have macOS smooth images.

12 Click **Flash screen when notification banner appears outside zoom view** (☐ changes to ☑) to get alerts for banners outside the zoom view.

13 Click **Follow keyboard focus** (☐ changes to ☑) if you want the zoomed area to follow the keyboard focus.

14 Click **Controls**.

The Controls tab appears.

15 Click to select (☑) or clear (➖) the top four check boxes to configure the zoom shortcuts you want to use.

16 Click **Use trackpad gesture to zoom** (☐ changes to ☑) to use three-finger gestures on the touchpad for zooming.

17 Drag **Maximum Zoom** to the appropriate level.

18 Drag **Minimum Zoom** to the appropriate level.

19 Click **OK**.

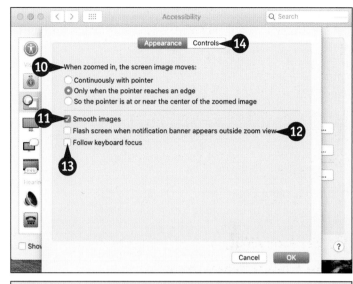

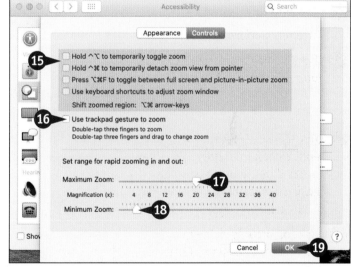

TIP

What is the quickest way to turn on the Universal Access features for seeing the screen?
Use keyboard shortcuts. Press Option+⌘+8 to toggle zoom on or off. With zoom turned on, press Option+⌘+= to zoom in by increments. Press Option+⌘+− to zoom out by increments. If you enable the Smooth Images feature by clicking **Smooth images** (☐ changes to ☑) in the Zoom options, you can press Option+⌘+\ to toggle Smooth Images on or off.

continued ▶

The Hover Text feature enables you to quickly zoom an item by moving the mouse pointer over it and pressing ⌘ or another key you specify. You can configure options for text entry using Hover Text.

If you tend to lose track of the pointer, you can turn on the Shake Mouse Pointer to Locate feature, which expands the pointer when you move the pointer back and forth quickly. You can also increase the cursor size to make the pointer more visible.

Make the Screen Easier to See (continued)

The Advanced dialog closes.

20 Click **Enable Hover Text** (☐ changes to ✓) if you want to be able to zoom the item under the pointer by pressing ⌘.

21 If you enable Hover Text, click **Options**.

The Options dialog opens.

22 Click **Text size** (⊡) and specify the text size.

23 Click **Text font** (⊡) and specify the font.

24 Click **Text-entry location** (⊡) and click the location, such as **Top left** or **Near current line**.

25 Click **Activation modifier** (⊡) and then click **Control**, **Option**, or **Command**.

Ⓐ You can click **Colors** to display extra controls for specifying the colors to use for hover text.

26 Click **OK**.

The Options dialog closes.

27 Click **Display** (🖥).

The Display options appear, with the Display tab shown at first.

28 Click **Invert colors** (☐ changes to ✓) if you want to invert the video colors for visibility. macOS does not invert the colors of images.

Ⓑ You can click **Classic Invert** (☐ changes to ✓) to invert the colors of images as well.

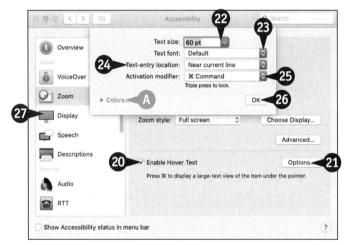

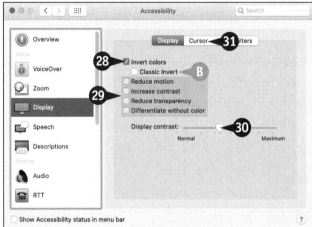

29 Click to enable or disable **Reduce motion**, **Increase contrast**, **Reduce transparency**, and **Differentiate without color**. See the Tip for details.

30 Drag the **Display contrast** slider to increase the contrast.

31 Click **Cursor**.

The Cursor tab appears.

32 Click **Shake mouse pointer to locate** (☐ changes to ☑) if you want to be able to enlarge the pointer temporarily by shaking it.

33 Drag the **Cursor size** slider to set the cursor size, such as the extreme size shown here.

34 Click **Color Filters**.

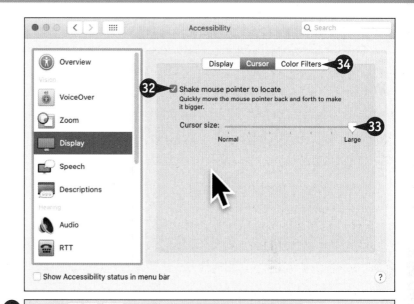

The Color Filters tab appears.

35 Click **Enable Color Filters** (☐ changes to ☑) if you want to apply a color filter.

36 Click **Filter type** (⬦) and then click the filter, such as **Grayscale**.

37 Click **Close** (⬤).

System Preferences closes.

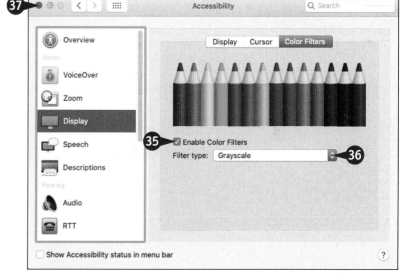

TIP

What do Reduce Motion, Increase Contrast, Reduce Transparency, and Differentiate Without Color do?
Click **Reduce motion** (☐ changes to ☑) to reduce 3D effects in the macOS user interface. Click **Increase contrast** (☐ changes to ☑) to increase the amount of contrast used in the interface. Click **Reduce transparency** (☐ changes to ☑) to reduce transparency, so that items in the foreground show less of the items behind them. Click **Differentiate without color** (☐ changes to ☑) to use non-color means of differentiating interface items that are differentiated using color by default.

Configure the Appearance

macOS has two systemwide appearances, the Light appearance and the Dark appearance. You can switch manually between appearances by using the Appearance setting in System Preferences. Alternatively, you can choose the Auto setting to have macOS switch automatically between Light appearance and Dark appearance to suit the time of day at your current location.

The Dark appearance, which is often called Dark Mode, can be easier on your eyes. If you use Dynamic wallpapers, the Dark appearance changes the wallpaper between the light still image and the dark still image.

Configure the Appearance

1 Click **Apple** (🍎).

The Apple menu opens.

2 Click **System Preferences**.

The System Preferences window opens.

3 Click **General** (▯).

The General pane opens.

A In the Appearance area, the current appearance has a blue outline.

4 Click **Light**, **Dark**, or **Auto** to set the appearance.

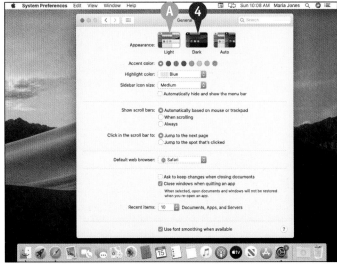

The appearance changes.

5 Click **Close** (●).

Note: The Dark appearance is a recent addition to macOS. The Dark appearance works with all the apps that come with your Mac, but some third-party apps may not support it.

System Preferences closes.

If you have a Dynamic wallpaper set, the wallpaper changes to suit the appearance.

How do I configure the time at which Auto changes the appearance?
Unlike on iOS devices, you cannot directly configure the schedule for changing the appearance: macOS uses the system time, the location, and the time of the year to set the schedule.

Configure the Keyboard

You can customize your MacBook's keyboard by adjusting the repeat rate and the delay until repeating starts, creating text shortcuts, and turning on automatic spell checking. If you have difficulty pressing the keys, you can turn on Sticky Keys or Slow Keys. Sticky Keys enables you to set a modifier key, such as ⌘, without having to hold it down. Slow Keys increases the delay between you pressing a key and macOS registering the keystroke.

Configure the Keyboard

1 Press `Control`+click **System Preferences** (⚙) on the Dock.

The contextual menu opens.

2 Click **Keyboard**.

System Preferences opens and displays the Keyboard pane.

3 Drag the **Key Repeat** slider to control how quickly a key repeats.

4 Drag the **Delay Until Repeat** slider to set the repeat delay.

5 If it appears, click **Adjust keyboard brightness in low light** (☐ changes to ☑) to have your MacBook adjust the keyboard brightness automatically.

6 To turn the keyboard backlight off automatically, click **Turn keyboard backlight off after [time] of inactivity** (☐ changes to ☑), click the pop-up menu (☉), and select the delay, such as **5 secs**.

Note: For a MacBook with a Touch Bar, click the **Touch Bar shows** pop-up menu (☉) and select App Controls with Control Strip, Expanded Control Strip, App Controls, or F1, F2, etc. Keys, as needed. You can also click the **Press Fn Key to** pop-up menu (☉), and then click **Show F1, F2, etc. Keys** or **Expand Control Strip**, as needed.

7 Click **Show keyboard and emoji viewers in menu bar** (☐ changes to ☑) to add an icon for the keyboard viewer and emoji viewer to the menu bar for quick access.

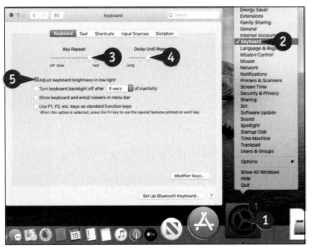

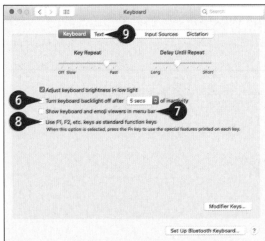

8 On a MacBook without a Touch Bar, click **Use F1, F2, etc. keys as standard function keys** (☐ changes to ☑) to use the dedicated keys as regular function keys.

9 Click **Text**.

The Text pane appears.

10 Click **Add** (+).

11 Type the text that will trigger the replacement.

12 Type the replacement text.

Note: macOS and iOS make your text shortcuts available to all your Macs and iOS devices using the same Apple ID.

13 Choose options for spelling and typing, such as **Correct spelling automatically** and **Capitalize words automatically**.

14 Click **Use smart quotes and dashes** (☐ changes to ☑) if you want macOS to replace regular quotes and dashes with smart quotes and dashes.

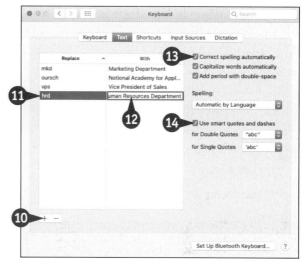

15 Press Control +click **System Preferences** (⚙) on the Dock.

The contextual menu opens.

16 Click **Accessibility**.

The Accessibility pane appears.

17 Click **Keyboard** (▦).

18 Click **Enable Sticky Keys** (☐ changes to ☑) if you want to press modifier keys separately from the keys they modify.

19 Click **Enable Slow Keys** (☐ changes to ☑) if you want to slow down macOS's registration of keystrokes.

20 Click **Enable Typing Feedback** (☐ changes to ☑) to have macOS announce the results of your typing.

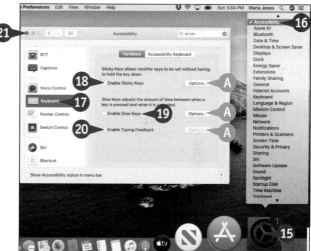

Ⓐ You can click **Options** to configure Sticky Keys, Slow Keys, or Typing Feedback.

21 Click **Close** (●).

System Preferences closes.

TIP

What is the purpose of the Shortcuts pane and the Input Sources pane in Keyboard preferences?
You use the Shortcuts pane to configure keyboard shortcuts for controlling macOS and apps directly from the keyboard. For example, you can set a keyboard shortcut to show Notification Center or to switch to a particular desktop. You use the Input Sources pane to load the keyboard layouts you want to use — for example, adding the Dvorak keyboard layout.

Configure the Trackpad or Other Pointing Device

You can customize the settings for your MacBook's trackpad to make it work the way you prefer. For example, you can adjust the firmness of the click, increase or decrease the tracking speed, and select which gestures to use. If you find the trackpad awkward, you can also connect a mouse or turn on the Mouse Keys feature, which enables you to control the pointer from the keyboard.

Configure the Trackpad or Other Pointing Device

1 Press ⌘+click **System Preferences** (⚙) on the Dock.

The contextual menu opens.

2 Click **Trackpad**.

System Preferences opens and displays the Trackpad pane.

3 Click each feature you want to use (☐ changes to ☑).

Ⓐ You can click a pop-up menu (∨) to choose options for a feature.

4 Drag the **Click** slider, if it appears, to set Light, Medium, or Firm clicks.

5 Drag the **Tracking speed** slider, if it appears, to adjust the tracking speed.

6 Click **Force Click and haptic feedback** (☐ changes to ☑), if it appears, to enable the Force Click feature and vibration feedback.

7 Click **Scroll & Zoom**.

The Scroll & Zoom pane appears.

8 Click **Scroll direction: Natural** (☐ changes to ☑) to have scrolling follow your finger movements.

9 Click **Zoom in or out** (☐ changes to ☑) to zoom by pinching in or out.

10 Click **Smart zoom** (☐ changes to ☑) to zoom by double-tapping with two fingers.

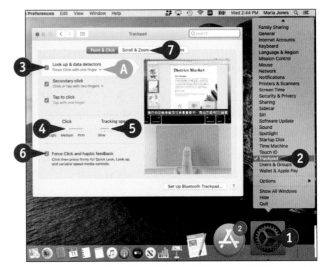

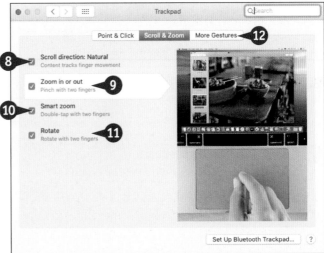

11 Click **Rotate** (☐ changes to ☑) to rotate objects by placing two fingers and rotating them.

12 Click **More Gestures**.

The More Gestures pane appears.

⑬ Click each feature you want to use
(☐ changes to ☑).

Ⓑ You can click a pop-up menu (⌄)
to choose options for a feature.

⑭ Click **Show All** (::::).

The System Preferences pane appears.

⑮ Click **Accessibility** (⊙).

The Accessibility pane appears.

⑯ Click **Pointer Control** (🖱).

⑰ Drag the **Double-click speed** slider to
adjust the double-click speed.

Ⓒ You can click **Ignore built-in
trackpad when mouse or wireless
trackpad is present** (☑ changes
to ☐) to deactivate the trackpad.

Ⓓ You can click **Alternate Control
Methods** and then click **Enable
Mouse Keys** (☐ changes to ☑) to
turn on Mouse Keys. With Mouse Keys
on, you press 7, 8, 9, U, I, O,
J, K, and L to move the pointer.

⑱ Click **Close** (●).

System Preferences closes.

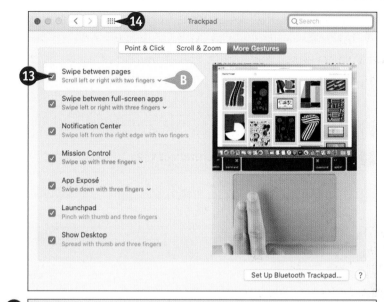

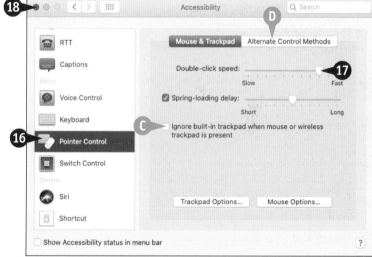

TIPS

How do I configure a mouse attached to my MacBook?
Press Control +click **System Preferences** (⚙) on the
Dock, and then click **Mouse** on the contextual menu.
The options in the Mouse preferences pane vary
depending on the mouse model, but you can always
adjust the tracking speed and the double-click speed.
You can also usually choose which mouse button to
use as the primary button.

**What does the Spring-Loading Delay setting do
in the Mouse & Trackpad pane in Accessibility
preferences?**
Spring-Loading Delay controls how long macOS waits
before opening a folder to which you have dragged
files in the Finder. The delay enables you either to
drop the files on the folder without opening it or
open the folder so you can navigate within it.

Configure iCloud Settings

Apple's iCloud service adds powerful online sync features to your MacBook. With iCloud, you can sync a wide variety of information via the Internet. You can also use the Find My Mac feature or the Find My app on iPhone or iPad to locate your MacBook if it goes missing — or even to erase the MacBook remotely.

To use iCloud, you set your user account to use your Apple ID, and then choose which features to use. If you added your iCloud account when first setting up your MacBook, iCloud is already configured, but you may want to select different settings for it.

Set Up iCloud and iCloud Keychain

1 Press **Control**+click **System Preferences** (⚙) on the Dock.

The contextual menu opens.

2 Click **Apple ID**.

System Preferences opens and displays the Apple ID pane.

Note: If the Sign In with Your Apple ID prompt appears, type your Apple ID and password, and then click **Sign In**.

3 Click each feature you want to use (☐ changes to ✓).

4 Click **Options** to the right of iCloud Drive.

The Options dialog for iCloud Drive opens.

5 Click **Desktop & Documents Folders** (☐ changes to ✓) to store your Desktop folder and Documents folder in iCloud.

6 Click each app (☐ changes to ✓) you want to enable to store documents and data in iCloud.

7 Click **Done**.

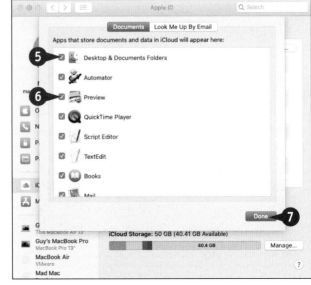

The Options dialog for iCloud Drive closes.

8 Click **Optimize Mac Storage** (☐ changes to ☑)
to store as much of your iCloud Drive on your
MacBook as possible.

9 Click **Manage**.

The Manage Storage dialog opens.

10 In the left pane, click the item you want to
manage. This example uses **Backups**.

The right pane shows the details for the item
you clicked.

11 Use the management features as needed.
For example, you can click a backup, and
then click **Delete** (☐) to delete it.

12 Click **Done**.

The Manage Storage dialog closes.

13 Click **Close** (⚫).

System Preferences closes.

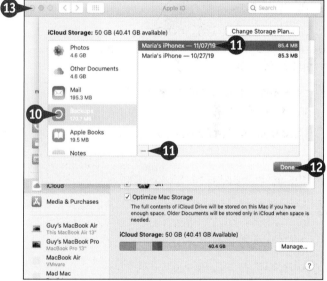

TIP

How do I change my iCloud password?

Click **Password & Security** (🔒) in the left pane of Apple ID preferences, click **Change Password** in the
Password & Security pane, and follow the prompts.

In the Password & Security pane, you can verify that Two-Factor Authentication is enabled for your iCloud
account, or enable it if it is not yet enabled. You can also edit the trusted phone numbers associated with
your Apple ID.

Add a Second Display

macOS enables you to add one or more external displays to your MacBook to give yourself more space for your apps. You connect the display to one of the USB-C/Thunderbolt 3 ports on the MacBook. If the display has a USB-C connector, you connect it directly; if not, you use a suitable adapter. Some displays that connect via USB-C can charge your MacBook; some provide additional ports.

After connecting the external display using a suitable cable, you use the Displays pane in System Preferences to set the resolution and specify the arrangement of the displays.

Add a Second Display

1 Connect the display to your MacBook.

Note: To connect an external display to the MacBook, you may need Apple's USB-C Digital AV Multiport Adapter or a functional equivalent. This adapter provides an HDMI port for connecting the external display.

2 Connect the display to power and turn it on.

3 Click **Apple** (🍎).

The Apple menu opens.

4 Click **System Preferences**.

The System Preferences window opens.

5 Click **Displays** (🖥).

Note: Your MacBook may automatically open the Displays pane of System Preferences after you connect the display and turn it on.

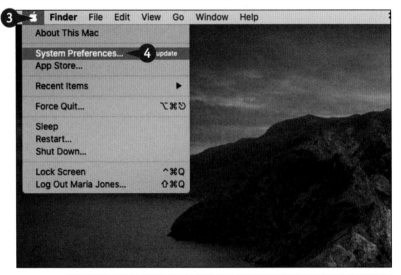

58

The Displays pane opens on each display.

6 In the Displays pane for the external display, click **Display**.

7 Click **Default for display** (○ changes to ●) to apply the display's best resolution.

Ⓐ You can click **Scaled** (○ changes to ●) and then click a different resolution.

Note: If the Scaled box does not show the resolution you want, press `Option`+click **Scaled** to display all available resolutions.

8 In the Displays pane for the MacBook's display, click **Arrangement**.

The Arrangement pane appears.

9 Drag either display thumbnail to match the displays' physical locations.

10 To move the menu bar and Dock, drag the menu bar from the icon for the MacBook's display to the icon for the external display.

11 Click **Close** (●).

System Preferences closes.

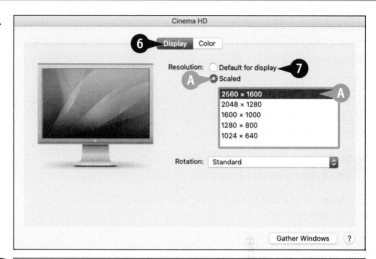

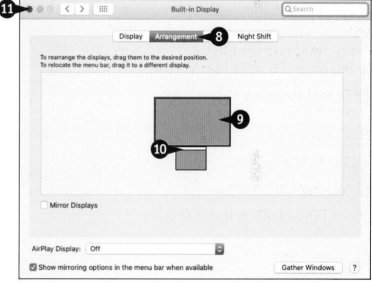

TIP

Can I add two external displays?
Current MacBook Air models and 13-inch MacBook Pro models can support two 4K external displays or one 5K external display. The 16-inch MacBook Pro supports four 4K external displays or two 6K external displays. Check the specifications for your MacBook model to verify how many external displays it can drive.

Using an Apple TV and HDTV as an Extra Display

With a second-generation or later Apple TV — any black model — you can wirelessly broadcast your MacBook's display on the device to which the Apple TV is connected. This is great for watching movies or videos on a big-screen TV, enjoying a shared web-browsing session, or giving presentations from your MacBook to a group of people. To broadcast to an Apple TV, your MacBook uses AirPlay. This technology enables Macs and iOS and iPadOS devices to send a signal to an Apple TV for it to display on a television.

Using an Apple TV and HDTV as an Extra Display

Note: If the Apple TV is not already set up, connect it to a power outlet, to your television, and to your wireless network. Enable AirPlay by opening the Apple TV's Settings screen, selecting **AirPlay**, and setting AirPlay to On.

① Click **Wi-Fi** (📶) on the menu bar.

The Wi-Fi menu opens.

② Click the network to which Apple TV is connected.

Note: Your MacBook and the Apple TV must be on the same network for AirPlay to work.

③ Click **AirPlay** (☐) on the menu bar.

The AirPlay menu opens.

④ Click **Open Displays Preferences**.

The Displays preference pane in the System Preferences app opens.

5 Click **AirPlay Display** ().

The AirPlay Display pop-up menu opens.

6 Click **Apple TV**.

Your MacBook's desktop appears on the television to which the Apple TV is connected. By default, the Apple TV mirrors the MacBook's screen, showing the same image.

7 Click **Show mirroring options in the menu bar when available** (☐ changes to ☑).

8 Click **Close** (●).

The AirPlay Device Code dialog opens.

9 Type the code displayed on the Apple TV.

10 Click **OK**.

System Preferences closes.

11 Click **AirPlay** (🖵) on the menu bar.

The AirPlay menu opens.

12 Click **Use As Separate Display** if you want to use the HDTV as a separate display.

13 When you finish using the Apple TV, click **AirPlay** (🖵) on the menu bar.

The AirPlay menu opens.

14 Click **Stop AirPlay**.

Your MacBook stops displaying content via the Apple TV.

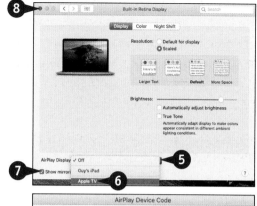

TIP

Why do I not see any AirPlay devices available on my MacBook?

First, check the network configuration of each device to make sure all devices are on the same network. Second, the network you are using may not support the protocols AirPlay uses; in some public areas, networks are designed to prevent streaming of content. If you cannot use a different network, see if the available one can be reconfigured to support AirPlay.

Using an iPad as an Extra Display

The Sidecar feature enables you to use an iPad as an extra display for your MacBook Pro or MacBook Air, giving you extra space for your work. Once you have connected your iPad to your MacBook, with both devices logged in to the same iCloud account, you can quickly move windows between the MacBook's screen and the iPad's screen, as needed. You can also show the sidebar and the Touch Bar on the iPad.

Verify Your iPad Is Supported for Sidecar

First, make sure that your iPad will work with Sidecar. The following list shows the iPad models that Sidecar supports:

- **iPad Pro.** All models.

- **iPad.** Sixth generation or later.

- **iPad mini.** Fifth generation or later.

- **iPad Air.** Third generation.

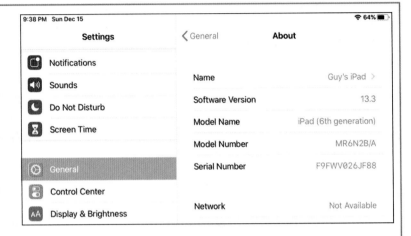

To determine which iPad model you have, tap **Settings** (⚙) on the Home screen to display the Settings screen, and then tap **General** (⚙). On the General screen, tap **About** to display the About screen, and then look at the Model Name readout in the top section.

Prepare for Connecting the iPad and the MacBook

Before trying to establish the Sidecar connection, make sure the following are true:

- The MacBook is running macOS Catalina or a later version.

- The iPad is running iPad OS 13 or a later version.

- The iPad and the MacBook are logged in to the same iCloud account.

- Two-Factor Authentication is enabled on that iCloud account.

- The iPad and the MacBook are connected to the same wireless network.

Bluetooth is enabled on both the iPad and the MacBook.

Connect the iPad and Configure Sidecar Preferences

You can use Sidecar Preferences to connect the iPad and the MacBook and to configure preferences for Sidecar.

Press Control+click **System Preferences** (⚙) on the Dock to display the contextual menu, and then click **Sidecar** to display the Sidecar pane in System Preferences.

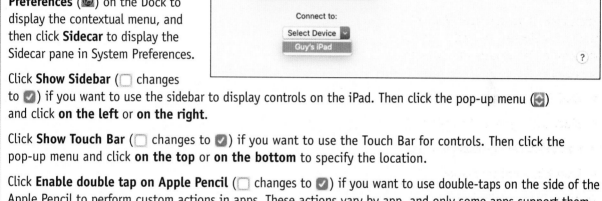

Click **Show Sidebar** (☐ changes to ☑) if you want to use the sidebar to display controls on the iPad. Then click the pop-up menu (⬍) and click **on the left** or **on the right**.

Click **Show Touch Bar** (☐ changes to ☑) if you want to use the Touch Bar for controls. Then click the pop-up menu and click **on the top** or **on the bottom** to specify the location.

Click **Enable double tap on Apple Pencil** (☐ changes to ☑) if you want to use double-taps on the side of the Apple Pencil to perform custom actions in apps. These actions vary by app, and only some apps support them.

Click **Connect to** (⬍) and then click the iPad to which you want to connect.

Move a Window to the iPad

You can move a window to the iPad quickly and easily by using the pop-up menu on the Zoom button in the upper-left corner of the window.

Hold the pointer over the Zoom button until the pop-up menu opens, and then click **Move to iPad** to move the window. macOS moves the window and resizes it to fit the iPad's screen.

You can also move windows to and from the iPad by dragging them. macOS does not resize these windows automatically, but you can resize them manually, as needed.

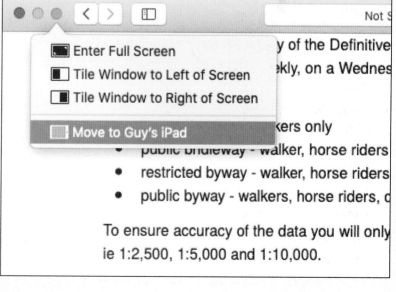

Connect External Devices

To extend your MacBook's capabilities, you can connect a wide variety of external devices. This section covers connecting speakers for audio output, connecting printers for creating hard-copy output from digital files, and connecting external drives for extra storage.

Connect Speakers

Each MacBook model has built-in speakers, but you can connect external speakers when you need greater volume. The easiest way to connect speakers is via the 3.5mm headphone jack that each MacBook model includes. On some models, the headphone jack can output only an analog signal. On other models, the headphone jack can output either an analog signal or a digital signal, and switch automatically between analog and digital depending on the type of cable you connect.

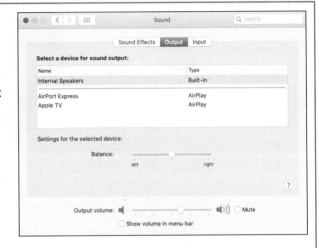

You can also connect speakers via a USB port. For any current MacBook, you need Apple's USB-C Digital AV Multiport Adapter or a similar adapter to provide a regular USB port instead of the USB-C port.

If you prefer not to connect your MacBook to speakers via a cable, you can use AirPlay or Bluetooth instead. For AirPlay, you need either speakers that are AirPlay-capable or speakers connected either to an AirPort Express wireless access point or to an Apple TV. For Bluetooth, you need either compatible Bluetooth speakers or a compatible Bluetooth audio receiver.

Whichever means of connection you use, you can use the Output pane in Sound preferences to specify which audio device to use. To give yourself easy control of audio inputs and outputs as well as the volume, click **Show volume in menu bar** (☐ changes to ☑).

You can then press Option+click **Volume** (◀)) to display a menu for selecting sound output and input options quickly. For example, you can click a device in the Output Device list on the menu to direct the sound output to that device. You can also click **Sound Preferences** at the bottom of the menu to display the Sound pane in System Preferences.

Connect a Printer

To print from your MacBook, you need to connect a printer and configure a *driver*, the software for the printer. macOS includes many printer drivers, so you may be able to connect your printer and simply start printing. But if your printer is a new model, you may need to locate and install the driver for it.

You can connect a printer directly to your MacBook by using a USB cable. Unless the printer has a USB-C cable, you will need Apple's USB-C Digital AV Multiport Adapter or a similar adapter to provide a regular USB port.

After connecting the printer to the MacBook and to power and turning on the printer, press **Control** + click **System Preferences** (⬚) on the Dock, and then click **Printers & Scanners** on the contextual menu to display the Printers & Scanners pane in System Preferences. See if the printer appears in the Printers list in the left pane. If not, click **Add** (+) and use the Add dialog to add the printer.

Connect an External Drive

To give yourself more disk space, you can connect an external drive to your MacBook via one of its USB-C/Thunderbolt ports. If the drive has a USB-C cable, you can connect it directly; if not, you will need Apple's USB-C Digital AV Multiport Adapter or a similar adapter to provide a regular USB port.

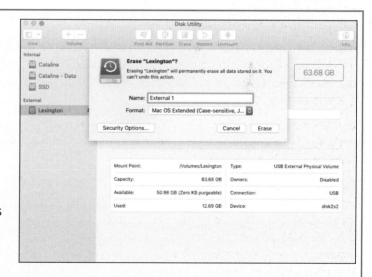

The drive can connect to your MacBook using either a USB standard or a Thunderbolt standard. USB-connected drives are ubiquitous and affordable, whereas Thunderbolt drives offer better performance than USB can provide, but they typically cost more. You can connect a USB drive to any computer, but relatively few non-Mac computers support Thunderbolt.

For best results, choose a drive that is designed for use with Macs. Normally, after connecting a drive, you will find that it appears in the Devices section of the sidebar in Finder windows; if so, you can simply start using the drive. But if you need to store large files on the drive, you may want to reformat the drive using the macOS Extended (Journaled) file system. You can do this by using Disk Utility, which you can launch by clicking **Launchpad** (🚀) on the Dock, typing **disk**, and then clicking **Disk Utility** (🖴).

Explore Other Important Settings

macOS is highly configurable, and the System Preferences app includes many settings beyond those you have met so far in this chapter. This section introduces you to five other categories of settings you may want to explore in order to get the most out of your MacBook: Language & Region, Extensions, Startup Disk, Dictation, and Speech.

To choose these settings, first display the System Preferences window by either clicking **System Preferences** (⚙) on the Dock or clicking **Apple** () on the menu bar, and then clicking **System Preferences** on the menu.

Choosing Language & Region Settings

Click **Language & Region** (🌐) to display the Language & Region preferences pane. Use the controls in the Preferred Languages pane to specify the languages you want to use, and then use the controls on the right side to specify the region, the first day of the week, the calendar type, whether to use 24-hour time, and which temperature scale to use.

Click **Advanced** to open the Advanced dialog box. Here, you can choose a wider variety of language and region settings. For example, you can click the **Dates** tab at the top and configure custom date formats as needed, or click the **Times** tab and set up exactly the time formats needed.

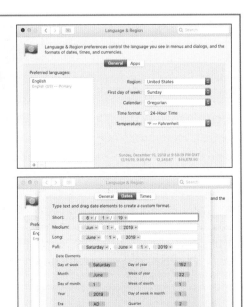

Choosing Extensions Settings

Click **Extensions** (🧩) to display the Extensions preferences pane, which enables you to manage extensions, add-on components that provide additional functionality to macOS.

In the left pane, click the category of extensions you want to configure. For example, click **Share Menu** in the left pane to display the Select Extensions for Sharing with Others list in the right pane, and then select (✔) or clear (☐) the check boxes to specify which items you want to have on the Share menu. Then click **Today** in the left pane to display the Select Widgets for the Today View in Notification Center list, and then select (✔) or clear (☐) the check boxes to specify which items to include in the Today view.

Choosing Startup Disk Settings

Click **Startup Disk** (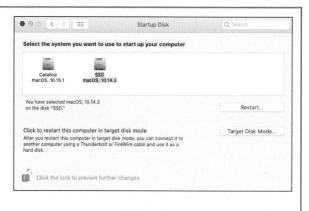) to display the Startup Disk preferences pane. Here, you can choose which disk to use for starting your MacBook. This functionality is useful for troubleshooting your MacBook and repairing its operating system — see Chapter 13 for more information — but it also enables you to switch among multiple operating systems installed on your MacBook. For example, if you configure your MacBook to run Windows as well as macOS, you can use the Startup Disk pane to choose which operating system to start.

Choosing Dictation and Speech Settings

Click **Keyboard** (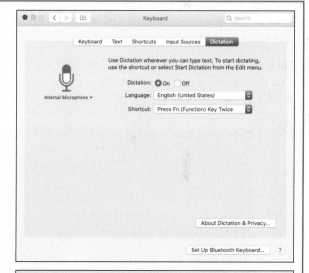) to display the Keyboard preferences pane, and then click the **Dictation** tab at the top to configure settings for dictation. On the Dictation line, click **On** (○ changes to ●) to enable dictation. Click the **Microphone** pop-up menu (▾) and select which microphone to use. Then click **Language** (⬍) and select the language to use. Last, click **Shortcut** (⬍) and specify the keyboard shortcut for invoking Dictation.

To configure Speech settings — having your MacBook speak selected text and notifications to you — click **Accessibility** (⬤) to display the Accessibility pane, and then click **Speech** (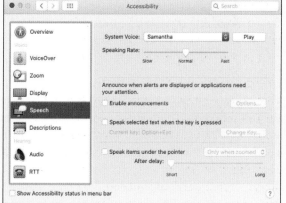) to display the Speech settings.

Click **System Voice** (⬍) to choose among different system voices; click **Customize** on the pop-up menu to download other voices, including novelty voices; and then drag the **Speaking Rate** slider to set the speaking speed.

CHAPTER 3

Sharing Your MacBook with Others

macOS makes it easy to share your MacBook with other people. Each user needs a separate user account for documents, e-mail, and settings.

Create a User Account

A user account is a group of settings that controls what a user can do in macOS. By creating a separate user account for each person who uses your MacBook regularly, you can enable users to have their own folders for documents and to use the settings they prefer. You can also use the Screen Time feature to apply limitations to the actions a child user can take.

When initially setting up your MacBook, you create an administrator account that you can use to configure macOS. You can also create a non-administrator account for yourself for day-to-day use.

Create a User Account

① Press **Control**+click **System Preferences** (⚙) on the Dock.

The contextual menu opens.

② Click **Users & Groups**.

Note: To create another account, you must provide administrator credentials, either by using an administrator account or — when using a non-administrator account — by entering an administrator name and password. To check whether you are an administrator, see if your account shows Admin in the Users & Groups pane.

The System Preferences window opens.

The Users & Groups pane appears.

③ Click the **lock** icon (🔒) to unlock System Preferences.

System Preferences displays a dialog asking you to type your password or — if you are not an administrator — to enter an administrator name and password.

Note: If your MacBook has the Touch Bar, use your fingerprint to authenticate yourself. Alternatively, click **Use Password** to use your password.

④ Type your password in the Password field.

⑤ Click **Unlock**.

Ⓐ System Preferences unlocks the preferences
(🔒 changes to 🔓).

6 Click **Add** (+).

The New Account dialog opens.

7 Click **New Account** (⬍) and then click **Standard**.

8 Type the user's full name, such as Kay or Kay
Renner, and account name, such as kay.

9 Click **Password Assistant** (🔑).

The Password Assistant dialog opens.

10 Click **Type** (⬍) and click the type, such as
Letters & Numbers.

11 Drag the **Length** slider to set the password length.

12 Click **Suggestion** (⌄) and then click a suggested
password.

The password appears in the Password box and the
Verify box.

13 Optionally, type a password hint. See the second
tip for details.

14 Click **Create User**.

The New Account dialog closes.

Ⓑ The new account appears in the Other Users list.

15 Click **System Preferences**.

The System Preferences menu opens.

16 Click **Quit System Preferences**.

The System Preferences app closes.

**Can I type a password instead of choosing one
from Password Assistant?**

Yes, you can type a password in the Password box.
Consider creating a simple password and then having
the user create a new password after she logs in.
This way, you do not know her password, making it
more secure.

Should I create a password hint?

This is entirely your decision. Apple recommends
creating a password hint, but it can be difficult to
create a hint that will help the user remember the
password but will not enable an attacker — who
perhaps knows the user and follows her social
media activities — to guess the password.

Configure Your MacBook for Multiple Users

A s well as letting any user log in individually from the login screen, macOS includes a feature called *Fast User Switching* that enables multiple users to remain logged in to your MacBook at the same time. After you enable Fast User Switching, another user can log in either directly from your macOS session or from the login screen. Your macOS session keeps running in the background, ready for you to resume it.

You can also enable the Guest User account to give a visitor temporary use of your MacBook without creating a dedicated account.

Configure Your MacBook for Multiple Users

1 Press **Control** + click **System Preferences** (⚙) on the Dock.

Note: You can click **Apple** (🍎) and then click **System Preferences** to open the System Preferences window. Then click **Users & Groups** (👥) to display the Users & Groups pane.

The contextual menu opens.

2 Click **Users & Groups**.

The System Preferences app opens and displays the Users & Groups pane at the front.

3 Click the **lock** icon (🔒).

System Preferences displays a dialog asking you to type your password.

Note: If you are using a standard account or managed account, the dialog prompts you to enter an administrator name and password.

Note: If your MacBook has the Touch Bar, you can use your fingerprint to authenticate yourself. Alternatively, click **Use Password** to use your password.

4 Type your password or credentials.

5 Click **Unlock**.

System Preferences unlocks the preferences (🔒 changes to 🔓).

6 Click **Login Options**.

The Login Options pane appears.

7 If Automatic Login is available, click **Automatic login** ( ) and click **Off** to ensure that whoever logs in must use his own user account.

8 Click **Show fast user switching menu as** (changes to).

9 Click **Show fast user switching menu as** ( ).

Ⓐ Guest User is a special account you can use to enable someone to use your MacBook temporarily without creating a dedicated account.

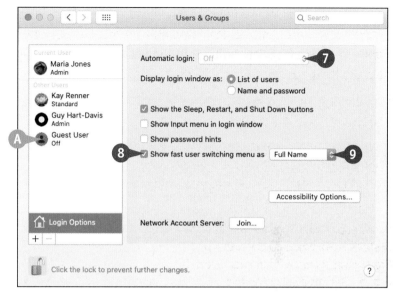

10 Click **Full Name** to show usernames, click **Account Name** to show account names, or click **Icon** to show icons.

Fast User Switching is now enabled.

11 Click **Close** ( ).

The System Preferences window closes.

Note: Fast User Switching uses more memory and resources, so it can make your MacBook run more slowly. If your MacBook runs too slowly, try turning Fast User Switching off. For some MacBook models, you may also be able to add RAM to improve performance.

TIP

How do I set up the Guest User feature?

In the left pane in Users & Groups preferences, click **Guest User** to display the Guest User pane. Click **Allow guests to log in to this computer** (changes to). Click **Limit Adult Websites** (changes to) if you want to limit the guest user's access to adult websites. Click **Allow guest users to connect to shared folders** (changes to) if you want to allow guests access to shared folders.

Share Your MacBook with Fast User Switching

With Fast User Switching enabled, multiple users can remain logged in to macOS on your MacBook. Only one user can use the keyboard, trackpad, and screen at any given time, but each other user's computing session keeps running in the background, with all her applications still open.

macOS automatically stops multimedia playing when you switch users. For example, if another user is still playing music in Music when you switch to your user account, Music stops playing the music.

Share Your MacBook with Fast User Switching

Log In to the MacBook

Note: If your MacBook has the Touch Bar, you can log in using Touch ID by placing one of your registered fingertips on the fingerprint scanner. You do not need to click your username or icon first.

Note: To scroll the list left or right, swipe left or right with two fingers on the trackpad.

1 On the login window, click your username or icon.

A If you have enabled the Guest User account, a guest can click **Guest User** to log in.

macOS prompts you for your password.

B You can click **Back** (◀) to return to the login window if you need to log in using a different account.

2 Type your password.

3 Click **Log In** (→) or press **Return**.

Your desktop appears.

Display the Login Window

1 When you are ready to stop using the MacBook, but do not want to log out, click your name, account name, or icon on the menu bar.

The Fast User Switching menu opens.

C You — or another user — can click the user's name to log that user in.

2 Click **Login Window**.

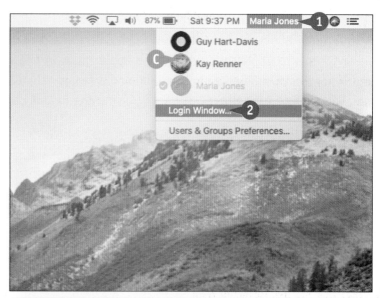

The login window appears.

D Your username shows a check mark icon (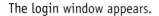), indicating that you have a session open.

Any of the MacBook's users can log in by clicking his username.

TIP

How can I log another user out so that I can shut down?
From the Fast User Switching menu, you can see what other users are logged in to the MacBook. If possible, ask each user to log in, and then log out before you shut down. If you must shut down the MacBook, and you are an administrator, click **Shut Down** (⏻) in the login window. macOS warns you that there are logged-in users. Type your name and password, and then click **Shut Down**.

Set Up Family Sharing

The Family Sharing feature lets you share purchases from the iTunes Store, the App Store, and the Apple Books service with your family members. You can also share an iCloud storage plan; subscriptions to Apple services, such as Apple Music, Apple TV, Apple Arcade, and Apple News+; and other items, such as a photo album and a family calendar. Family Sharing also enables family members to find each other's devices by using the Find My app.

Understand How Family Sharing Works

The Family Sharing group consists of one organizer plus up to five family members. This section assumes that you are the organizer. The family members can be either adults or children.

Each family member must have an Apple ID, an e-mail address and password credential used to identify users to Apple services. Any family member aged 13 or over who does not yet have an Apple ID can create one online at https://appleid.apple.com or by using various mechanisms built into macOS, iOS, and iPadOS. You, the organizer, can create an Apple ID for a family member aged under 13.

You add the family members to Family Sharing by using their Apple IDs. You can either send an invitation via e-mail or, if the family member is present, have her enter her Apple ID details on a device you use for administering Family Sharing, such as your MacBook.

You can administer Family Sharing on a Mac, on an iPad, on an iPhone, or on an iPod touch.

For the services shared with family members, you can specify which members can purchase items, such as songs and movies, freely and which members need your approval. You can designate adult family members as parents/guardians who can approve requests to purchase content.

Access the Family Sharing Controls

You access the Family Sharing controls via the Family Sharing preferences pane in the System Preferences app. The quick way to open the Family Sharing preferences pane is to `Control`+click **System Preferences** (⚙) on the Dock, and then click **Family Sharing** on the contextual menu. Alternatively, click **Apple** (🍎) and then **System Preferences** to open the System Preferences window, and then click **Family Sharing** (☁).

Add a Person to Family Sharing

To add a person to Family Sharing, click **Add** (+) in the Family category of the Family Sharing preferences pane. In the Add a Family Member dialog, you can either add a person who has an Apple ID or set up a new Apple ID for a child who does not yet have one.

For a person with an Apple ID, click **Enter a family member's name, email address or Game Center nickname** (○ changes to ◉), click **Continue**, and follow the steps to authenticate yourself and send the invitation.

For a child without an Apple ID, click **Create an Apple ID for a child who doesn't have an account** (○ changes to ◉), and then click **Continue**. Follow the prompts for authenticating yourself; providing the information needed to set up the child's account; and accepting terms and conditions, such as the Parental Privacy Disclosure conditions.

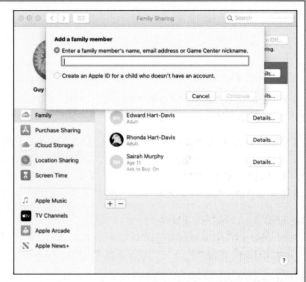

Configure Ask to Buy for a Family Member

To control whether a family member needs permission to purchase items and services from Apple, you configure the Ask to Buy setting. In the Family Sharing preferences pane, click the Family category to display the list of family members, and then click **Details** on the row for the family member you want to affect. In the dialog that opens, go to the Ask to Buy line; click **On** (○ changes to ◉) or **Off** (○ changes to ◉), as needed; and then click **Done** to close the dialog.

continued ▶

If you turn on the Ask to Buy feature for some of your family members, you as the organizer will receive notifications of their requests to buy items. You may want to designate some adult family members as parents/guardians who can approve or deny such requests.

After setting up Family Sharing, you can use the Screen Time feature to apply restrictions to what child family members can do on Macs, iPads, and iOS devices on which they sign in using their Apple ID. The following sections explain how you can set "downtime" for a user, set limits on app and website usage, and apply content restrictions.

Designate an Adult Family Member as a Parent/Guardian

You can designate an adult family member as a parent/guardian who can approve or deny purchases from the services you enable in Family Sharing. In the Family Sharing preferences pane, click the Family category to display the list of family members, and then click **Details** on the row for the family member you want to make a parent/guardian. In the dialog that opens, click **Parent/Guardian** (changes to ✓), and then click **Done**.

Remove a Person from Family Sharing

To remove a person aged 13 or over from Family Sharing, click the person's name in the Family category in the Family Sharing pane, and then click **Remove** (−). The Are You Sure You Want to Remove *Person*? dialog opens. Click **Remove**.

Alternatively, you can click **Details** for the family member, click **Remove from Family Sharing** in the dialog that opens, and then click **Remove** in the Are You Sure You Want to Remove *Person*? dialog.

Once you have added a child under 13 to Family Sharing, you cannot remove them from your family except by transferring them to another family. To transfer a child, the organizer of another family group must request the transfer. You, the organizer of your family group, receive a notification of the requested transfer, which you then approve to effect the transfer.

Set Up the Services Available in Family Sharing

Once you have added your family members and designated any parents/guardians needed, set up the services available to the family members through Family Sharing. Click **Purchase Sharing** (), **iCloud Storage** (), **Location Sharing** (), **Apple Music** ( ), **TV Channels** (), **Apple Arcade** (), and **Apple News+** () in turn, and use the controls that appear to set up the services you want to share with your family members.

Approve a Purchase

When a family member who does not have authority to make purchases tries to buy an item, the macOS app involved prompts them to ask permission to make the purchase. If the family member clicks **Ask**, macOS sends a notification to the organizer and to each parent/guardian. The organizer or parent/guardian can review the purchase and click **Decline** to refuse it, click **Buy** to authorize payment for an item, or click **Get** to authorize a free item.

Turn On Screen Time and Set Downtime

The Screen Time feature in macOS, iOS, and iPadOS enables you to track how much time a person spends using his or her devices. You can use Screen Time to monitor your own usage and set limits on it, such as enforcing "downtime," but you may find it more useful for monitoring and setting limits on what other family members do.

Once you have enabled Family Sharing, you can manage Screen Time through Family Sharing using either the same Mac, iPad, or iOS device that a family member uses or a different Mac or device.

Turn On Screen Time and Set Downtime

1 Press **Control** +click **System Preferences** (⚙) on the Dock.

The contextual menu opens.

2 Click **Screen Time**.

The System Preferences app opens and displays the Screen Time pane at the front.

Note: The first time you access the Screen Time settings, macOS displays an informational dialog. Read the contents and click **Continue**.

3 Click the pop-up menu (↕) and then click the user for whom you want to turn on Screen Time.

4 Click **Options** (⚙).

The Options screen appears.

5 Click **Turn On**.

Other controls appear in the Screen Time pane.

6 Verify **Include Website Data** is selected (✓) to make Screen Time monitor the user's web activity.

7 Click **Use Screen Time Passcode** (☐ changes to ✓).

A dialog opens, prompting you to set a Screen Time passcode.

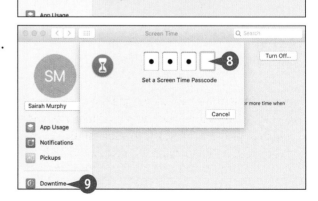

8 Type a four-digit passcode, and then type it again when prompted.

The dialog closes.

9 Click **Downtime** (⏳).

The Downtime pane appears.

⑩ Click **Turn On**.

The Turn Off button replaces the Turn On button.

⑪ If you want to apply the same downtime hours for each day, click **Every Day** (◯ changes to ◉), and then set the hours. If you want to set different hours for different days, click **Custom** (◯ changes to ◉).

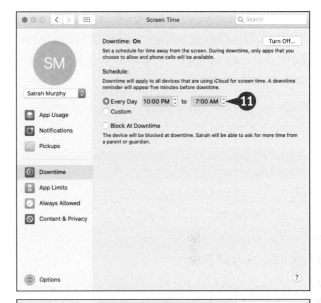

Ⓐ If you click **Custom**, use the controls to specify the downtime schedule. Click to deselect (☐) the check box for any day on which you do not want to use downtime. For each other day, use the time controls to set the hours for downtime — for example, from 9:00 PM on Sunday to 7:00 AM on Monday.

⑫ Click **Block At Downtime** (☐ changes to ☑) if you want to block the user from using devices when downtime starts.

Now that Screen Time is enabled, you can configure other aspects of it, as explained in the following sections.

TIP

Should I enable the Block At Downtime setting?

Normally, it is best to enable the Block At Downtime setting if you want to enforce the downtime schedule you set. The user receives a five-minute warning of impending downtime and can then request more time, which any parent/guardian in your Family Sharing group can grant. For example, you might allow a child an extra 30 minutes to complete homework.

Set Time Limits for Apps and Websites

S creen Time enables the Family Sharing organizer to set time limits for a child's use of apps and websites. These limits apply to all the devices with which the child uses her Apple ID for Screen Time. For example, you might allow the child only a short time for games but allow a longer time for apps in the Creativity category.

You can use the App Limits controls, like the other Screen Time controls, to set limits for your own account if you want.

Set Time Limits for Apps and Websites

1 Press **Control**+click **System Preferences** (⚙) on the Dock.

The contextual menu opens.

2 Click **Screen Time**.

The System Preferences app opens and displays the Screen Time pane at the front.

3 Click the pop-up menu (⬍), and then click the user for whom you want to configure app limits.

4 Click **App Limits** (⏳).

The App Limits category appears.

5 Click **Turn On**, and then type the Screen Time passcode if prompted to do so.

Screen Time enables the App Limits controls.

6 Click **Add** (+).

The Create a New App Limit dialog opens.

Ⓐ You can click **Search** (🔍) and type a search term.

Ⓑ You can click **All Apps & Categories** (☐ changes to ✅) to set time limits for all apps and categories in one move.

Ⓒ You can click an app category (☐ changes to ✅) to affect all apps in the category.

7 Click **Expand** (▶ changes to ▼).

The app category expands.

8 Click the check box (☐ changes to ✅) for the app.

9 In the Time area, either click **Every Day** (○ changes to ◉) and click the spin button (⬍) to set the same time limit for each day, or click **Custom** (○ changes to ◉) to customize the schedule.

Note: Screen Time records the length of time an app is open, regardless of whether the app is being actively used. This blunt measurement method makes it difficult to set effective time limits, because users typically run multiple apps at once and switch among them as needed.

10 If you clicked **Custom**, click **Edit**.

The Daily Time Limit dialog opens.

11 Set the time limit for each day.

Note: The Daily Time Limit dialog does not let you set a limit of 0 hours 0 minutes for a day, but you can set 0 hours 1 minute, if necessary.

12 Click **Done**.

The Daily Time Limit dialog closes.

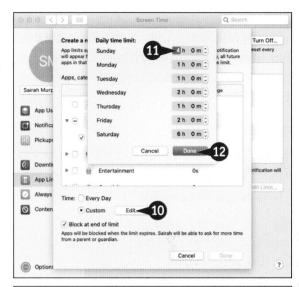

13 To set daily time limits for websites, click **Expand** (▶ changes to ▼) next to Websites.

The Websites category opens.

14 Click **Add Website** (⊕).

An edit box opens.

15 Type the website's address, such as www.wiley.com, and press Return.

16 In the Time area, either click **Every Day** (◯ changes to ◉) and click the spin button (⬦) to set the same time limit for each day, or click **Custom** (◯ changes to ◉) and click **Edit** to create a custom schedule.

17 Click **Block at end of limit** (☐ changes to ☑) if you want to block the apps when the user reaches the time limit.

18 Click **Done**.

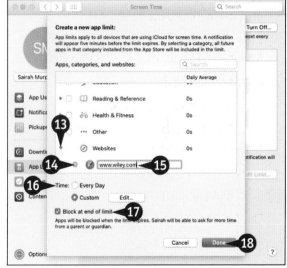

TIP

Why is the Done button not available while I am adding a website?
As of this writing, the mechanism for adding websites is somewhat awkward. After typing the address of the website you are adding, press Return to add the entry to the list. With the new website selected, you can either click **Every Day** (◯ changes to ◉) and set a standard limit for each day; or click **Custom** (◯ changes to ◉), click **Edit**, and set a limit for each day. Every day must have a limit above 0 hours 0 minutes; if any day has a 0 hours 0 minutes value, the Done button is unavailable.

Make Apps Always Available to a User

The Always Allowed feature in Screen Time enables you to make specific apps always available for a user to use even during downtime. You can use Always Allowed to make sure the user always has those communications apps and features she needs to stay in contact and stay safe. You may also want to provide productivity and creativity apps for the user to use when she is blocked from entertainment apps, social networking, and other time-sinks.

Make Apps Always Available to a User

1 Click **Apple** (🍎).

The Apple menu opens.

2 Click **System Preferences**.

The System Preferences window opens.

3 Click **Screen Time** (⏳).

The Screen Time pane appears.

4 Click the pop-up menu (⬍) and then click the user for whom you want to make apps always available.

5 Click **Always Allowed** (✓).

The Always Available category appears.

A You can click **Search** (🔍) and type a search term to find an app quickly.

6 To make the list of apps easier to navigate, click **Sort by Name** (⌄).

The Sort By pop-up menu opens.

Note: The Sort by State option sorts the apps by whether they are allowed or not, putting the allowed apps at the top of the list.

7 Click **Sort by Daily Usage**.

Screen Time reorders the list, putting the most used apps at the top.

8 Click each app (☐ changes to ☑) you want to make always available to the user.

TIP

Which apps should I always allow?

At a minimum, you should always allow Phone, Messages, Mail, and Contacts. Normally, Screen Time prevents you from disallowing Phone to avoid you inadvertently rendering your child incommunicado; likewise, Screen Time discourages you from disallowing Messages, because the child may need to reach emergency contacts. Similarly, you should make the Mail app always available in case of important messages, and keep Contacts available so that your child can stay in touch at any time.

Apply Content and Privacy Restrictions

The Content & Privacy category in Screen Time enables you to choose settings to limit the content a user can access online. After turning on Content & Privacy Restrictions, you can choose settings on the Content tab, the Stores tab, the Apps tab, and the Other tab of the Content & Privacy category.

The Content tab includes controls for limiting access to web content. You can either set Safari to limit access to adult websites or allow a user access to only the websites on an approved list.

Apply Content and Privacy Restrictions

Display the Content & Privacy Pane and Enable Restrictions

1 Press **Control** + click **System Preferences** (⚙) on the Dock.

The contextual menu opens.

2 Click **Screen Time**.

The System Preferences app opens and displays the Screen Time pane at the front.

3 Click the pop-up menu (⬍) and then click the user for whom you want to configure Content & Privacy settings.

4 Click **Content & Privacy** (🚫).

The Content & Privacy category appears.

5 Click **Turn On**, and then type the Screen Time passcode if prompted to do so.

Screen Time enables the Content & Privacy Restrictions controls.

Allow Access to Only Specific Websites

1 Click **Content**.

The Content tab appears.

A Click **Unrestricted Access** (◯ changes to ⦿) if you want to impose no restrictions on the user's access to websites. Normally, this is not wise for a child.

2 Click **Allowed Websites** (◯ changes to ⦿).

3 Click **Customize**.

Note: When you permit a user to visit only certain websites, those sites appear on the Bookmarks bar in Safari.

A dialog opens, showing a prepopulated list of child-friendly websites.

Ⓑ You can click **Remove** (—) to remove the selected website.

Ⓒ You can click **Settings** (⚙) to change the display name or address for the selected website.

④ Click **Add** (+).

A dialog opens for adding a website.

⑤ Type the name under which you want to list the website.

⑥ Type or paste the website address.

⑦ Click **OK** to close the second dialog.

Note: You can now add other websites, as needed.

⑧ Click **Done** to close the first dialog.

Specify Allowed and Blocked Sites

① Click **Content**.

The Content tab appears.

② Click **Limit Adult Websites** (○ changes to ⦿).

③ Click **Customize**.

TIP

How effective is the blocking of adult websites?
The blocking of adult websites is only partly effective. macOS, iOS, and iPadOS can block sites that identify themselves as adult sites using standard rating criteria, but many adult sites either do not use ratings or do not rate their content accurately. Because of this, do not rely on Screen Time to block all adult material. It is much more effective to choose **Allow access to only these websites** and provide a list of permitted sites. You can add to the list by vetting and approving extra sites when the user needs to access them.

continued ▶

Apart from controlling website access, the Content tab of the Content & Privacy category also enables you to choose whether to allow explicit language in Siri and the Dictionary app, web search content in Siri, music profiles — artist information — in the Music app, multiplayer games in Game Center, and the ability to add friends in Game Center.

On the Stores tab, you can choose ratings limits for movies, TV shows, and apps; restrict explicit books, music, podcasts, and news; set app restrictions on iOS and iPadOS; and require a password for every purchase on Apple's stores and services.

Apply Content and Privacy Restrictions (continued)

A dialog opens.

D The Allow list box shows allowed websites.

E The Restricted list box shows restricted — blocked — websites.

F You can click **Remove** (−) to remove the selected website.

G You can click **Settings** (✪) to change the address for the selected website.

4 Click **Add** (+) below the Allow list box or the Restricted list box. This example uses Restricted.

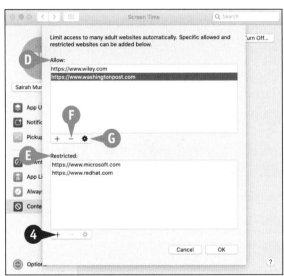

A dialog opens for adding a website.

5 Type or paste the website address.

Note: Although the setting on the Content tab of Content & Privacy preferences is called Limit Adult Websites, you can put any websites you wish on the Allow list and the Restricted list.

6 Click **OK**.

The dialog closes.

Screen Time adds the website to the appropriate list.

7 When you finish adding websites to the lists, click **OK**.

The dialog closes.

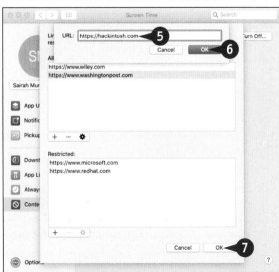

Choose Which Content to Allow

1 Click **Content**.

The Content tab appears.

2 Select (☑) or deselect (☐) **Explicit Language in Siri & Dictionary**, as needed.

3 Select (☑) or deselect (☐) **Web Search Content in Siri**, as needed.

4 Select (☑) or deselect (☐) **Music Profiles**, as needed.

5 Select (☑) or deselect (☐) **Multiplayer Games in Game Center**, as needed.

6 Select (☑) or deselect (☐) **Adding Friends in Game Center**, as needed.

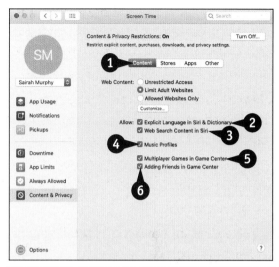

Set Store Restrictions

1 Click **Stores**.

The Stores tab appears.

2 Click **Ratings for** (⬍), and then click the appropriate country, such as **United States**.

3 Click **Movies** (⬍) and then click the highest certification to allow, such as **PG-13** or **R**.

Note: To block movies, TV shows, or apps completely, click **Don't Allow Movies**, **Don't Allow TV Shows**, or **Don't Allow Apps**.

4 Click **TV Shows** (⬍) and then click the highest certification to allow, such as **TV-PG** or **TV-14**.

5 Click **Apps** (⬍) and then click the highest age rating to allow, such as **12+**.

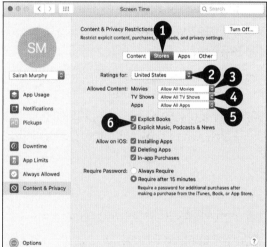

6 Select (☑) or deselect (☐) **Explicit Books** and **Explicit Music, Podcasts & News**, as needed.

TIP

Which Require Password setting should I choose?

For a child, choose **Always Require** (◯ changes to ◉) to make your Macs, iPads, and iOS devices require a password for every single purchase from Apple's services. Otherwise, authorizing a single purchase gives the child 15 minutes to purchase other apps or items with few restrictions. Free-to-play games marketed to children often include in-app purchases that can rack up costs quickly, especially if implemented in a predatory way.

continued ▶

The Other tab in Content & Privacy preferences enables you to control whether the user can configure various key features on iOS and iPadOS devices for themselves. For example, you can prevent the user from changing his passcode; altering Cellular Data settings, such as Data Roaming; or messing with the Do Not Disturb While Driving settings.

Apply Content and Privacy Restrictions (continued)

Set Store Restrictions (continued)

7 Select (☑) or deselect (☐) **Installing Apps**, as needed.

8 Select (☑) or deselect (☐) **Deleting Apps**, as needed.

9 Select (☑) or deselect (☐) **In-app Purchases**, as needed.

10 In the Require Password section, click **Always Require** (◯ changes to ◉) or **Require after 15 minutes** (◯ changes to ◉), as needed.

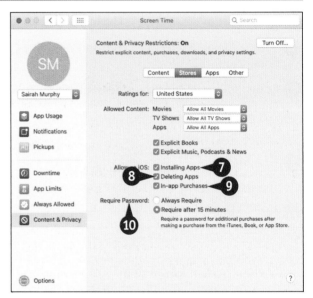

Control Access to Apps and Features

1 Click **Apps**.

The Apps tab appears.

2 Select (☑) or deselect (☐) **Camera** to control whether apps the user runs can access the device's camera or cameras.

3 Select (☑) or deselect (☐) **Books Store** to control whether the user can access the Book Store.

4 Select (☑) or deselect (☐) **Siri & Dictation** to control whether the user can use the Siri and Dictation features.

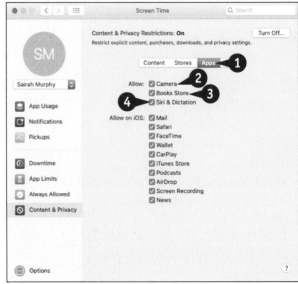

⑤ In the Allow on iOS section, select (✓) or deselect (☐) each item to control whether the user can access them on iOS and iPadOS devices.

Apply Other Content & Privacy Restrictions

① Click **Other**.

The Other tab appears.

② Select (✓) or deselect (☐) **Passcode Changes** to control whether the user can change his passcode.

③ Select (✓) or deselect (☐) **Account Changes** to control whether the user can make account changes.

④ Select (✓) or deselect (☐) **Cellular Data Changes** to control whether the user can change the cellular data plan.

⑤ Select (✓) or deselect (☐) **Do Not Disturb While Driving** to control whether the user can configure Do Not Disturb While Driving.

⑥ Select (✓) or deselect (☐) **TV Provider** to control whether the user can change the TV Provider setting.

⑦ Select (✓) or deselect (☐) **Background App Activities** to control whether the user can change the settings for what apps can do when in the "background."

TIP

What are background app activities?
On iOS devices, the app you are using is considered to be in the foreground; on iPadOS devices, you can have two or more foreground apps at once. Any non-foreground apps visible in the App Switcher are considered to be running in the background; other apps not visible in the App Switcher may also be performing actions, such as tracking your location. iOS and iPadOS enable you to allow apps to perform activities while in the background. For example, Mail synchronizes your e-mail messages with your e-mail providers while in the background, Messages synchronizes your messages, and the Phone app listens for incoming phone calls.

Review a User's Actions

After you, as the Family Sharing organizer, enable Screen Time for a child user, Screen Time logs the actions that user takes when logged in to devices using her Apple ID. You can review the logs of a user's actions to see what the user has done and what she has tried to do. Using this information, you can decide whether you need to adjust the Screen Time settings to allow more freedom or tighter control. You can review the Screen Time logs either from your MacBook or from another device you log in to using your Apple ID.

Review a User's Actions

① Press **Control**+click **System Preferences** (⚙) on the Dock.

The contextual menu opens.

② Click **Screen Time**.

The System Preferences app opens and displays the Screen Time pane at the front.

③ Click the pop-up menu (◉) and then click the user whose Screen Time data you want to view.

④ Click **App Usage** (▣).

The App Usage category appears.

⑤ Click the pop-up menu (◉) and then click the Mac or device for which you want to view data.

⑥ Navigate to the date you want to view:

Ⓐ You can click **Today** to display the current date.

Ⓑ You can click **Choose Date** (◌) and then click the date on the pop-up panel.

Ⓒ You can click **Previous** (‹) to display the previous day.

Ⓓ You can click **Next** (›) to display the next day.

Ⓔ The user's usage data for the day appears.

Ⓕ This readout shows when the data was last updated.

Ⓖ You can click **Apps** to display the usage data by apps.

⑦ Click **Categories**.

Screen Time sorts the usage data by categories, such as the Productivity category and the Reading & Reference category.

⑧ Click **Notifications** (▣).

The Notifications category appears.

H You can see how many notifications the user has received.

9 Click **Pickups** (img).

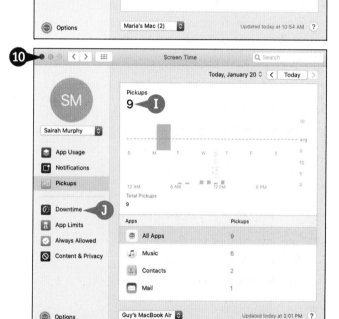

The Pickups category appears.

I You can see how many times the user unlocked an iOS device, iPad, or Mac.

Note: Pickups includes restarts of the Mac, iPad, or iOS device. Pickups appears to be intended as a proxy metric that gives you an idea of roughly how much a user uses his devices, but it is arguably too imprecise to be useful.

J You can click another category, such as **Downtime** (img) or **App Limits** (img), if you need to change Screen Time settings.

10 Click **Close** (img).

System Preferences closes.

Does receiving many notifications indicate a problem?

Not necessarily. Various apps raise a large number of notifications under normal circumstances. For example, the Music app raises a notification displaying the details of each song it starts playing, so it may raise around 15–20 notifications per hour if the user is playing popular music.

However, if a child is receiving so many notifications as to distract him from the computer tasks you encourage, you may want to explore what is causing the notifications and consider changing notification settings, or limiting problematic apps or categories of apps, to reduce the onslaught of notifications.

CHAPTER 4

Running Apps

macOS includes many apps, such as the TextEdit word processor, the Preview viewer for PDF files and images, and the Music app for playing music. You can install other apps as needed. Whichever apps you run, you can switch among them easily, quit them when you finish using them, and force them to quit if they crash.

Open an App and Quit It

macOS enables you to open your MacBook's apps in several ways. The Dock is the quickest way to launch apps you use frequently. Launchpad is a handy way to see all the apps installed in your MacBook's Applications folder and its subfolders. You can also launch an app from the Applications folder, but typically you do not need to do so.

When you finish using an app, you quit it by giving a Quit command. You can quit an app either from the menu bar or by using a keyboard shortcut.

Open an App and Quit It

Open an App from the Dock

1 Click the app's icon on the Dock.

Note: If you do not recognize an app's icon, position the pointer over it to display the app's name.

Ⓐ The app opens.

Open an App from Launchpad

1 Click **Launchpad** (🚀) on the Dock.

The Launchpad screen appears.

To scroll to another screen, swipe left or right with two fingers on the trackpad.

Ⓑ You can also click a dot to move to another screen.

2 Click the app.

The app opens.

Note: To launch an app you have used recently, click **Apple** (), highlight **Recent Items**, and then click the app in the Applications list.

Open an App from the Applications Folder

1 Click **Finder** (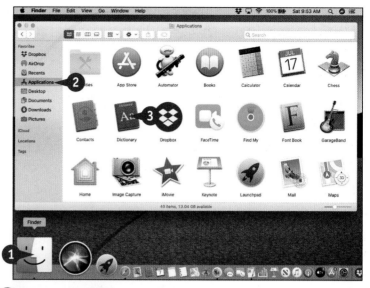) on the Dock.

A Finder window opens.

2 Click **Applications** in the left column.

An icon appears for each app.

3 Double-click the app you want to run.

The app opens.

Note: You can also open an app by clicking **Spotlight** (Q), starting to type the app's name, and then clicking the appropriate search result.

Quit an App

1 Click the app's menu, the menu with the app's name — for example, **Dictionary**.

The menu appears.

2 Click the Quit command from the menu that has the app's name — for example, **Quit Dictionary**.

Note: You can also quit the active app by pressing ⌘ + Q.

Note: You can quit some single-window apps, such as System Preferences and Dictionary, by clicking **Close** (●). But for most apps, clicking **Close** (●) closes the window but leaves the app running.

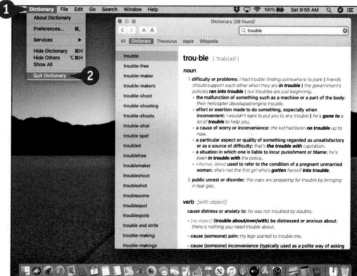

How do I add an app to the Dock?

Open the app as usual — for example, by using Launchpad. Press Control +click its Dock icon, highlight **Options** on the contextual menu, and then click **Keep in Dock**. You can also click an app in Launchpad or the Applications folder and drag it to the Dock.

What happens if a document in the app I quit contains unsaved changes?

Some apps automatically save your changes when you quit the app. Other apps display a dialog asking if you want to save the changes. Click **Save** to save the changes or **Delete** to discard the changes.

Install an App from the App Store

Your MacBook comes with many useful apps already installed, such as Safari for browsing the Web, Mail for reading and sending e-mail, and iTunes for enjoying music and video.

To get your work or play done, you may need to install other apps on your MacBook. You can install apps in three ways: by downloading them from Apple's App Store; by downloading them from other websites and then installing them; or by installing them from CD, DVD, or other removable media.

Install an App from the App Store

1 Click **App Store** (⊛) on the Dock.

A The App Store window opens.

The Discover screen includes various categories, including Apps and Games We Love Right Now and Top Free Apps & Games.

2 In the sidebar on the left, click the category you want to browse. This example uses **Work** (✈).

The screen for the category appears — in the example, the Work category.

B Most categories contain multiple lists, such as the Stay on Task list in the Work category. Scroll down the screen to browse the categories.

C You can click **See All** to see all the apps in a list.

3 Click the app you want to view.

The app's screen appears.

Ⓓ You can view screenshots of the app.

Ⓔ You can read ratings and reviews of the app.

④ Click the app's price button, and then click the **Buy** button that replaces the price button. For a free app, click **Get** and then click **Install**.

Note: If the Sign In Required dialog opens, type your Apple ID and password, and then click **Get** for a free app or **Buy** for a pay app.

The download begins.

⑤ Click **Launchpad** (🚀).

The Launchpad screen appears.

Ⓕ A blue dot indicates a new app installed from the App Store or a recently updated app.

⑥ Click the app's icon.

The app opens.

TIP

How do I update apps downloaded from the App Store?
Click **App Store** (Ⓐ) on the Dock or on the Launchpad screen, or click **Apple** (), and then click **App Store** to open the App Store app. Click **Updates** (🔽) in the sidebar on the left to display the Updates screen. If any updates appear, click **Update All** to download and install them all, or click **Update** for an app to update just that app. App Store checks for app updates as well as operating system updates.

Install an App from a Disc or the Internet

If an app is not available on Apple's App Store, you can acquire it either on a CD, DVD, or other removable medium or as a file that you download. To install an app from a downloaded file, you open the file. To install an app from a CD or DVD, you must either connect an optical drive to your MacBook or use the Remote Disc feature to access an optical drive on another Mac.

Install an App from a Disc or the Internet

Install an App

1 Open the disc or file that contains the app.

If the app is on a CD or DVD, connect an optical drive to your MacBook, and insert the disc in it.

If the app is in a file, double-click the file. This example uses a file.

If the file is a disk image, macOS mounts the image as a disk.

Ⓐ The disk icon appears on the desktop unless you have configured Finder not to show external disks on the desktop.

A Finder window opens showing the contents of the disc or file.

Note: If the Finder window shows a file containing installation instructions, follow those instructions. If there are no installation instructions but there is an installer icon, double-click the installer icon and follow the prompts.

2 If the app uses the drag-and-drop installation method, drag the app's icon to the Applications folder icon.

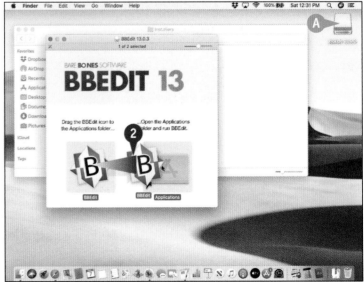

macOS copies the app to the Applications folder.

Ⓑ A new Finder window opens showing the Applications folder.

Ⓒ You can double-click the new app to launch it.

③ If macOS has mounted a disk, drag it to the Trash. The Trash icon changes to an Eject icon (⏏) when you are dragging a removable disk.

macOS unmounts the disk.

The Finder window showing the disk's contents closes automatically.

④ Click **Close** (●).

The Applications window closes.

⑤ Click **Close** (●).

The Finder window containing the installation file closes.

Run the App You Installed

Note: If the app used an installer, it may have added an icon for the app to the Dock. If so, click that icon to run the app.

① Click **Launchpad** (🚀) on the Dock.

Ⓓ Click the dot to display another Launchpad screen if necessary.

② Click the app's icon.

The app opens.

How do I use Remote Disc?

Put the CD or DVD in the sharing Mac's optical drive. This must be an internal optical drive, not an external drive. Click **Apple** (🍎) and **System Preferences**, then click **Sharing** (●). In the Sharing pane, go to the left box and click **DVD or CD Sharing** (☐ changes to ☑).

On your MacBook, click **Finder** (🙂) on the Dock to open a Finder window. Position the pointer over Locations in the sidebar and click **Show** to display the Devices list. Click **Remote Disc**, and then click the appropriate optical drive.

Run an App Full Screen

macOS enables you to run an app full screen instead of in a window. Running an app full screen helps you focus on that app, removing the distraction of other open apps.

You can instantly switch the active app to full-screen display. When you need to use another app, you can switch to that app full screen as well — and then switch back to the previous app. When you finish using full-screen display, you can switch back to displaying the app in a window.

Run an App Full Screen

Switch the Active App to Full Screen

1 Click **Zoom** (⬤).

Note: In many apps, you can also switch to full screen by clicking **View** on the menu bar and selecting **Enter Full Screen** or pressing Control + ⌘ + F.

The app expands to take up the full screen.

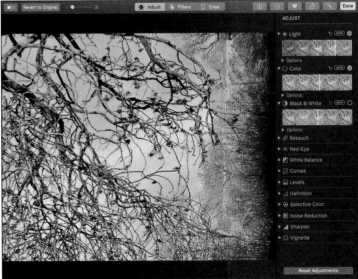

102

Switch to Another App

1️⃣ Swipe left or right with three fingers on the trackpad.

Note: You can also switch apps by using Application Switcher or Mission Control.

The next app or previous app appears.

2️⃣ Swipe in the opposite direction.

The app you were using before you switched appears.

Return from Full-Screen Display to a Window

1️⃣ Move the pointer to the upper-left corner of the screen.

The menu bar and the app's title bar appear.

2️⃣ Click **Zoom Back** (🔵).

The app appears in a window again.

Note: In many apps, you can also move the pointer to the top of the screen, click **View**, and then click **Exit Full Screen** on the View menu.

TIPS

How do I display the Dock when an app is in full-screen view?

Move the pointer to the bottom of the screen; the Dock slides into view. If you have positioned the Dock at the left side or right side of the screen, move the pointer to that side to display the Dock.

Can I exit full-screen display by using the keyboard?

Yes. Press Esc once or twice to return from full-screen view to windowed view. In many apps, you can also press ⌘+Control+F to exit full-screen display.

Run Apps at Login

macOS enables you to set apps to open automatically each time you log in to your MacBook. By opening your most-used apps automatically, you can save time getting started with your work or play. Opening apps at login does make the login process take longer, so it is best to run only those apps you always use. You can configure an app to open automatically either from the Dock or by using the Login Items pane in Users & Groups preferences.

Run Apps at Login

Use the Dock to Set an App to Run at Login

1. If the app does not have a Dock icon, click **Launchpad** ( ) on the Dock, and then click the app.

   The app's icon appears on the Dock.

2. Press **Control**+click the app's Dock icon.

   The contextual menu opens.

3. Click **Options**.

Note: You can also highlight **Options** without clicking.

   The Options submenu opens.

4. Click **Open at Login**.

   A check mark appears next to Open at Login.

Use System Preferences to Set an App to Run at Login

1. Press **Control** + click **System Preferences** ( ) on the Dock.

   The contextual menu opens.

2. Click **Users & Groups**.

   The Users & Groups pane appears, showing your user account.

3. Click **Login Items**.

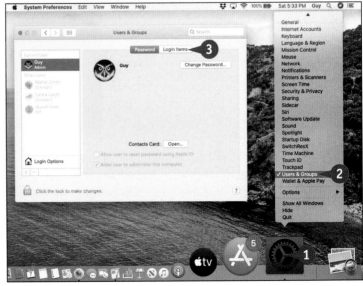

The Login Items pane appears.

Note: If you need to run an app in the background, click **Hide** (☐ changes to ☑) next to the app.

④ Click **Add** (+).

A dialog opens showing a list of the apps in the Applications folder.

Note: You can also add documents to the list for automatic opening. To do so, navigate to the document, click it, and then click **Add**. macOS opens the document in its default app at login.

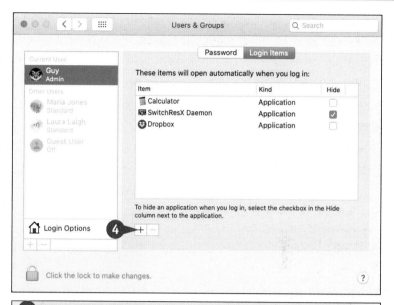

⑤ Click the app you want to run automatically at login.

Note: To select multiple apps, click the first, and then press ⌘+ click each of the others.

⑥ Click **Add**.

The dialog closes.

The app appears in the list.

⑦ Click **Close** (●).

System Preferences closes.

TIP

How else can I add an app to the Login Items pane?
Instead of clicking **Add** (+) and using the dialog to pick the apps, you can drag the apps from a Finder window. Click **Finder** (🙂) on the Dock to open a Finder window, and then click **Applications** in the sidebar. Click the app you want, and then drag it across to the Login Items pane of Users & Groups preferences.

Using Split View

macOS includes Split View, which enables you to divide the screen between two apps. When you need to view two apps simultaneously, using Split View can save time and effort over resizing and positioning app windows manually.

Depending on the apps you choose and the screen resolution on your MacBook, the split in Split View may not be equal. As of this writing, only some apps work in Split View, but macOS clearly identifies windows that are not available in Split View.

Using Split View

① Hold the pointer over Zoom (●) in the window of the first app you want to use in Split View.

The pop-up menu opens.

② Click Tile Window to Left of Screen (◧) or Tile Window to Right of Screen (◨), as needed.

macOS snaps the window to that side of the screen and resizes the window to occupy that section of the screen.

Your other open windows appear on the opposite side of the screen.

Note: The message No Available Windows appears if none of the other open app windows are available in Split View.

Ⓐ A small thumbnail indicates that the window is not available in this split view. If you move the pointer over such a window, the message Not Available in This Split View appears.

③ Click the window you want to position on the other section of the screen.

macOS snaps the window to the side of the screen and resizes the window to occupy the other section of the screen.

You can then work in the app windows as normal.

B You can resize the windows by dragging the handle on the separator bar between them.

4 When you are ready to finish using Split View, move the pointer to the upper-left corner of a window.

The title bar for each window appears.

5 Click **Zoom Back** ( ).

macOS restores the windows to their previous sizes and positions.

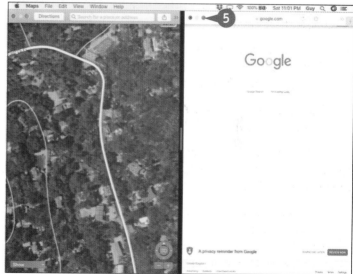

How do I move an app to the other side in Split View?

Move the pointer to the top of the app's window. When the title bar appears, click it and drag it to the other side of the screen. macOS switches the two windows.

Are there other ways to switch to Split View?

If you are using an app full screen, swipe up with three fingers on the trackpad to open Mission Control. You can then drag a window onto the full-screen app's thumbnail in the Spaces bar at the top of the screen. macOS switches the app to Split View on the thumbnail. Click the space's thumbnail to display that space full screen.

Switch Quickly Among Apps

macOS enables you to switch quickly among your open apps by using either the trackpad or the keyboard.

If you have several apps displayed on-screen, you may be able to switch by clicking the window for the app you want to use. If the app is not visible, you can click the app's icon on the Dock. If the app has multiple windows, you can then select the window you need.

Switch Quickly Among Apps

Switch Apps Using the Trackpad

1 If you can see a window for the app to which you want to switch, click anywhere in that window.

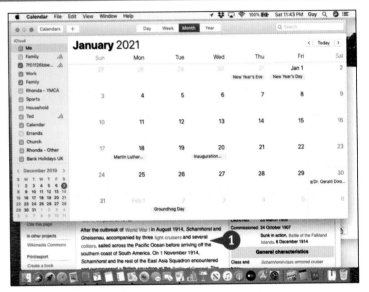

2 If you cannot see a window to which you want to switch, click the app's icon on the Dock.

All the windows for that app appear in front of the other apps' windows.

3 Click **Window** on the menu bar.

The Window menu opens.

4 Click the window you want to bring to the front.

Note: To bring a specific window to the front, press [Control] +click the app's icon on the Dock to display the contextual menu, and then click the window you want to see. You can also click and hold the app icon on the Dock to display the contextual menu.

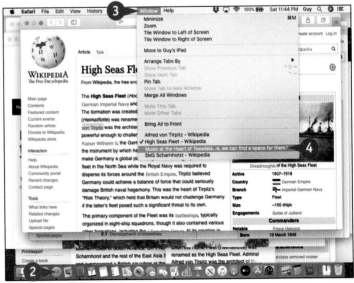

Switch Among Apps Using the Keyboard

1 Press and hold ⌘ and press Tab.

Ⓐ Application Switcher opens, showing an icon for each open app.

2 Still holding down ⌘, press Tab one or more times to move the highlight to the app you want.

Note: Press and hold ⌘ + Shift and press Tab to move backward through the apps.

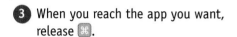

3 When you reach the app you want, release ⌘.

Application Switcher closes, and the selected app comes to the front.

4 If necessary, click **Window** and select the window you want.

Note: You can press ⌘ + ` to switch among the windows in the current app.

TIPS

Are there other ways of switching among apps?
You can use the keyboard and the trackpad — or mouse, if you have connected one — together. Press and hold ⌘, press Tab once to open Application Switcher, and then click the app you want to bring to the front.

Can I do anything else with Application Switcher other than switching to an app?
You can also hide an app or quit an application from Application Switcher. Press and hold ⌘, press Tab to open Application Switcher, and then press Tab as many times as needed to select the app you want to affect. Still holding ⌘, press H to hide the app or press Q to quit the app.

Switch Apps Using Mission Control

The Mission Control feature helps you manage your desktop and switch among apps and windows. When you activate Mission Control, it shrinks the open windows so that you can see them all and click the one you want. You can use Mission Control to display all open windows in all apps or just the windows in a particular app.

Mission Control also shows different desktop spaces, enabling you to switch among desktop spaces or move an app window from one desktop space to another.

Switch Apps Using Mission Control

Switch Among All Your Open Apps and Windows

1. Swipe up on the trackpad with three fingers.

Note: On some Mac keyboards, you press `F3` to launch Mission Control. You can also press `Control` + `↑` on any Mac.

Note: You can also launch Mission Control by using a hot corner. See Chapter 2 for instructions on setting and using hot corners.

Mission Control opens and displays all open apps and windows.

Ⓐ The Spaces bar at the top of the window shows the open desktops and any apps that are full screen.

Ⓑ The current desktop or app is highlighted.

2. Move the pointer over the Spaces bar.

Thumbnails of the desktops and full-screen apps appear.

C To preview a window in an app, position the pointer over the window so that a blue outline appears around it. Then press `Spacebar` to preview the window. Press `Spacebar` again to close the preview.

3 Click the window you want to use.

The window appears, and you can work with it.

Switch Among All the Windows in the Active App

1 Click the Dock icon of the app you want to see.

2 Press `Control` + ⬇.

Note: On some MacBooks, you can also press `Control` + `F3` to display the windows of the active app.

macOS displays thumbnails of that app's windows.

3 Click the window you want to see.

macOS restores all the windows from all the apps, placing the window you clicked at the front.

TIP

What other actions can I take with Mission Control?
After pressing `Control` + ⬇ or `Control` + `F3` to show all windows of the current app, you can press `Tab` to show all windows of the next app. Press `Shift` + `Tab` to show all windows of the previous app. You can press ⌘ + `F3` to move all open windows to the sides of the screen to reveal the desktop. Press ⌘ + `F3` when you want to see the windows again.

Set Up Dictation and Speech

The Dictation feature enables you to dictate text, which can be a fast and accurate way of entering text into documents. The Speech feature enables you to have the system voice read on-screen items to you.

Before using Dictation and Speech, you use Dictation preferences and Speech preferences to enable the features. You can select your dictation language and the system voice, define keyboard shortcuts for starting dictation and having your MacBook speak text, and choose whether to have Speech announce when alerts are displayed or apps need your attention.

Set Up Dictation and Speech

1. Press **Control**+click **System Preferences** (⚙) on the Dock.

   The contextual menu opens.

2. Click **Keyboard**.

   The System Preferences window opens and displays the Keyboard pane.

3. Click **Dictation**.

   The Dictation pane appears.

4. Click **Input** (⌄) and select the correct input.

5. Click **On** (○ changes to ◉).

   The When You Dictate Text, What You Say Is Sent to Apple to Be Converted to Text dialog opens.

   Ⓐ You can click **About Dictation and Privacy** to understand how Apple protects your privacy while processing your speech.

6. Click **Enable Dictation**.

Note: If the Improve Siri & Dictation dialog opens, asking you to allow Apple to temporarily store audio of your use of Siri and Dictation, click **Share Audio Recordings** or **Not Now**, as appropriate.

7. Click **Language** (⬦) and select your language.

8. Click **Shortcut** (⬦) and select the shortcut for starting dictation.

9. Click **Show All** (⠿).

   The main System Preferences pane appears.

10. Click **Accessibility** (♿).

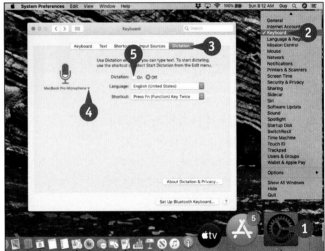

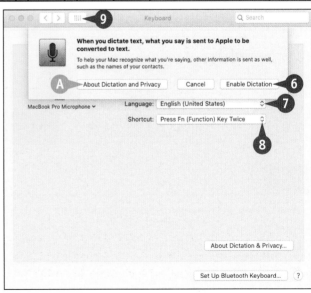

The Accessibility pane opens.

11 Click **Speech**.

The Speech pane opens.

12 Click **System Voice** (⬦) and select the voice you prefer.

Note: You can install other voices by clicking **Customize** on the System Voice pop-up menu.

13 Click **Play** to hear the voice.

14 Drag the **Speaking Rate** slider to adjust the speed if necessary.

15 Click **Enable announcements** (☐ changes to ☑) to hear alerts.

B You can click **Options** to choose the voice, phrase, and delay for alerts.

16 Click **Speak selected text when the key is pressed** (☐ changes to ☑) to make your MacBook speak selected text.

C You can click **Change Key** to set the keystroke.

17 Click **Speak items under the pointer** (☐ changes to ☑) to make your MacBook speak items when you hold the mouse pointer over them.

D You can click the pop-up menu (⬦) and choose **Only when zoomed** or **Always**.

E You can drag the **After delay** slider to set the delay.

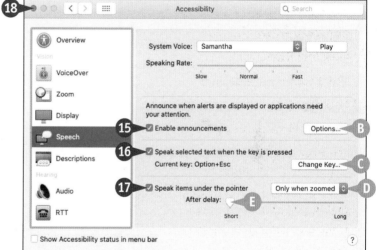

18 Click **Close** (●).

System Preferences closes.

Should I share my audio recordings with Apple?

Whether you share your audio recordings with Apple is entirely up to you. If you do choose to share the recordings, Apple uses the recordings only to improve Siri, Dictation, and its voice-recognition system, not to create a profile of you. Apple stores the recordings only for a limited period and does not associate them with your Apple ID.

Using Dictation and Speech

With the Dictation and Speech features enabled and configured on your MacBook, you can use them freely as you work or play. When you are using an app that accepts text input, you can press your keyboard shortcut to turn on Dictation, and then dictate text into a document.

To make Speech read to you, you select the text you want to hear and then press the appropriate keyboard shortcut. If you have enabled the announcing of alerts, your MacBook automatically speaks their text as well.

Using Dictation and Speech

Use Dictation

1 Open the app into which you want to dictate text. For example, click **Notes** ( ) on the Dock to open Notes.

2 Open the document into which you will dictate text. For example, in Notes, click the appropriate note.

3 Position the insertion point.

4 Press the keyboard shortcut you set for starting Dictation.

Note: The default keyboard shortcut is pressing **Fn** twice.

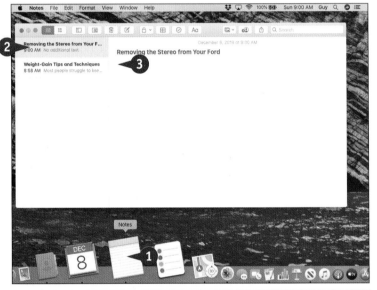

Ⓐ The Dictation window opens.

5 Speak into your microphone.

Note: To enter a word with an initial capital letter, say "cap" followed by the word — for example, say "cap director" to enter "Director." To enter punctuation, say the appropriate word, such as "period," "comma," or "semicolon." To create a new paragraph, say "new paragraph."

Ⓑ Dictation inserts the text in the document.

6 Click **Done**.

The Dictation window closes.

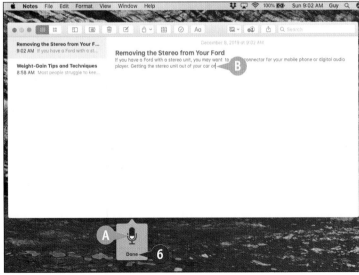

Make the Speech Feature Read Text Aloud

1 In an app that contains text, select the text you want to hear.

2 Press the keyboard shortcut you set for Speech.

Note: The default keyboard shortcut is `Option`+`Esc`.

Speech reads the selected text to you.

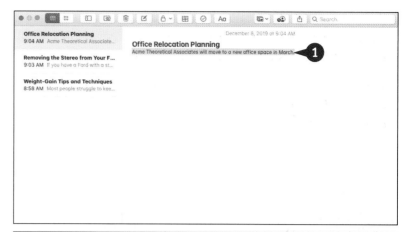

Hear Alerts from Speech

C After an alert appears, Speech waits as long as specified in Dictation & Speech preferences.

If you have not dismissed the alert, Speech announces the app and then reads the text of the alert.

1 Click **Close** or **Snooze**, as appropriate, to dismiss the alert.

How accurate is Dictation?

Dictation can be highly accurate, but your results depend on how clearly you speak and how faithfully your microphone transmits the sound. For best results, use a headset microphone and position it to the side of your mouth, outside your breath stream, to avoid distortion.

When reviewing dictated text, read it for sense to identify incorrect words and phrases. Because all the text is spelled correctly, it can be easy to overlook mistakes caused by Dictation inserting the wrong words or phrases instead of what you said.

Configure and Invoke Siri

The powerful Siri feature on your MacBook enables you to take essential actions by using your voice to tell your MacBook what you want. Siri requires an Internet connection, because the speech recognition runs on servers in Apple's data centers. You can configure several settings to specify how to invoke Siri and to make Siri work your way.

Configure and Invoke Siri

Configure Siri

1 Press **Control**+click **System Preferences** (🔘) on the Dock.

The contextual menu opens.

2 Click **Siri**.

The System Preferences window opens and displays the Siri pane.

3 Select **Enable Ask Siri** (☑) to be able to trigger Siri by saying "Hey, Siri!"

4 Click **Listen for "Hey Siri"** (☑) to be able to launch Siri by voice.

5 Click **Allow Siri when locked** (☑) to use Siri from the lock screen.

6 Click **Keyboard Shortcut** (🔘) and then click the shortcut you want to use. The default shortcut is to hold down **⌘**+**Spacebar**.

7 Click **Language** (🔘) and then click your language, such as **English (United States)**.

8 Click **Siri Voice** (🔘) and then click the voice, such as **American (Female)**.

9 On the Voice Feedback line, select **On** (🔘) or **Off** (🔘), as needed.

10 Click **Show Siri in menu bar** (☐ changes to ☑) if you want the Siri icon in the menu bar.

11 Click **Siri Suggestions & Privacy**.

116

The Siri Suggestions & Privacy dialog opens.

12 In the left pane, click the app or feature you want to configure.

The settings for that app or feature appear.

13 Select (☑) or clear (☐) **Show Siri Suggestions in App**, as needed.

14 Select (☑) or clear (☐) **Learn from this App**, as needed.

15 Repeat steps **12** through **14** for each app.

16 Click **Done**.

The Siri Suggestions & Privacy dialog closes.

17 Click **Close** (●).

The System Preferences window closes.

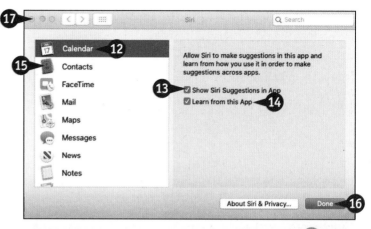

Invoke Siri

1 Click **Siri** (●) on the Dock.

Ⓐ You can also click **Siri** (●) on the menu bar if you chose to display this icon.

Ⓑ The Siri window opens, asking how Siri can help you.

A tone plays to tell you that Siri is ready to help.

Note: If you invoke Siri unintentionally, press Esc to close the Siri window.

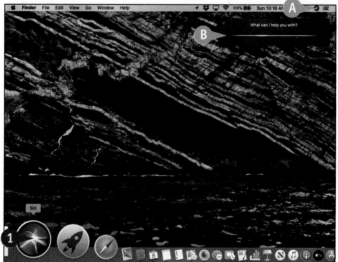

2 Tell Siri what you want to do or research. See the next section for some of your options.

TIPS

Are there other methods of invoking Siri?
If your MacBook has the Touch Bar, you can tap **Siri** (●) toward the right end of the Touch Bar to invoke Siri.

What does the Delete Siri & Dictation History button in Siri preferences do?
This button enables you to delete the data on your use of Siri and Dictation from Apple's servers. Click this button to open the Delete Siri & Dictation History dialog, then click **Delete** to confirm the deletion.

Perform Tasks with Siri

You can use Siri either with the MacBook's built-in microphone or with a headset microphone. You can get good results from the built-in microphone if you are in a quiet environment and you speak loudly and clearly, or if you can speak as close to the built-in microphone as possible. Otherwise, use a headset microphone, which will usually provide better results.

This section gives examples of the many uses to which you can put Siri.

Send an E-Mail Message

Say "E-mail" and the contact's name, followed by the message. Siri creates an e-mail message to the contact and enters the text. Review the message, and then click **Send** to send it.

You can also say "E-mail" and the contact's name and have Siri prompt you for the various parts of the message. This approach gives you more time to collect your thoughts.

If your Contacts list has multiple e-mail addresses for the contact, Siri prompts you to choose the address to use.

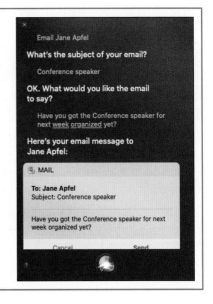

Send a Text Message

Say "Tell" or "Text" and the contact's name. When Siri responds, say the message you want to send. For example, say "Tell Kelli Wilson" and then "I'm stuck in traffic, but I should be there in about 15 minutes. Please start the meeting without me." Siri creates a text message to the contact, enters the text, and sends the message when you say "Send" or click **Send**.

You can also say "Tell" and the contact's name followed immediately by the message. For example, "Tell Bill Sykes the package will arrive at 10AM."

Set a Reminder for Yourself

Say "Remind me" and the details of what you want Siri to remind you of. For example, say "Remind me to take the wireless transmitter to work tomorrow morning." Siri listens to what you say and creates a reminder. Check what Siri has written; if the reminder is correct, you need do nothing more, but if it is incorrect, click **Remove** to remove it.

Set Up a Meeting

Say "Meet with" and the contact's name, followed by brief details of the appointment. For example, say "Meet with Don Williamson for lunch at noon on Friday." Siri listens and warns you of any scheduling conflict. Siri then displays the appointment for you to check.

If you click **Confirm**, Siri sends a meeting invitation to the contact if it finds an e-mail address. Siri adds the meeting to your calendar.

Gather Information with Siri

You can use Siri to research a wide variety of information online — everything from sports and movies to restaurants worth visiting or worth avoiding. Here are three examples:

* "Siri, when's the next Patriots game?"
* "Siri, where is the movie *Spies in Disguise* playing in Indianapolis?"
* "Where's the best Mexican food in Spokane?"

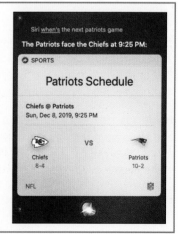

Remove Apps

macOS enables you to remove apps you have added, but not apps included with the operating system. If you no longer need apps you have installed, you can remove them to reclaim the disk space they occupy and to prevent them from causing your MacBook to run more slowly.

You can remove most apps by simply moving them to the Trash. But if an app has an uninstall utility, you should run that utility to remove the app and its ancillary files.

Remove Apps

Remove an App by Moving It to the Trash

1 Click **Launchpad** (⊙) on the Dock.

Note: You can also place four fingers on the trackpad and pinch them together to display the Launchpad screen.

The Launchpad screen appears.

Ⓐ If necessary, click a dot to move to another screen in Launchpad. You can also swipe left or right with two fingers on the trackpad.

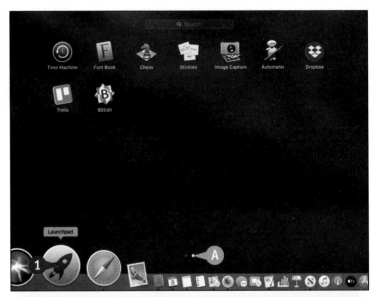

2 Click the app and drag it to the Trash.

A confirmation dialog opens.

3 Click **Delete**.

Finder places the app in the Trash.

Note: You can also drag an app to the Trash from the Applications folder. Alternatively, click the app in the Applications folder, click **Action** (⊛ ⌄), and then select **Move to Trash**.

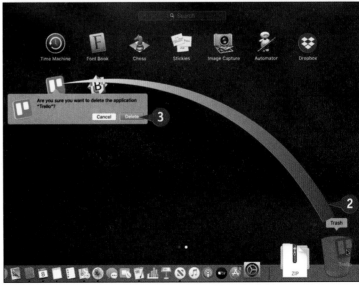

Remove an App by Using an Uninstall Utility

1 Click **Finder** () on the Dock.

A Finder window opens.

2 Navigate to the folder that contains the uninstall utility.

Note: With the Finder active, you can press ⌘ + Shift + A to open a window showing the Applications folder.

Note: See the tip for instructions on where to find the utility.

3 Press Option + double-click the uninstall utility.

The uninstall utility opens, and the Finder window closes.

4 Follow the steps of the uninstall utility. For example, click **Uninstall**.

5 When the uninstall utility finishes running, quit it. For example, press ⌘+Q.

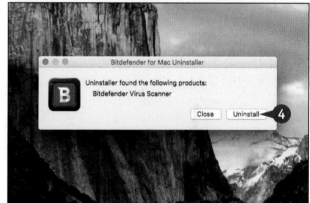

TIP

Where do I find the uninstall utility for an app?
If the app has a folder within the Applications folder, look inside that folder for an uninstall utility. It may also be in the Utilities folder. If there is no folder, open the disk image file, CD, or DVD from which you installed the app and look for an uninstall utility there. Some apps use an installer for both installing the app and uninstalling it, so if you do not find an uninstall utility, try running the installer and see if it contains an uninstall option. For some apps, you may need to download an uninstall utility from the app developer's website.

Identify Problem Apps

Sometimes you may find that your MacBook starts to respond slowly to your commands, even though no app has stopped working. When this occurs, you can use the Activity Monitor utility to see what app is consuming more of the processors' cycles than it should. To resolve the problem, you can quit that app and then restart it.

If you cannot quit the app normally, you can force quit it. You can force quit it either from Activity Monitor or by using the Force Quit Applications dialog.

Identify Problem Apps

1 Click **Launchpad** (🚀) on the Dock.

The Launchpad screen appears.

2 Type **ac**.

Launchpad displays only those items whose names include words starting with *ac*.

3 Click **Activity Monitor** (■).

The Activity Monitor window opens, listing all your running apps and processes.

Ⓐ The title bar shows (My Processes) to indicate you are viewing only your processes.

4 Click **View**.

The View menu opens.

5 Click **All Processes**.

Note: You should view all processes because another user's processes may be slowing your MacBook.

122

B The title bar shows (All Processes).

C Other users' processes and system processes appear as well.

6 Click **CPU**.

The details of your MacBook's central processing units, or CPUs, appear.

D The CPU Load graph shows how hard the CPU is working.

7 Click **% CPU** once or twice, as needed, so that Descending Sort (⌄) appears on the column heading.

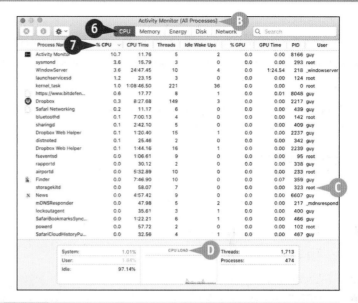

Activity Monitor sorts the processes by CPU activity in descending order.

8 Identify the app that is using the most processor cycles.

9 Click that app's Dock icon.

The app appears.

10 Save your work in the app, and then quit it.

11 Click the Activity Monitor window.

12 Click the **Activity Monitor** menu and click **Quit Activity Monitor** to close Activity Monitor.

TIP

How do I see whether my MacBook is running short of memory?

Click **Memory** on the Activity Monitor tab bar and then look at the Memory Pressure readout. Click the **Memory** column heading to sort the processes by the amount of memory they are using.

Force a Crashed App to Quit

When an app is working normally, you can quit it by clicking the Quit command on the app's menu or by pressing `Control`+`Q`. But if an app stops responding to the trackpad and keyboard, you cannot quit it this way. Instead, you use the Force Quit command that macOS provides for this situation.

When an app stops responding, it may freeze, so that the window does not change, or it may display the spinning cursor for a long time, indicating that the app is busy.

Force a Crashed App to Quit

Force Quit an App from the Dock

① Pressing and holding `Option`, click the app's icon on the Dock. Keep holding down the trackpad button until the Dock menu appears.

② Click **Force Quit**.

macOS forces the app to quit.

Force Quit an App from the Force Quit Applications Dialog

① Click **Apple** (🍎).

The Apple menu opens.

② Click **Force Quit**.

Note: You can open the Force Quit Applications dialog from the keyboard by pressing `Option`+`⌘`+`Esc`.

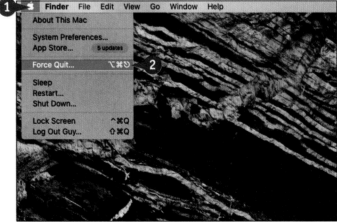

The Force Quit Applications dialog opens.

3 Click the app you want to force quit.

4 Click **Force Quit**.

A dialog opens to confirm that you want to force quit the app.

5 Click **Force Quit**.

macOS forces the app to quit.

6 Click **Close** (●).

The Force Quit Applications dialog closes.

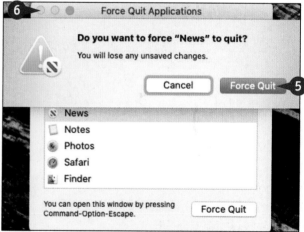

TIP

How do I recover the unsaved changes in a document after force quitting the app?
When you force quit an app, you normally lose all unsaved changes in the documents you were using in the app. However, some apps automatically store unsaved changes in special files called *recovery files*, which the apps open when you relaunch them after force quitting. For some apps, you may also be able to return to an earlier version of the document.

Revert to an Earlier Version of a Document

macOS includes a feature called *versions* that enables apps to save different versions of the same document in the same file. You can display the different versions of the document at the same time and go back to an earlier version if necessary.

Only apps written to work specifically with the macOS versions feature enable you to revert to an older version of a document in this way. Such apps include TextEdit — the text editor and word processor included with macOS — and the apps in Apple's iWork suite.

Revert to an Earlier Version of a Document

① In the appropriate app, open the document. For example, open a word processing document in TextEdit.

② Click **File** on the menu bar.

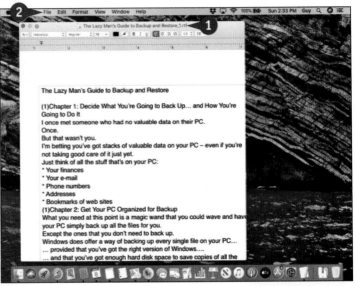

The File menu opens.

③ Click **Revert To**.

Note: You can also highlight Revert To without clicking.

The Revert To submenu opens.

Ⓐ You can click a version on the menu to go straight to that version.

④ Click **Browse All Versions**.

Ⓑ The current version appears on the left.

Ⓒ macOS displays earlier versions of the document on the right, with newer versions at the front, and older versions at the back.

⑤ Position the pointer over the time bars, and then click the version you want.

The version comes to the front.

⑥ Click **Restore**.

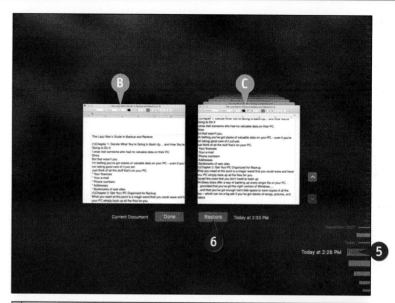

macOS restores the version of the document.

The version opens in the app so that you can work with it.

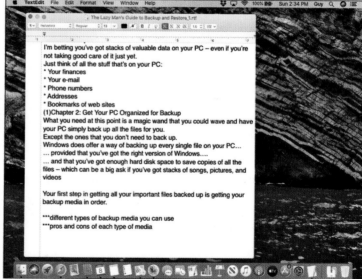

How can I tell whether an app supports versions?
With the app open, click **File** and see if the Revert To command appears on the menu. If the command appears, the app supports versions; if not, it does not.

How can I examine a document more closely before reverting to it?
When macOS displays the document versions, click the document you want to examine. The document's window enlarges so that you can see the document better. Click the background when you want to return the document window to its previous size.

CHAPTER 5

Managing Your Files and Folders

The Finder enables you to manage your files, folders, drives, and even your iPhone or iPad. You can take many actions in the Finder, including copying, moving, and deleting files and folders.

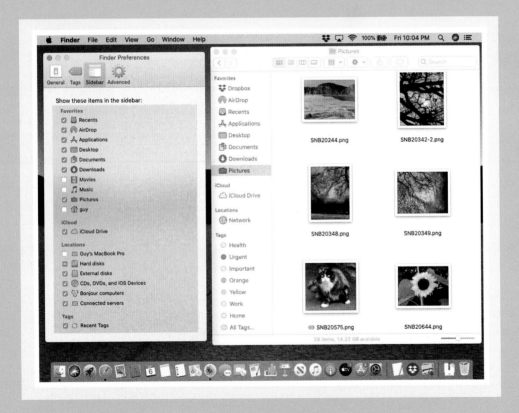

Understanding Where to Store Files

In macOS, your local home base is your Home folder, which is stored on your MacBook and contains folders such as Downloads, Music, and Pictures. Your online home base is your iCloud account, which macOS recommends you use to sync your Desktop folder and your Documents folder across your Macs and your iOS and iPadOS devices. If you choose not to use iCloud, the Desktop folder and Documents folder appear in the Home folder on your MacBook. You can easily navigate among your folders by using the sidebar or the Go menu.

Understanding Where to Store Files

1 Click **Finder** ( ) on the Dock.

A Finder window opens to your default folder or view.

2 Click **Recents**.

The Finder window displays the Recents view, which shows the files you have used most recently.

3 Click **Documents**.

Note: Documents appears in the iCloud list if you accept macOS' suggestion to store your documents in iCloud, which syncs your documents automatically across devices. If you decline this suggestion, Documents is located on your MacBook and appears in the Favorites list.

The contents of the Documents folder appear.

A The Desktop folder contains items on your desktop.

Note: The Documents folder is intended to be your storage place for word processing documents, spreadsheets, and similar files.

4 Click **Go**.

The Go menu opens.

5 Click **Home**.

The contents of your Home folder appear.

Ⓑ The Downloads folder contains files you download via apps such as Safari or Mail.

Ⓒ The Movies folder contains movies, such as iMovie projects.

Ⓓ The Pictures folder contains images.

Ⓔ The Public folder is for sharing files with others.

6 Double-click **Music**.

The contents of your Music folder appear.

Ⓕ The Music folder contains your music library.

Ⓖ The GarageBand folder appears if you have used GarageBand, the music-composition app.

Ⓗ The Audio Music Apps folder contains support files for GarageBand and other music apps.

Ⓘ You can click **Back** (❮) to move back along the path of folders you have followed.

7 Click **Close** (⬤).

The Finder window closes.

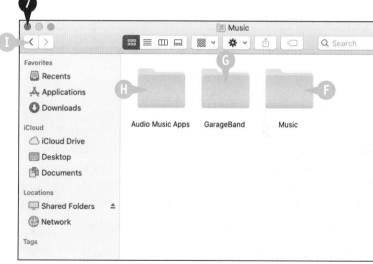

TIP

How do I choose what folder the Finder opens by default?

Click the desktop to activate the Finder. Click **Finder** to open the Finder menu, and then click **Preferences**. Click **General** (▣) to display the General pane. Click the **New Finder windows show** pop-up menu (◆), and then select the folder you want new Finder windows to display. Click **Close** (⬤) to close the Finder Preferences window.

Using the Finder's Views

The Finder provides four views to help you find, browse, and identify your files and folders. You can switch views by using the View buttons, the View menu or the contextual menu, or keyboard shortcuts.

Icon view shows each file or folder as a graphical icon. List view shows folders as a collapsible hierarchy. Column view enables you to navigate quickly through folders and see where each item is located. Gallery view is great for identifying files visually by looking at a preview of their contents.

Using the Finder's Views

Using Icon View

1 Click **Finder** ( ) on the Dock.

A Finder window opens showing your default folder or view.

2 Click the folder you want to display.

The folder appears — in this case, the Pictures folder.

3 Click **Icons** ( ) on the toolbar.

The files and folders appear in Icon view.

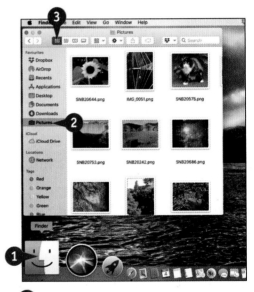

Using List View

1 Click **List** (≡) on the toolbar.

The files and folders appear in List view.

2 Click **Expand** (▶ changes to ▼) next to a folder.

The folder's contents appear.

Note: If the disclosure triangles do not appear next to folders, click **View**, highlight **Arrange By** without clicking, and click **None**.

3 When you need to hide the folder's contents again, click **Collapse** (▼ changes to ▶).

Note: Click a column header in List view to sort by that column. You can click the same column header again to reverse the sort order.

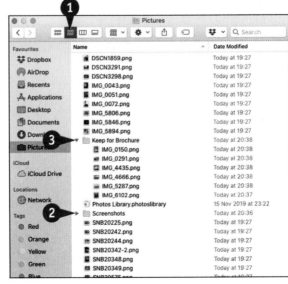

Using Column View

1. In the Finder window, click **Columns** (⊞) on the toolbar.

   The files and folders appear in Column view.

2. Click a folder in the first column after the sidebar.

   The folder's contents appear in the next column.

Note: You can click another folder if necessary.

3. Click a file.

A. A preview of the file appears.

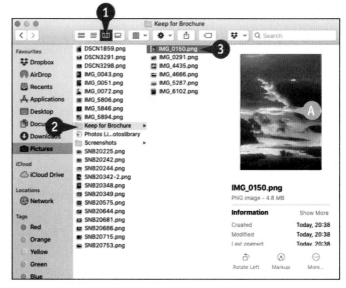

Using Gallery View

1. In the Finder window, click **Gallery** (⊡) on the toolbar.

   The files and folders appear in Gallery view.

2. Click a file in the thumbnail bar.

B. A preview or icon appears.

C. Information about the selected file appears in the right pane.

Note: You can also swipe left or right on the trackpad with two fingers to move through the thumbnails on the thumbnail bar.

TIP

Can I change the size of icons used in Icon view?

Yes. The easiest way to change the size is to drag the slider on the right side of the status bar. To display the status bar, click **View** and **Show Status Bar**.

To set a default size for Icon view, switch to Icon view, and then click **View** and **Show View Options**. In the View Options window, drag the **Icon size** slider to make the icons the size you want, and then click **Use as Defaults**. Click **Close** (●) to close the View Options window.

Work with Finder Tabs

The Finder enables you to open multiple tabs within the same window. This capability is useful when you need to work in multiple folders at the same time. You can navigate quickly among the tabs by using the tab bar.

Finder tabs are especially useful if you switch a Finder window to full-screen mode. You can drag files or folders from one Finder tab to another to copy or move the items.

Work with Finder Tabs

1 Click **Finder** ( ) on the Dock.

A Finder window opens.

2 Click the folder you want to view in the window.

3 Press ⌘+T or click **File** and **New Tab**.

Note: The Finder hides the tab bar by default when only one tab is open. You can display the tab bar by clicking **View** and clicking **Show Tab Bar** or pressing Shift+⌘+T.

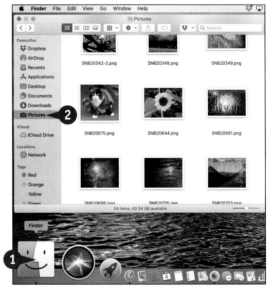

Ⓐ The tab bar appears.

Ⓑ A new tab opens, showing your default folder or location.

4 Click the folder you want to view.

Note: You can use a different view in each tab.

5 Click **New Tab** ( ).

Note: To close a tab, position the pointer over it and then click **Close** ( ). You can also press ⌘+W or click **File** and select **Close Tab**.

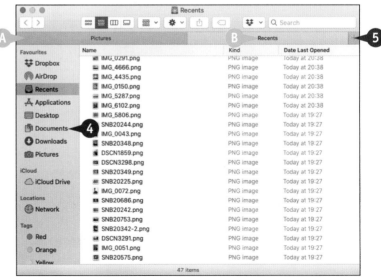

A new tab opens.

6 Drag the tab along the tab bar to where you want it.

Note: You can drag a tab to another Finder window if you want. You can also drag a tab out of a Finder window to turn it into its own window.

7 Click **View** and **Enter Full Screen**. Alternatively, press `Control` + `⌘` + `F`.

The Finder window appears full screen, giving you more space for working with files, folders, and tabs.

Note: To exit full-screen view, move the pointer to the top of the screen so that the menu bar appears, and then click **View** and **Exit Full Screen**. Alternatively, press `Esc` or press `Control` + `⌘` + `F` again.

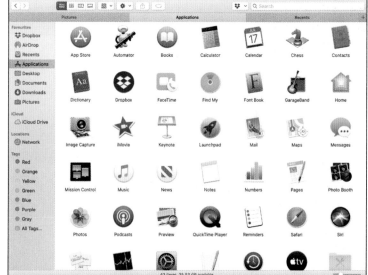

TIP

How do I copy or move files using Finder tabs?

Select the files in the source tab, and then drag them to the destination tab on the tab bar. To put the files into the folder open in the destination tab, drop the files on the destination tab in the tab bar. To navigate to a subfolder, position the pointer over the destination tab until its content appears, and then drag the items to the subfolder.

View a File with Quick Look

The Quick Look feature enables you to preview files in Finder windows without actually opening the files in their apps. You can use Quick Look to determine what a file contains or to identify the file for which you are looking. You can preview a file full screen with Quick Look or preview multiple files at the same time. Quick Look works for many widely used types of files, but not for all types.

View a File with Quick Look

1 Click **Finder** (😀) on the Dock.

A Finder window opens to your default folder or view.

2 Click the file you want to look through.

3 Click **Action** (❋ ⌄).

The Action pop-up menu opens.

Note: You can also press Spacebar to open a Quick Look window for the selected item.

4 Click **Quick Look**.

A Quick Look window opens, showing a preview of the file or the file's icon.

Note: When you use Quick Look on an audio file or a video file, macOS starts playing the file.

5 If you need to scroll to see more of the file, click another page thumbnail or swipe up on the trackpad.

Ⓐ You can click **Open with** to open the file in its default app.

6 To view the file as a full-screen preview, click **Full Screen** (◉).

136

The Quick Look window expands to fill the screen.

Note: To see more of the file in full-screen view, scroll down, swipe up with two fingers, or press Page down.

7 Click **Exit Full Screen** (⬚) when you finish using full-screen view.

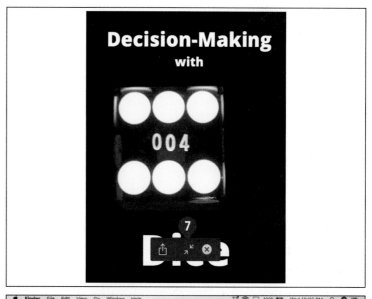

8 Click **Close** (⊗) to close the Quick Look window.

Note: Instead of closing the Quick Look window, you can press ➡, ⬅, ⬆, or ⬇ to display another file or folder.

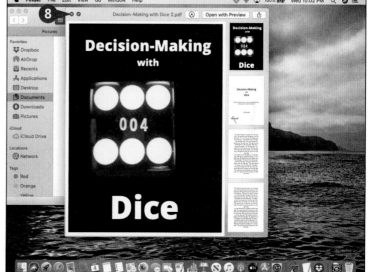

How do I use Quick Look on more than one file at a time?
Use Quick Look's full-screen view, which enables you to browse the files easily. Select the files you want to view with Quick Look, launch Quick Look, and click **Full Screen** (◉) to enter full-screen view. Click **Play** (▶) to play each preview for a few seconds, or click **Next** (➡) and **Previous** (⬅) to move from preview to preview. Click **Index Sheet** (⬛) to see the index sheet showing all previews, and then click the item you want to see.

Organize Your Desktop Files with Stacks

Many people find the desktop a handy place to save files that they need to be able to access quickly. But saving many files to the desktop can clutter up the desktop and make files hard to find quickly.

To solve this problem, macOS provides the Stacks feature, which organizes the desktop's files by the criteria you choose. By turning on Stacks, you create a series of stacks that are easier to navigate. You can browse a stack quickly, find the file you need, and open it.

Organize Your Desktop Files with Stacks

Turn On Stacks and Choose the Grouping

1 Click anywhere on the desktop.

The Finder becomes active, and the Finder menus appear.

Note: The desktop is technically a Finder window, although it looks and behaves very differently from most Finder windows. This is why the Finder becomes active when you click the desktop.

2 Click **View**.

The View menu opens.

3 Click **Use Stacks**.

Finder sorts the documents into stacks using the default grouping, Kind. This grouping creates stacks such as Documents, PDF Documents, and Images.

4 If you want to change the grouping, click **View**.

The View menu opens.

5 Highlight **Group Stacks By** without clicking.

The Group Stacks By submenu opens.

6 Click the grouping you want, such as **Date Last Opened**.

Finder sorts the stacks by the new grouping.

Browse a Stack and Open a File

1 Click the stack.

The stack's contents appear.

2 Click the file you want to open.

The file opens in its default app.

Note: You can also take other actions after displaying a stack's contents. For example, you can `Ctrl`+click a file and then click **Quick Look** on the contextual menu to view the file's contents using Quick Look.

What other moves can I use with Stacks?

You can quickly browse a stack by moving the pointer over the stack and dragging left or right with two fingers on the trackpad. The topmost item on the stack grows larger, so you can see its preview a little better, and its filename appears in place of the stack name. Drag left or right with two fingers to locate the item you want, and then click the item to open it.

Search for a File or Folder

macOS includes a powerful search feature called *Spotlight* that enables you to find the files and folders you need. Spotlight automatically indexes the files on your MacBook and connected drives so that it can deliver accurate results within seconds when you search.

You can use Spotlight either directly from the desktop or from within a Finder window. Depending on what you need to find, you can use either straightforward search keywords or complex search criteria.

Search for a File or Folder

Search Quickly from the Desktop

1️⃣ Click **Spotlight** (🔍).

The Spotlight pop-up window opens.

2️⃣ Type one or more keywords.

Spotlight displays a list of matches.

3️⃣ In the left pane, click the result you want to preview.

🅐 The right pane shows a preview.

4️⃣ Double-click the file you want to open.

The file opens in the application associated with it.

Search from a Finder Window

1 Click **Finder** ( ) on the Dock.

A Finder window opens.

2 Click the folder or location you want to search.

3 Click in the search field.

4 Type the keywords for your search.

Ⓑ The Finder window's title bar changes to *Searching* and the folder or location.

Ⓒ A list of search results appears.

Ⓓ You can click a suggested search criterion on the pop-up menu to restrict the search.

5 To change where Spotlight is searching, click a button on the Search bar.

Ⓔ You can quickly view a file by Control +clicking it, and then clicking **Quick Look** or by clicking it and pressing Spacebar .

Ⓕ You can open a file by double-clicking it.

Ⓖ You can click **Save** to save the search for future use.

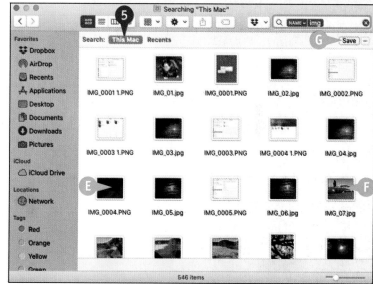

TIPS

What does Spotlight index?

Spotlight indexes both the metadata and the contents of files. Metadata includes information such as the filename, file extension, and file label; the date created, date received, and date last viewed; and the subject, title, and comment assigned to the file. Contents include any text, enabling you to search by keyword in documents that contain text.

Can I change where Spotlight searches for files?

You can customize the list of folders that Spotlight searches. See the next section for instructions on customizing Spotlight.

Control Which Folders Spotlight Searches

macOS's Spotlight feature indexes your MacBook's files so that you can easily search them from either the Spotlight icon on the menu bar or from a Finder window. To improve the search results that Spotlight returns, you can customize the folders that Spotlight searches. You can exclude folders you do not want to search and choose whether to use Spotlight Suggestions in Spotlight itself and in the Look Up feature, which enables you to look up words in documents or web pages.

Control Which Folders Spotlight Searches

1 Press Control+click **System Preferences** (⚙) on the Dock.

The contextual menu opens.

2 Click **Spotlight**.

Note: Alternatively, click **Apple** (🍎), click **System Preferences**, and then click **Spotlight** (🔍).

The System Preferences window opens with the Spotlight pane at the front.

3 Click **Search Results**.

The Search Results pane appears.

4 Click the check box for any item you want to exclude from search results (☑ changes to ☐).

5 Click **Allow Spotlight Suggestions in Look up** (☐ changes to ☑) if you want Spotlight suggestions to appear in Look Up.

A You can click **Keyboard Shortcuts** to display the Spotlight category in the Shortcuts pane in Keyboard preferences. Here, you can disable or change the keyboard shortcuts for Spotlight.

6 Click **Privacy**.

The Privacy pane appears.

7 Click **Add** (+).

Note: Adding a folder to the exclusion list prevents even a search in a Finder window showing that folder's contents from finding matches. This can be confusing to users, because the files are right there and clearly match the search criteria.

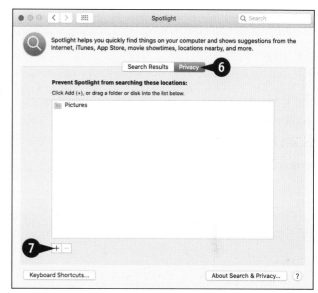

A dialog opens.

8 Click the folder you want to add.

Note: You can select two or more folders by clicking the first and then ⌘+clicking each of the others.

9 Click **Choose**.

The dialog closes, and the folder appears in the list.

10 Click **Close** (●).

System Preferences closes.

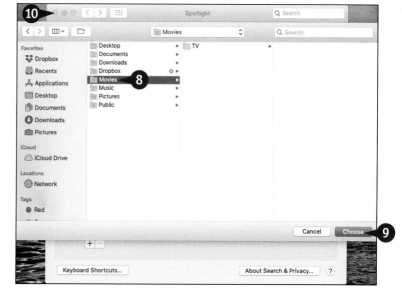

TIP

Is there another way to add locations to the Privacy list?
Instead of using the dialog to build the list of locations you do not want Spotlight to search, you can work from a Finder window. Click **Finder** (🙂) on the Dock to open a Finder window, and position it so that you can see both it and the Privacy pane in Spotlight preferences. Drag from the Finder window to the Privacy pane the folders or disks you want to protect, adding them to the list. You can select multiple items to save time.

Create a New Folder

Y ou can customize the hierarchy of folders in your user account by creating as many new folders and subfolders as you need. You can create folders and subfolders in your user account or in other parts of the file system, such as on an external drive connected to your MacBook or in your iCloud account. macOS blocks you from creating folders in folders or locations for which you do not have permission.

If you want to sync your folders automatically across your devices, create the folders in your iCloud account.

Create a New Folder

1 Click **Finder** (🙂) on the Dock.

A Finder window opens to your default folder.

2 Click the folder in which you want to create the new folder.

3 Click **Action** (✴ ⌄) on the toolbar.

The Action pop-up menu opens.

4 Click **New Folder**.

Note: You can also create a new folder by pressing 🟦+ Shift + N or by clicking **File** on the Finder menu bar and clicking **New Folder**.

Ⓐ A new folder appears in the Finder window.

The new folder shows an edit box around the default name, Untitled Folder.

5 Type the name you want to give the folder.

6 Press Return .

The folder takes on the new name.

7 Click or double-click the folder, depending on the view you are using.

The folder opens. You can now add files to the folder or create subfolders inside it.

Rename a File or Folder

The Finder enables you to rename any file or folder you have created. To keep your MacBook's file system well organized, it is often helpful to rename files and folders.

macOS prevents you from renaming system folders, such as the System folder itself, the Applications folder, or the Users folder. macOS also prevents you from renaming the standard folders in each user account, such as the Documents folder and the Pictures folder, because apps expect these folders to be available.

Rename a File or Folder

1 Click **Finder** (🙂) on the Dock.

A Finder window opens to your default folder.

2 Navigate to the folder that contains the file or folder you want to rename. For example, click **Documents** and then click a subfolder in the Documents folder.

3 Click the file or folder. This example uses a folder.

4 Press **Return**.

Note: You can also display the edit box by clicking the file's name to select it, pausing, and then clicking again. You must pause between the clicks; otherwise, the Finder registers a double-click and opens the file.

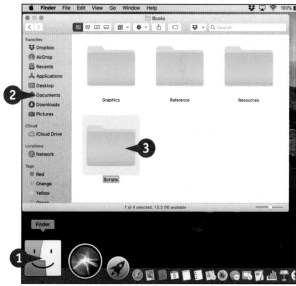

An edit box appears around the filename.

5 Edit the file's current name, or simply type the new name over the current name.

6 Press **Return**.

The file takes on the new name.

Note: Finder does not provide a convenient way to rename several files or folders at the same time, but various third-party scripts and utilities offer extensive renaming options.

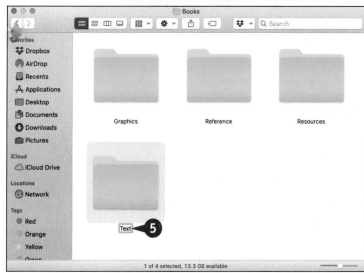

Copy a File

The Finder enables you to copy a file from one folder to another. Copying is useful when you need to share a file with other people or when you need to keep a copy of the file safe against harm.

You can copy either by clicking and dragging or by using the Copy and Paste commands. You can copy a single file or folder at a time or copy multiple items.

Copy a File

Copy a File by Clicking and Dragging

1 Click **Finder** (🙂) on the Dock.

A Finder window opens.

2 Click the folder that contains the file you want to copy.

3 Click **File**.

The File menu opens.

4 Click **New Finder Window**.

A new Finder window opens.

5 In the second Finder window, navigate to the destination folder.

6 Arrange the Finder windows so that you can see both.

7 Select the file or files.

8 Press and hold Option while you click the file and drag it to the destination folder.

Note: Pressing and holding Option while dragging causes macOS to copy the file on a local drive instead of moving the file.

Note: The pointer displays a plus sign (🝣) to indicate copying.

The copy or copies appear in the destination folder.

Copy a File Using Copy and Paste

① Click **Finder** (![icon]) on the Dock.

A Finder window opens.

② Click the folder that contains the file you want to copy.

③ Click the file.

Note: You can also copy the selected item by pressing ⌘+C and paste the copied or cut item by pressing ⌘+V.

④ Click **Action** (✱ ⌄).

The Action pop-up menu opens.

⑤ Click **Copy**.

Finder copies the file's details to the clipboard.

⑥ Click the folder in which you want to create the copy.

⑦ Click **Action** (✱ ⌄).

The Action pop-up menu opens.

⑧ Click **Paste Item**.

A copy of the file appears in the destination folder.

Note: You can use the Paste command in either the same Finder window or tab or another Finder window or tab — whichever you find more convenient.

How do I copy a folder?

Use the same techniques as for files: Either press Option +drag the folder or folders to the destination folder, or use the Copy command to copy the folder and the Paste command to paste it into the destination folder.

Can I make a copy of a file in the same folder as the original?

Yes. To do this, click the file, click **Action** (✱ ⌄), and then click **Duplicate**. Finder automatically adds *copy* to the end of the copy's filename to distinguish it from the original.

Move a File

The Finder makes it easy to move a file from one folder to another. You can move a file quickly by clicking it in its current folder and then dragging it to the destination folder.

When the destination folder is on the same drive as the source folder, the Finder moves the file to that folder. But when the destination folder is on a different drive, the Finder copies the file by default. To override this and move the file, you press ⌘ as you drag.

Move a File

Move a File Between Folders on the Same Drive

1 Click **Finder** (🙂) on the Dock.

A Finder window opens.

2 Click the folder that contains the file you want to move.

3 Click **File**.

The File menu opens.

4 Click **New Finder Window**.

A new Finder window opens.

5 In the second Finder window, open the destination folder.

6 Arrange the Finder windows so that you can see both.

7 Click the file and drag it to the destination folder.

The file appears in the destination folder and disappears from the source folder.

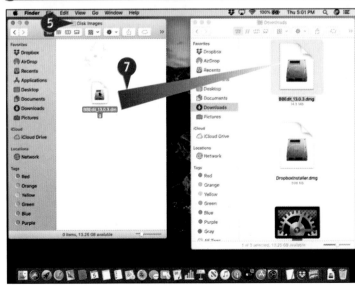

Move a File from One Drive to Another

1 Click **Finder** ( ) on the Dock.

A Finder window opens.

2 Click the folder that contains the file you want to move.

3 Press Control + click **Finder** ( ) on the Dock.

The contextual menu opens.

4 Click **New Finder Window**.

A new Finder window opens.

5 In the second Finder window, click the drive to which you want to copy the file.

6 Click the destination folder.

7 Arrange the Finder windows so that you can see both.

8 Press and hold ⌘ while you click the file and drag it to the destination folder.

The file appears in the destination folder and disappears from the source folder.

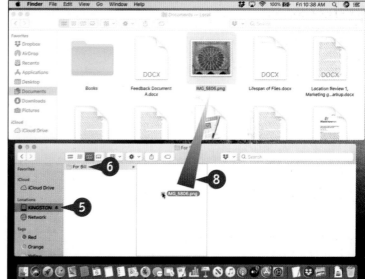

TIP

Can I move files by using menu commands rather than clicking and dragging?
If you find it awkward to drag files from one folder to another, you can use menu commands instead. Select the file or files you want to move, and then click **Edit** and **Copy** to copy them. Open the destination folder and click **Edit** to open the Edit menu. Press and hold Option and click **Move Item Here** or **Move Items Here**.

View the Information About a File or Folder

macOS keeps a large amount of information about each file and folder. When you view the file or folder in most Finder views, you can see the item's name and some basic information about it, such as its kind, size, and date last modified.

To see more information about the file or folder, you can open the Info window. This window contains multiple sections that you can expand by clicking **Expand** (▶) or collapse by clicking **Collapse** (▼).

View the Information About a File or Folder

1 Click **Finder** (🙂) on the Dock.

A Finder window opens.

2 Click the folder that contains the file whose info you want to view.

3 Click the file.

4 Click **Action** (✳ ▾).

The Action pop-up menu opens.

5 Click **Get Info**.

Note: You can also open the Info window for the selected item by pressing ⌘+Ⓘ.

The Info window opens.

6 View the preview.

7 Review the tags. Press Return to add tags.

Note: If your MacBook has the Touch Bar, you can apply tags using the Touch Bar.

Note: See the next section, "Organize Your Files with Tags," for more on tags.

8 Review the general information: *Kind* shows the file's type. *Size* shows the file's size on disk. *Where* shows the folder that contains the file. *Created* shows when the file was created. *Modified* shows when the file was last changed.

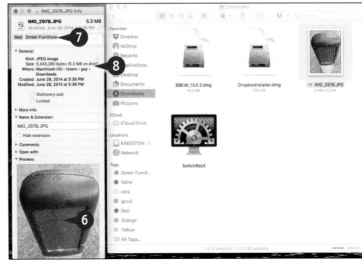

9 Review the details in the More Info section.

Note: The More Info details are especially useful for photos.

Ⓐ You can change the filename or extension. Normally, though, it is best not to change the extension.

10 Click **Hide extension** (☐ changes to ☑) if you want to hide the extension.

11 Type any comments to help identify the file.

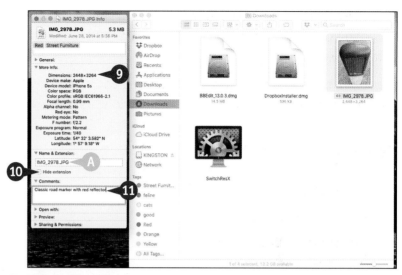

12 Click **Open with** (⬦) and select the app with which to open this file.

13 Click **Change All** if you want to use the app for all files of this type.

14 Click **Close** (●).

The Info window closes.

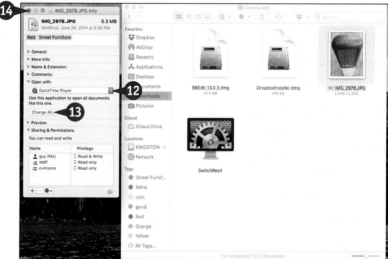

TIP

How do I use the Sharing & Permissions settings?
To adjust the permissions for the file or folder, click the Privilege row for the user or group you want to affect. You can then select the appropriate level of permissions: **Read & Write**, **Read only**, or **No Access**. Click **Add** (+) to add a user or group to the list. Click **Remove** (−) to remove the selected user or group from the list.

Organize Your Files with Tags

You can organize your files and folders by giving them descriptive names and storing them in appropriate places. But macOS and its apps give you another means of organizing your files and folders: tags.

macOS includes a set of default tags that you can customize to better describe your projects. You can then apply one or more tags to a file to enable you to locate it more easily either on your MacBook or in iCloud.

Organize Your Files with Tags

Customize Your Tags

1 Click the desktop.

The Finder becomes active.

2 Click **Finder**.

The Finder menu opens.

3 Click **Preferences**.

The Finder Preferences window opens.

4 Click **Tags** ( ).

The Tags pane appears.

5 Click a tag you want to rename, type the new name in the edit box that appears, and then press Return.

6 Click the check box (☐ changes to ✓) to make the tag appear in the list in the Finder.

7 Drag the tags into the order in which you want them to appear.

8 Drag tags to the Favorite Tags list at the bottom to control which tags appear in Finder menus.

Ⓐ You can click **Add** (+) to add a new tag to the list.

9 Click **Close** ( ).

The Finder Preferences window closes.

Apply Tags to Files and Folders

1 If the Tags section of the sidebar is not displayed, position the pointer over Tags and click **Show**.

2 Click the file or folder and drag it to the appropriate tag.

Finder applies the tag.

Note: You can also apply tags from the File menu or from the contextual menu.

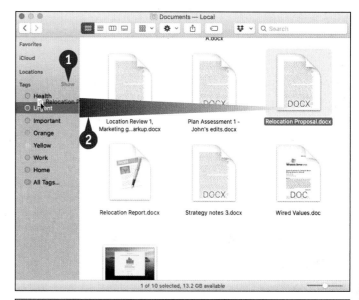

View Files and Folders by Tags

1 If the Tags section of the sidebar is not displayed, position the pointer over Tags and click **Show** when it appears.

2 Click the appropriate tag.

B The Finder window shows the tagged files and folders.

How do I apply tags to a new document I create?

In the app, click **File** and **Save** or press ⌘ + S to display the Save As dialog. Type the filename, then click **Tags** and click each tag you want to apply. You can then choose the folder in which to save the document and click **Save** to save it.

Work with Zip Files

macOS includes a compression tool that enables you to shrink files. Compression is especially useful for files you need to transfer across the Internet, place on a limited-capacity medium such as a USB drive, or archive for storage.

Using the Finder, you can compress a single file or multiple files. Compressing creates a compressed file in the widely used Zip format, often called a *Zip file*, that contains a copy of the files. The original files remain unchanged.

Work with Zip Files

Compress Files to a Zip File

1. Click **Finder** (⬚) on the Dock.

   A Finder window opens.

2. Click the folder that contains the file or files you want to compress.

3. Select the file or files.

4. Click **Action** (✳ ⌄).

   The Action pop-up menu opens.

5. Click **Compress**.

Ⓐ The compressed file appears in the folder.

Note: If you selected one file, macOS gives the file the same name with the .zip extension. If you selected multiple files, macOS names the Zip file Archive.zip.

6. Click the file and press Return.

   An edit box appears.

7. Type the new name and press Return.

   The file takes on the new name.

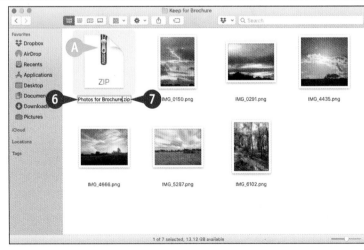

Extract Files from a Zip File

1 Click **Finder** ( ) on the Dock.

A Finder window opens.

2 Click the folder that contains the Zip file.

Note: If you receive the Zip file attached to an e-mail message, save the file as explained in Chapter 7.

3 Double-click the Zip file.

Archive Utility unzips the Zip file, creates a folder with the same name as the Zip file, and places the contents of the Zip file in it.

4 Click the new folder to see the files extracted from the Zip file.

TIP

When I compress a music file, the Zip file is bigger than the original file. What have I done wrong?
You have done nothing wrong. Compression removes extra space from the file, and can squeeze some graphics and text files down by as much as 90 percent. But if you try to compress an already compressed file, such as an MP3 audio file or an MPEG video file, Archive Utility cannot compress it further — and the Zip file packaging adds a small amount to the file size.

Using the Trash

macOS provides a special folder called the Trash in which you can place files and folders you intend to delete. Like a real-world trash can, the Trash retains files until you actually empty it. So if you find you have thrown away a file that you need after all, you can recover the file from the Trash. The Trash icon appears at the right end of the Dock by default, giving you quick access to the Trash and an easy way to eject removable media, which you must remove from the macOS file system before physically disconnecting.

Using the Trash

Place a File in the Trash

1 Click **Finder** (🙂) on the Dock.

A Finder window opens to your default folder or view.

2 Click the folder that contains the file you want to throw in the Trash.

3 Click the file you want to delete.

4 Click **Action** (✳ ⌄).

The Action pop-up menu opens.

5 Click **Move to Trash**.

🅐 The file disappears from the folder and moves to the Trash.

Note: You can also place a file in the Trash by clicking and dragging it to the Trash icon on the Dock, or from the keyboard by clicking the file and then pressing ⌘+Del.

Recover a File from the Trash

1 Click **Trash** (🗑) on the Dock.

The Trash window opens.

Note: You can use Quick Look to examine a file in the Trash. For example, click the file and press `Spacebar` to open the Quick Look window. However, you cannot open a file from the Trash; to open a file, you must first remove it from the Trash, putting it in either its original folder or another folder.

2 Click the file you want to recover.

3 Click **Action** (⚙ ⌄).

The Action pop-up menu opens.

4 Click **Put Back**.

The Finder restores the file to its previous folder.

Note: If you want to put the file in a different folder, drag it to that folder. For example, drag the file to the desktop.

5 Click **Close** (●) or press ⌘+W.

The Trash window closes.

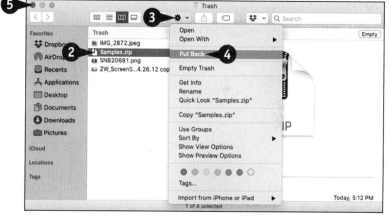

TIP

What else can I do with the Trash?

You can use the Trash to eject a removable disk, CD, or DVD in an optical drive you have connected to your MacBook. When you click a removable disk, CD, or DVD and drag it toward the Trash, the Trash icon changes to an Eject icon (⏏). Drop the item on the Eject icon to eject it. When you drag a recordable CD or DVD to which you have added files toward the Trash, macOS displays a Burn icon (☢). Drop the disc on the Burn icon to start burning it.

Customize the Finder Toolbar

The toolbar that appears at the top of the Finder window contains buttons that you can use to access commands quickly and easily. For example, the various View buttons appear there along with the Action menu button. The Finder toolbar includes a useful set of buttons by default, but you can configure the toolbar so that it contains the buttons you use most frequently.

Customize the Finder Toolbar

1 Click **Finder** () on the Dock.

A Finder window opens to your default folder or view.

2 Click **View**.

The View menu opens.

3 Click **Customize Toolbar**.

The Customize Toolbar dialog opens.

4 To add a button to the toolbar, drag it from the Customize Toolbar dialog and drop it on the toolbar where you want it to appear.

Note: You can click a button on the toolbar and drag it to a new position.

A If you need to restore the toolbar to its original state, click the **. . . or drag the default set into the toolbar** box and drag it to the toolbar.

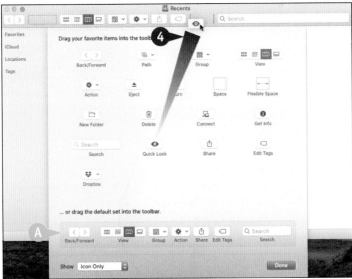

The button appears on the toolbar.

5 To remove a button from the toolbar, drag its icon from the toolbar into the Customize Toolbar dialog.

6 Click **Show** (⬦) and then click the appearance you want: **Icon and Text**, **Icon Only**, or **Text Only**.

7 Click **Done**.

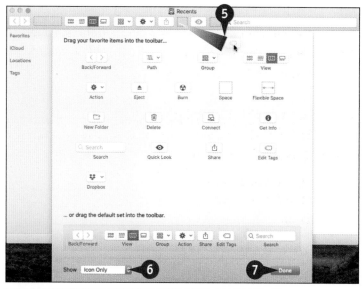

The Customize Toolbar dialog closes.

The Finder toolbar appears in its customized form.

Note: If your MacBook has the Touch Bar, you can customize its contents by clicking **View**, clicking **Customize Touch Bar**, and then working in the Customize Touch Bar dialog that opens. Click **Done** when you are finished.

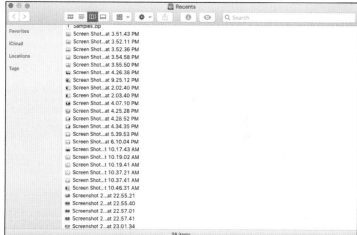

What does the Path button do?

The Path button enables you to easily see and navigate the path to the folder the Finder window is displaying. The path appears as a vertical menu of locations starting from the active folder — for example, New : Documents : Maria : Users : Macintosh HD : MacBook Air. You can also display the path by pressing ⌘+clicking the location name in the title bar.

How do I use the Space item and the Flexible Space item?

Drag a Space item to where you need a fixed amount of space on the toolbar. Drag a Flexible Space item to where you need a space whose width will adjust automatically depending on the number of other controls on the toolbar.

Customize the Sidebar

The sidebar on the left side of Finder windows gives you quick access to files, folders, and apps. You can customize the sidebar from its default contents to make it contain only the items you find most useful.

The sidebar contains four sections. Favorites are items you access frequently. iCloud includes your iCloud Drive, plus your Desktop folder and Documents folder if you choose to store these in iCloud. Locations include your MacBook, hard disks, external disks and optical drives, computers running the Bonjour sharing protocol, and connected servers. Tags shows your list of tags for identifying and accessing items.

Customize the Sidebar

1 Click **Finder** ( ) on the Dock.

A Finder window opens to your default folder or view.

Note: If the sidebar does not appear, click **View**, and then click **Show Sidebar**. Alternatively, press ⌘ + Option + S.

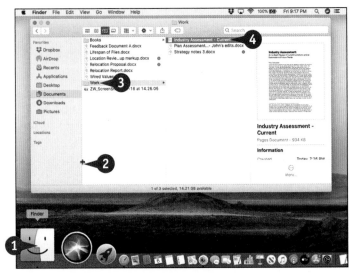

2 Optionally, move the pointer over the border of the sidebar, then drag to change the width.

3 Click the folder that contains the item you want to add to the sidebar.

4 Click the item you want to add.

5 Click **File**.

The File menu opens.

6 Click **Add to Sidebar**.

The item appears at the bottom of the sidebar.

7 Optionally, click the item and drag it to a different position on the sidebar.

The item appears in its new position.

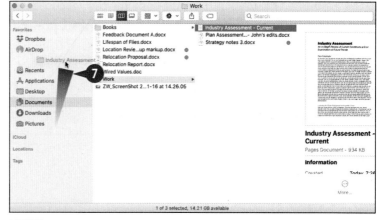

8 To remove an item from the sidebar, press **Control** +click the item.

The contextual menu opens.

9 Click **Remove from Sidebar**.

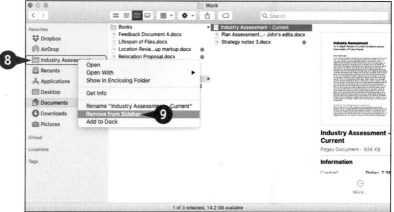

Which items can I add to the sidebar?
You can add most any item you can access through the Finder. To find out whether you can add a particular item, click it in a Finder window, click **File** to open the File menu, and see if the Add to Sidebar command appears. If so, click **Add to Sidebar** to add the item to the sidebar.

Configure Finder Preferences

The Finder is the application that controls the macOS desktop, how files and folders are managed, and many other aspects of the way your MacBook operates. Like most applications, the Finder has a set of preferences you can configure to change the way it looks and works. You change Finder preferences using its Preferences command. The Preferences window has several tabs that you use to configure specific aspects of how the Finder looks and behaves.

Configure Finder Preferences

1 Click the desktop.

The Finder becomes active.

2 Click **Finder**.

The Finder menu opens.

3 Click **Preferences**.

The Finder Preferences window opens.

4 Click **General** ( ).

The General tab appears.

5 In the Show These Items on the Desktop list, select ( ) each item you want to appear on the desktop.

6 Click **New Finder windows show** ( ) and select the default location for new Finder windows, such as **Documents**.

7 Select **Open folders in tabs instead of new windows** ( ) if you want each folder to open in a new tab in the current window rather than in a new window.

8 Click **Sidebar** ( ).

The Sidebar tab appears.

Note: The Sidebar tab in Finder preferences displays the default list of items for the sidebar. To add or remove individual locations or files, use the technique explained in the previous section.

9 Select ( ) each item you want the sidebar to show.

10 Deselect ( ) each item you want to remove from the sidebar.

11 Click **Advanced** ( ).

The Advanced tab appears.

12 Select (☑) **Show all filename extensions** to make the Finder always display all filename extensions.

13 Select (☑) **Show warning before changing an extension** to receive a warning when you change a filename extension. This is normally helpful.

14 Select (☑) **Show warning before removing from iCloud Drive** to receive a warning when you move a file so that it will no longer be synced by iCloud Drive.

15 Select (☑) **Show warning before emptying the Trash** to confirm emptying the Trash.

16 Select (☑) **Remove items from the Trash after 30 days** if you want macOS to delete items automatically after 30 days.

17 In the Keep Folders on Top area, select (☑) each check box if you want folders to remain at the top of windows when sorting items by name or on the Desktop.

18 Click **When performing a search** (◌) and then click **Search This Mac**, **Search the Current Folder**, or **Use the Previous Search Scope**, as needed.

19 Click **Close** (●).

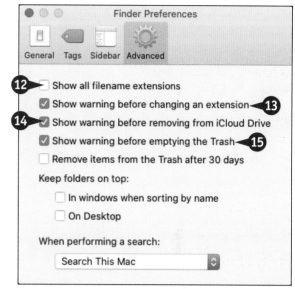

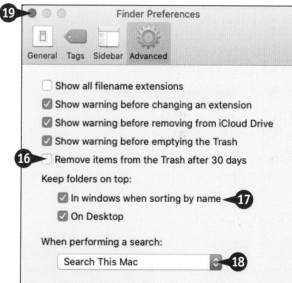

TIP

Which folder should I use as my start folder for new Finder windows?
Choose whichever folder you find most convenient — for example, the folder you keep your most important documents in. Click **New Finder windows show** (◌) and select **Other.** In the dialog that opens, click the folder you want to use, and then click **Close.**

CHAPTER 6

Surfing the Web

If your MacBook is connected to the Internet, you can browse or *surf* the sites on the World Wide Web. For surfing, macOS provides a web browser app called Safari. Using Safari, you can quickly move from one web page to another, search for interesting sites, and download files to your MacBook.

Open a Web Page

The Safari app included with macOS enables you to browse the Web in various ways. The most straightforward way to reach a web page is to type or paste its unique address, which is called a *uniform resource locator* or *URL*, into the address box in Safari.

This technique works well for short addresses but is slow and awkward for complex addresses. Instead, you can click a link or click a bookmark for a page you have marked. If you do not have a bookmark, you can use a search engine, such as Google or Bing, to locate the address.

Open a Web Page

1 Click **Safari** () on the Dock.

Safari opens.

2 Click anywhere in the address box or press ⌘+L.

Safari selects the current address.

3 Type the URL of the web page you want to visit.

Note: You do not need to type the http:// or https:// part of the address. Safari adds this automatically for you when you press Return.

4 Press Return.

Safari displays the web page.

Note: To search, click the address box and start typing your search terms. If the Suggestions list displays a result that is what you want, click that result to go to the page. Otherwise, finish typing your search terms and press Return to display a page of search results, then click the result you want to see.

Follow a Link to a Web Page

Y ou can click a link on a web page in Safari to navigate to another page or another marked location on the same page. Most web pages contain multiple links to other pages, which may be either on the same website or on another website. Some links are underlined, whereas others are attached to graphics or to different-colored text. When you position the pointer over a link, the pointer changes from the standard arrow ( ) to a hand with a pointing finger ( ).

Follow a Link to a Web Page

1 In Safari, position the pointer over a link (changes to).

Note: If you want to see the address of a link over which you move the pointer, display the status bar by clicking **View**, and then clicking **Show Status Bar**. The address appears in the status bar.

2 Click the link.

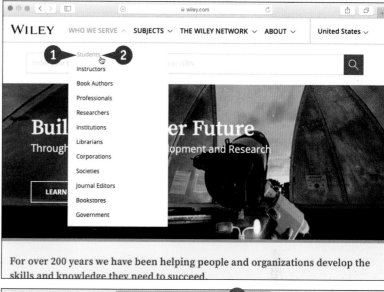

Safari shows the linked web page.

A You can click the address box to see the full address of the web page to which you have navigated.

Note: The address box in Safari normally shows the base name of the website you are visiting, such as wiley. com, rather than the full address of the web page.

Open Several Web Pages at Once

Safari enables you to open multiple web pages at the same time, which is useful for browsing quickly and easily. You can open multiple pages either on separate tabs in the same window or in separate windows. You can drag a tab from one window to another.

Use separate tabs when you need to see only one of the pages at a time. Use separate windows when you need to compare two pages side by side.

Open Several Web Pages at Once

Open Several Pages on Tabs in the Same Safari Window

1 Go to the first page you want to view.

Note: You can also click **Add** (+) or press ⌘+T to open a new tab showing your home page. Type a URL in the address box, and then press Return to go to the page.

2 Press Control+click a link.

The contextual menu opens.

3 Click **Open Link in New Tab**.

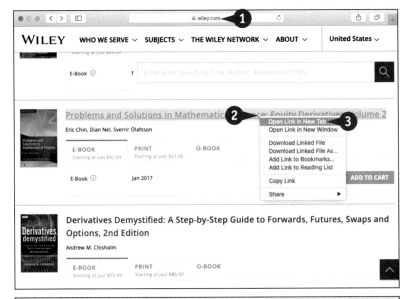

A Safari opens the linked web page in a new tab.

Note: You can repeat steps **2** and **3** to open additional pages on separate tabs.

4 To change the page Safari is displaying, click the tab for the page you want to see.

Note: If your MacBook has the Touch Bar, you can navigate by tapping the tab icons on the Touch Bar.

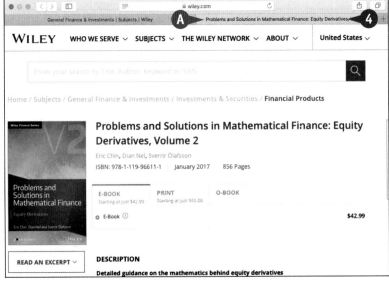

Open Several Pages in Separate Safari Windows

1 Go to the first page you want to view.

2 Press **Control**+click a link.

The contextual menu opens.

3 Click **Open Link in New Window**.

Note: You can also open a new window by pressing ⌘+N.

B Safari opens the linked web page in a new window.

4 To move back to the previous window, click it. If you cannot see the previous window, click **Window** and then click the window on the Window menu.

Note: You can also move back to the previous window by closing the new window you just opened.

Note: Press ⌘+` to cycle forward through windows and ⌘+Shift+` to cycle backward.

Note: You can click **Window** and **Merge All Windows** to merge all windows onto tabs in a single window.

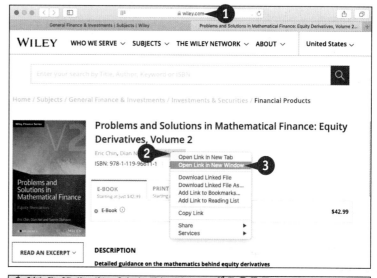

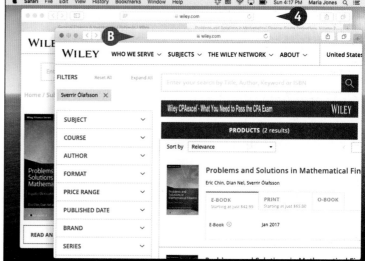

TIP

Can I change the way Safari tabs and windows behave?

Yes. Click **Safari** and select **Preferences** to open the Preferences window, and then click **Tabs** (▭). Click **Open pages in tabs instead of windows** (◌) and then click **Never**, **Automatically**, or **Always**, as needed. Click **⌘+click to open a link in a new tab** (☐ changes to ☑) to use ⌘ for opening a new tab. Click **When a new tab or window opens, make it active** (☐ changes to ☑) if you want to switch to the new tab or window on opening it. Click **Use ⌘+1 through ⌘+9 to switch tabs** (☐ changes to ☑) to switch tabs quickly by pressing shortcuts. Click **Show website icons in tabs** (☐ changes to ☑) to include website icons for visual reference in tabs. Click **Close** (⬤) to close the Preferences window.

Navigate Among Web Pages

Safari makes it easy to navigate among the web pages you browse. Safari tracks the pages that you visit, so that the pages form a path. You can go back along this path to return to a page you viewed earlier; after going back, you can go forward again as needed.

Safari keeps a separate path of pages in each open tab or window, so you can move separately in each tab or window. You can also navigate using the browser history, as explained in the next section, "Return to a Recently Visited Page."

Navigate Among Web Pages

Go Back One Page

1 In Safari, click **Previous Page** (‹).

Note: You can also swipe right with two fingers on the trackpad to go back to the previous page. You must start the movement from the left side of the window.

> Safari displays the previous page you visited in the current tab or window.

Go Forward One Page

1 Click **Next Page** (›).

Note: The Next Page button is available only when you have gone back. Until then, there is no page for you to go forward to.

Note: You can also swipe left with two fingers on the trackpad to go forward to the next page. You must start the movement from the right side of the window.

> Safari displays the next page for the current tab or window.

Note: If your MacBook has the Touch Bar, you can tap ‹ to go back and › to go forward.

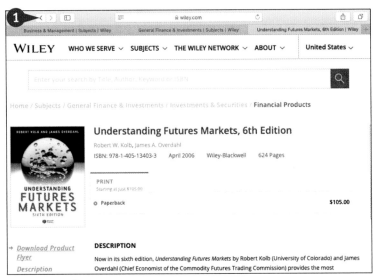

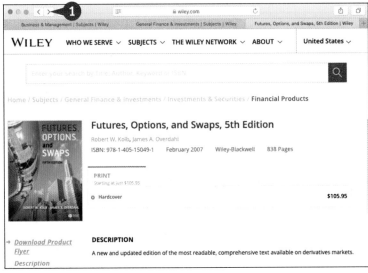

Go Back Multiple Pages

1 Click **Previous Page** (**<**) and keep holding down the trackpad button.

A pop-up menu opens showing the pages you have visited in the current tab or window.

2 Click the page you want to visit.

Safari displays the page.

Go Forward Multiple Pages

1 Click **Next Page** (**>**) and keep holding down the trackpad button.

A pop-up menu opens showing the pages further along the path for the current tab or window.

2 Click the page you want to visit.

Safari displays the page.

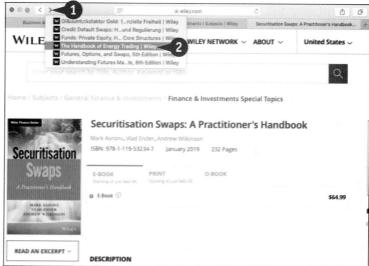

TIP

How can I navigate with the keyboard?

You can use these following keyboard shortcuts:

- Press ⌘+[to display the previous page.
- Press ⌘+] to display the next page.
- Press ⌘+Shift+H to display your home page.
- Press ⌘+Shift+[to display the previous tab.
- Press ⌘+Shift+] to display the next tab.

- Press ⌘+W to close the current tab and display the previous tab. If the window has no tabs, this command closes the window.
- Press ⌘+Shift+W to close the current window and display the previous window, if there is one.
- Press ⌘+1 to display the first tab, ⌘+2 to display the second tab, and so on up to ⌘+9.

Return to a Recently Visited Page

To help you return to web pages you have visited before, Safari keeps the History list of all the pages you have visited recently.

Normally, each person who uses your MacBook has a separate user account, so each person has his own History. But if you share a user account with other people, you can clear the History list to prevent them from seeing what web pages you have visited. You can also shorten the length of time for which History tracks your visits.

Return to a Recently Visited Page

Return to a Page on the History List

1 In Safari, click **History**.

The History menu opens.

A If a menu item for the web page you want appears on the top section of the History menu, before the day submenus, simply click the item.

2 Highlight or click the day on which you visited the web page.

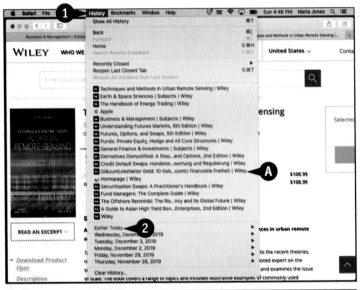

The submenu opens, showing the sites you visited on that day.

3 Click the web page to which you want to return.

Safari displays the web page.

Clear Your Browsing History

1 Click **History**.

The History menu opens.

Note: You may have to scroll down the History menu to reach the Clear History command.

2 Click **Clear History**.

The Clearing History Will Remove Related Cookies and Other Website Data dialog opens.

3 Click **Clear** () and then click **the last hour**, **today**, **today and yesterday**, or **all history** to specify what you want to clear.

4 Click **Clear History**.

Safari clears the History list for the period you chose.

Note: If you want to browse without History storing the list of web pages you visit, click **File**, and then click **New Private Window**. Any sites you browse in the Private Browsing window will not be stored.

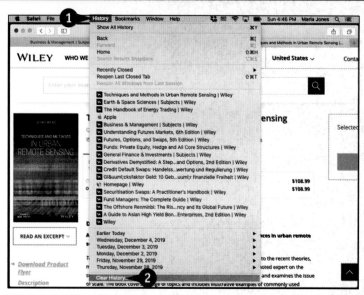

Clearing history will remove related cookies and other website data.

History will also be removed on other devices signed into your iCloud account.

Clear all history

Cancel   Clear History

TIP

What does the Show All History command do?
Click **History** and select **Show All History** to open a History window for browsing and searching the sites you have visited. Type a term in the Search box in the upper-right corner to search. Click the disclosure triangle (▶ changes to ▼) to expand the list of entries in a day. Double-click a history item to open its page in the same window, or press `Control` +click a history item and click **Open in New Tab** or **Open in New Window** to open the page in a new tab or a new window.

Play Music and Videos on the Web

Many websites contain music files or video files that you can play directly in the Safari browser. Safari can play many widely used types of audio files and video files, and most sites provide easy-to-use buttons — such as a Play/Pause button and a volume slider — to enable you to control playback. This section shows the SoundCloud music website and the YouTube video website as examples.

You can play music and videos either directly on your MacBook or via AirPlay to a supported device, such as an Apple TV.

Play Music and Videos on the Web

Play Music

1 In Safari, navigate to a music website and browse to find a song you want to play.

Note: This example uses the SoundCloud site, www.soundcloud.com. There are many other music sites.

2 Click **Play** (such as ▶).

The song starts playing.

A The progress indicator shows playback progress.

Note: If your MacBook has the Touch Bar, you may be able to use the Touch Bar to move the playhead and control playback, depending on the music website.

3 Click **Pause** (such as ⏸) if you want to pause the music.

B Some sites enable you to comment on the music.

C The Audio icon (🔊) appears on a tab that is playing audio. Click **Audio** (🔊 changes to 🔇) to mute the audio.

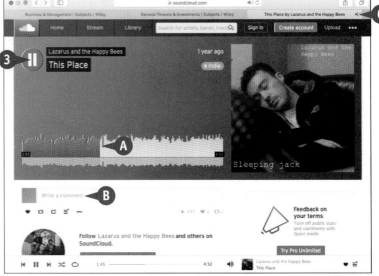

Play Videos

1 In Safari, navigate to a video website and browse to find a video you want to play.

Note: This example uses the YouTube website, www.youtube.com. There are various other video websites; see the tip for information on some.

2 Click the video to open it.

The video starts playing automatically.

D You can click **Settings** (⚙) to change the playback speed or the quality.

3 Click **Full Screen** (⬛).

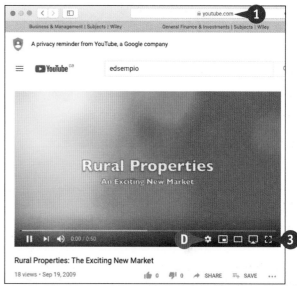

The video appears full screen.

4 Move the pointer over the video.

The playback controls appear, and you can use them to control playback.

E You can click **Share** (➡) to share the video with others.

F You can click **Exit Full Screen** (⊞) to return from full screen to a window.

G You can click **AirPlay** (▤) to play the video to a TV connected to an Apple TV.

TIPS

What are the main video sites on the Web?
As of this writing, the most popular video websites include YouTube (www.youtube.com), Netflix (www.netflix.com), Vimeo (www.vimeo.com), and Dailymotion (www.dailymotion.com). Alternatively, search for videos using a search engine, such as Google's Videos search filter.

How do I prevent a site from playing videos automatically?
Go to the site, click **Safari** on the menu bar, and then click **Settings for This Website**. In the pop-up panel that opens, click **Auto-Play** (⬍), and then click **Stop Media with Sound** or **Never Auto-Play**, as appropriate.

Set Your Home Page and Search Engine

When you open a new window, Safari automatically displays your *home page*, the page it is configured to show at first. You can set your home page to any web page you want or to an empty page. You can also control what Safari shows when you open a new tab or a new window: the Favorites screen, your home page, an empty page, or the page from which you opened the new tab or window.

You can also specify which search engine Safari uses and configure settings for it.

Change Your Home Page

1. In Safari, navigate to the web page that you want to make your home page.

2. Click **Safari**.

   The Safari menu opens.

3. Click **Preferences**.

Note: You can also press ⌘+, to open the Preferences window.

   The Preferences window opens.

4. Click **General** ( ).

   The General pane opens.

5. Click **Set to Current Page**.

   Safari changes the Home Page text field to show the page you chose.

6. Click **New windows open with** ( ) and click **Favorites**, **Homepage**, **Empty Page**, or **Same Page**, as appropriate.

7. Click **New tabs open with** ( ) and select **Top Sites**, **Homepage**, **Favorites**, **Empty Page**, or **Same Page**, as appropriate.

8. Click **Search** ( ).

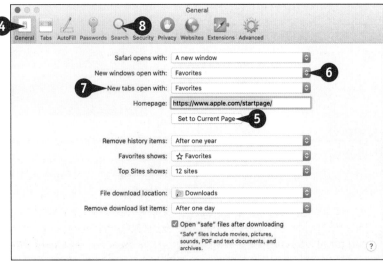

The Search tab appears.

9 Click **Search engine** (🔽) and then click the search engine you want to use.

10 Click **Include search engine suggestions** (☐ changes to ✅) to have Safari show suggestions from the search engine.

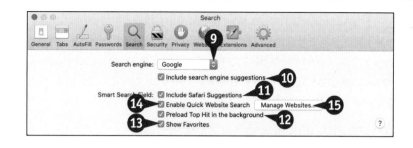

11 Click **Include Safari Suggestions** (☐ changes to ✅) to include Safari suggestions in the Smart Search Field.

12 Click **Preload Top Hit in the background** (☐ changes to ✅) to have Safari preload the Top Hit for the search to enable you to view it more quickly.

13 Click **Show Favorites** (☐ changes to ✅) to include your Favorites in the Smart Search Field.

14 Click **Enable Quick Website Search** (☐ changes to ✅) to enable the Quick Website Search feature.

15 Click **Manage Websites**.

The Manage Websites dialog opens.

16 To remove a website, click it, and then click **Remove**.

A To remove all websites, click **Remove All**.

17 Click **Done**.

The Manage Websites dialog closes.

18 Click **Close** (⬤).

The Preferences window closes.

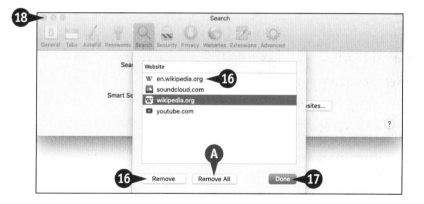

TIPS

How can I display my home page in the current window?

Click **History** on the menu bar and then click **Home**. Alternatively, press ⌘+Shift+H.

What does Quick Website Search do?

Quick Website Search enables you to search quickly for content in some websites you have previously visited. For example, if you have previously visited the wikipedia.org web encyclopedia, you can type **wikipedia** and a search term in the address box to search for that term on Wikipedia.

Create Bookmarks for Web Pages

Safari enables you to create markers called *bookmarks* for the addresses of web pages you want to be able to revisit easily. When you find such a web page, you can create a bookmark for its address, assign the bookmark a descriptive name, and store it on the Favorites bar, on the Bookmarks menu, or in a Bookmark folder. You can then return to the web page's address by clicking its bookmark. The content of the web page may have changed by the time you return.

Create Bookmarks for Web Pages

Create a New Bookmark

① In Safari, navigate to a web page you want to bookmark.

② Click **Bookmarks**.

The Bookmarks menu opens.

③ Click **Add Bookmark**.

Note: You can also press ⌘+D to open the Add Bookmark dialog.

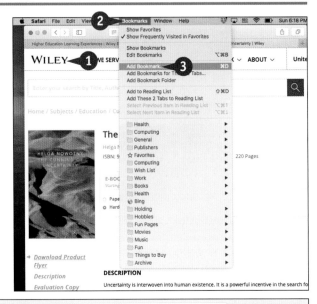

The Add Bookmark dialog opens, with the web page's title added to the upper box.

④ Click **Add this page to** (⬍) and select the location or folder in which to store the bookmark.

⑤ Edit the default bookmark name — the web page's title — to create a descriptive name.

⑥ Optionally, click **Description** and type a description to help you identify the bookmark by searching.

⑦ Click **Add**.

The Add Bookmark dialog closes.

Safari creates the bookmark.

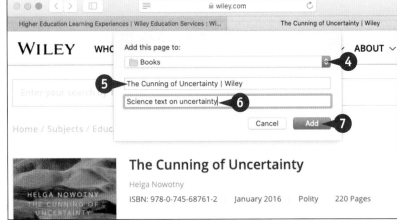

Organize Your Bookmarks

1 Click **Bookmarks**.

The Bookmarks menu opens.

2 Click **Edit Bookmarks**.

Note: You can also press ⌘ + Option + B to display the Bookmarks screen.

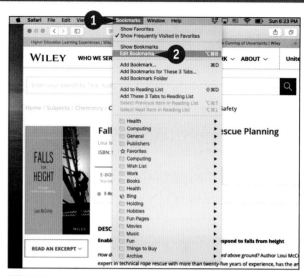

The Bookmarks screen appears.

A You can click **New Folder** to create a new folder, type the name for the folder, and then press Return.

3 Double-click a collapsed folder to display its contents, or double-click an expanded folder to collapse it to the folder.

4 Drag a bookmark to the folder in which you want to place it.

Note: You can drag the bookmark folders into a different order. You can also place one folder inside another folder.

5 Click **Previous Page** (〈).

Safari returns you to the page you were viewing before.

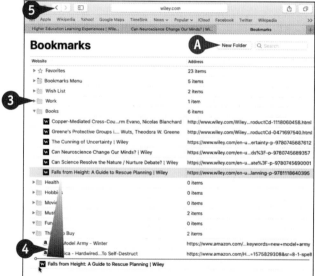

<hr />

TIP

How do I go to a bookmark I have created?

If you placed the bookmark on the Favorites bar, click the bookmark on the Favorites bar; if the Favorites bar is not displayed, click **View** and **Show Favorites Bar** to display it. If you put the bookmark on the Bookmarks menu, click **Bookmarks**, and then click the bookmark on the Bookmarks menu or one of its submenus. If you cannot easily locate the bookmark, click **Show sidebar** (▢) to display the sidebar, and then click **Bookmarks** (▢) to display the bookmarks. Locate the bookmark, and then double-click it.

Using Reader View and Reading List

Safari's Reader View enables you to minimize distractions by displaying only the text of a web page in an easily readable format. Reader View works on many, but not all, web pages.

Safari also enables you to save a web page in its current state so that you can read it later. You can quickly add the current web page to Reading List, which you can then access via the Reading List pane in the sidebar.

Using Reader View and Reading List

Switch a Web Page to Reader View

1 In Safari, navigate to a web page you want to read.

2 Click **Show Reader View** (☰).

Note: If the Show Reader View button does not appear, it is because Safari has determined that the page does not have content suitably formatted for Reader View.

Note: You can also switch to Reader View by clicking **View** and **Show Reader** and switch back by clicking **View** and **Hide Reader**. Alternatively, press ⌘+Shift+R to toggle Reader View on or off.

Safari switches the web page to Reader View.

Ⓐ The web page's contents appear in easy-to-read fonts.

Ⓑ Links are easier to see but work as usual.

3 When you finish using Reader View, click **Hide Reader View** (☰).

Safari switches the web page back from Reader View.

Add a Web Page to Reading List

1 Navigate to a web page.

2 Move the pointer over the Show Reader View button (≡).

3 Click **Add Page to Reading List** (⊕).

Safari displays a brief animation showing the page moving from the address box to the Show Sidebar button (▢).

Note: You can also click **Bookmarks** and select **Add to Reading List** or press ⌘+Shift+D.

Note: You can click **Bookmarks** and select **Add These Tabs to Reading List** to add all the tabs in the current window to Reading List.

Open Reading List and Display a Page

1 Click **Show sidebar** (▢).

Safari displays the sidebar.

2 Click **Reading List** (∞).

The Reading List pane opens.

3 Click the item you want to read.

The item appears.

C When you are ready to remove an item from Reading List, press Control+click its entry and click **Remove Item**.

TIP

Can I make a site always open in Reader View?

Yes — when Reader View is available for the site's pages. Go to the site, click **Safari** on the menu bar, and then click **Settings for This Website**. In the pop-up panel that opens, click **Use Reader when available** (☐ changes to ☑).

Download a File

M any websites provide files to download, and Safari makes it easy to download files from websites to your MacBook's file system. For example, you can download apps to install on your MacBook, pictures to view on it, or songs to play.

macOS includes apps that can open many file types, including music, graphic, movie, document, and PDF files. To open other file types, you may need to install extra apps or add plug-in software components to extend the features of the apps you already have.

Download a File

① In Safari, go to the web page that contains the link for the file you want to download.

② Click the link.

Note: For safety, download files only from sites that you trust, and use an anti-malware app or antivirus app to scan downloaded files before you open them.

③ If the Do You Want to Allow Downloads? dialog opens, click **Allow**.

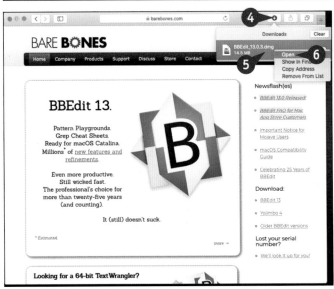

Safari starts the download.

Note: The indicator on the Downloads button (⬇) shows the progress of the download.

④ Click **Downloads** (⬇) to open the Downloads window.

⑤ When the download is complete, press Control +click the file in the Downloads window.

The contextual menu opens.

⑥ Click **Open**.

Note: Depending on the file type and the preferences you have set, Safari may open the file automatically for you.

The file opens.

Depending on the file type, you can then work with the file, enjoy its contents, or install it.

Note: If the file is an app, you can install it, as discussed in Chapter 4. If the file is a data file, such as a document or a picture, macOS opens the file in the app for that file type.

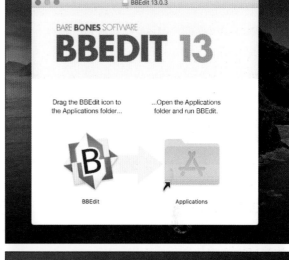

⑦ If the file disappears from the Downloads window and Safari does not open the file for you, click **Downloads** on the Dock.

The Downloads stack opens.

⑧ Click the file you downloaded.

The file opens.

TIP

What should I do when clicking a download link opens the file instead of downloading it?
If clicking a download link on a web page opens the file instead of downloading it, press Control + click the link to display the contextual menu. Click **Download Linked File** if you want to save the file in your Downloads folder. If you prefer to save the file in a different folder or under a different name of your choice, click **Download Linked File As**, and then specify the folder and filename in the dialog that opens.

Configure Safari for Security and Privacy

The Web is packed with fascinating sites and useful information, but it is also full of malefactors and criminals who want to attack your MacBook and steal your valuable data.

To keep your MacBook safe, you can prevent Safari from automatically opening supposedly safe files you download. Safari also enables you to choose which websites can use WebGL, a technology for displaying three-dimensional graphics in the browser. You can also choose which Internet plug-ins to use and which websites can use them.

Configure Safari for Security and Privacy

1 With the Safari app running, click **Safari**.

The Safari menu opens.

2 Click **Preferences**.

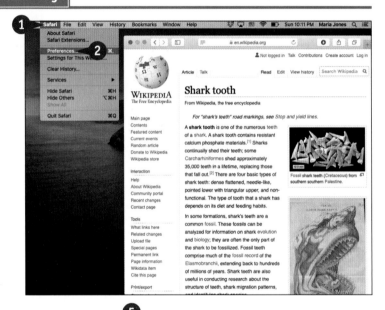

The Preferences window opens.

3 Click **General** ( ).

The General pane opens.

4 Click **Open "safe" files after downloading** (changes to).

5 Click **Security** ( ).

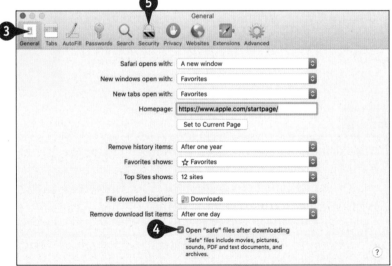

The Security pane opens.

6 Click **Warn when visiting a fraudulent website** (☐ changes to ☑).

7 Click **Enable JavaScript** (☑ changes to ☐) if you want to disable JavaScript. See the tip for advice.

8 Click **Privacy** (✋).

The Privacy pane appears.

9 Click **Prevent cross-site tracking** (☐ changes to ☑) to have Safari try to prevent sites tracking your movements from one site to another.

10 Click **Allow websites to check for Apple Pay and Apple Card** (☐ changes to ☑) to allow websites to determine whether you have Apple Pay and Apple Card as payment options.

11 Click **Block all cookies** (☐ changes to ☑) if you want to block all cookies. This is not usually helpful.

12 Click **Manage Website Data**.

The Manage Website Data dialog opens.

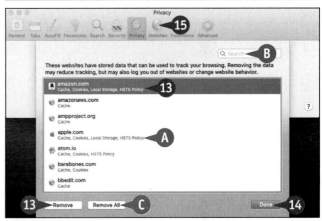

Ⓐ Each entry lists the types of data the site has stored about you.

Ⓑ You can search to locate a site.

13 To remove the data a website has saved about you, click the site, and then click **Remove**.

Ⓒ You can click **Remove All** to remove all the sites' saved data.

14 Click **Done**.

The Manage Website Data dialog closes.

15 Click **Websites** (🌐).

TIP

What is JavaScript, and should I disable it?

JavaScript is a scripting language used by many websites to provide interactive features. While it is possible for malefactors to perform some unwelcome actions with JavaScript, such as borrowing your computer's processing power to "mine" cryptocurrency, the language is widely used for positive purposes and is required for many websites to be usable. What is more of a threat to your MacBook's security is Java, a full-featured programming language that can run on many computer platforms and is often used by Web-delivered services. JavaScript is completely different from Java but is sometimes tainted by association with Java.

continued ▶

I n the Websites pane of Safari preferences, you can configure various aspects of how Safari interacts with websites you visit for security, privacy, and usability. For example, you can control which sites can automatically play media and which sites can send you notifications.

For each category of settings, you can choose custom settings for individual websites you visit and a global setting that applies to all websites for which you have not chosen custom settings. For example, you might allow specific sites to play videos automatically but block all other websites from doing so.

Configure Safari for Security and Privacy (continued)

The Websites pane appears.

16 In the General pane, click the category you want to customize first. To follow this example, click **Auto-Play** (⊙).

17 In the Currently Open Websites list, click 🔄 for a site you want to configure, and then click **Allow All Auto-Play**, **Stop Media with Sound**, or **Never Auto-Play**, as needed.

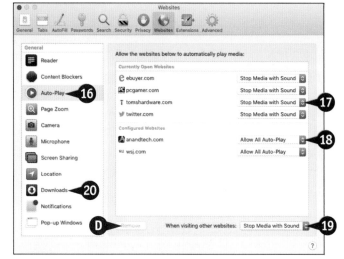

18 Adjust the settings for sites in the Configured Websites list, as needed.

19 Click **When visiting other websites** (🔄) and click the setting to use for all other websites.

Ⓓ You can click a website and then click **Remove** to remove it from the list.

20 Click **Downloads** (⊙).

The Downloads pane appears. This pane enables you to control which sites Safari can download content from.

21 In the Currently Open Websites list, click 🔄 for a site you want to configure, and then click **Ask**, **Deny**, or **Allow**, as needed.

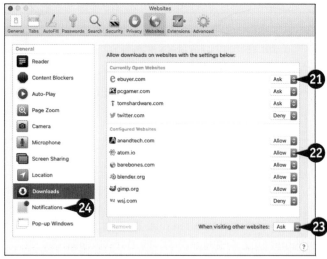

22 Adjust the settings for sites in the Configured Websites list, as needed.

23 Click **When visiting other websites** (🔄) and click the setting to use for all other websites.

24 Click **Notifications** ( ).

The Notifications pane appears. This pane enables you to control which sites can send notifications in Notification Center.

25 In the These Websites Have Asked for Permission to Show Alerts in Notification Center list, click ⬍ for a site you want to configure, and then click **Allow** or **Deny**, as needed.

26 Select (☑) or clear (☐) **Allow websites to ask for permission to send notifications**, as needed.

27 Click other categories and choose settings, as needed. For example, click **Camera** (📷) and specify which websites can use your MacBook's camera.

28 Click **AutoFill** (✎).

The AutoFill pane appears.

29 In the AutoFill Web Forms list, click to select (☑) or deselect (☐) **Using information from my contacts**, **User names and passwords**, **Credit cards**, and **Other forms**, to specify the items for which you want to use AutoFill.

E You can click **Edit** to view the stored information.

Note: Clicking **Edit** for Using Information from My Contacts opens the Contacts app.

30 Click **Close** (⬤).

The Safari Preferences window closes.

TIP

What are cookies, and should I block them?

A *cookie* is a small text file that a website uses to store information about what you do on the site — for example, what products you have browsed or added to your shopping cart. Cookies from sites you visit are usually helpful to you. Be aware that blocking all cookies may prevent many websites from working as they are supposed to.

CHAPTER 7

Sending and Receiving E-Mail

macOS includes Mail, a powerful e-mail app. After setting up your e-mail accounts, you can send and receive e-mail messages and files.

Set Up Your E-Mail Accounts

The Mail app enables you to send and receive e-mail messages easily using your existing e-mail accounts. If you add an iCloud account to your user account during initial setup or in System Preferences, macOS can automatically set up e-mail in Mail. After setup, you can add other e-mail accounts manually. For some accounts, you need only your e-mail address and your password. For other accounts, you also need to enter the addresses and types of your provider's mail servers.

Set Up Your E-Mail Accounts

1 Click **Mail** (✉) on the Dock.

Mail opens.

2 Click **Mail**.

The Mail menu opens.

3 Click **Add Account**.

The Choose a Mail Account Provider dialog opens.

4 Click the account type (○ changes to ●).
Your choices are **iCloud**, **Exchange**, **Google**, **Yahoo!**, **AOL**, or **Other Mail Account**.

Note: For an Office 365 account, click **Exchange** (○ changes to ●) and use the server name **outlook.office365.com**.

5 Click **Continue**.

A dialog opens that allows you to sign in to the account. This example shows the Sign In dialog that appears for a Google account.

6 Type your e-mail address.

7 Click **Next**.

The service prompts you for your password.

8 Type your password.

Ⓐ For some services, you can click **Show Password** (👁) to reveal the characters you typed.

9 Click **Next**.

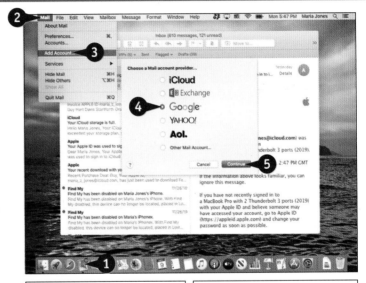

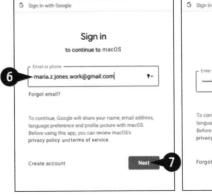

If you use two-factor authentication for the account, a dialog opens prompting you to provide the second form of authentication.

10 Enter the code.

11 Click **Next**.

The Select the Apps You Want to Use with This Account dialog opens.

12 Click the check box (☐ changes to ☑) for each app you want to use with this account.

13 Click **Done**.

Mail displays your inbox, and you can begin reading and sending e-mail.

B You can click a message in the message list to display its contents.

C Mail automatically identifies possible events and contacts in e-mail messages you receive. Move the pointer over an event's details and then click the pop-up button (⊙). In the panel that appears, you can click **Add to Calendar** to add the event to your calendar.

Note: When you receive a calendar invitation, the message includes the name of the event and the Calendar icon. You can click **Accept**, **Maybe**, or **Decline** to give your response.

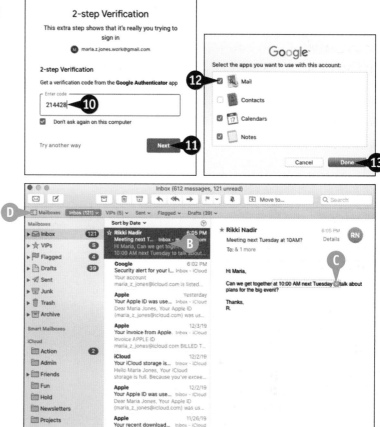

D You can click **Mailboxes** (▦) to toggle the display of the Mailboxes pane.

What extra information must I provide when I select Other Mail Account?

When you select Other Mail Account, you must choose between IMAP and POP for your incoming mail server type and enter the mail server's address. Check your ISP's website or call customer service to find out what type of mail server to use. Most ISPs use either POP (Post Office Protocol) or IMAP (Internet Mail Access Protocol), but others use Exchange or Exchange IMAP. You may also need to provide the outgoing mail server's address.

Send an E-Mail Message

The Mail app enables you to send an e-mail message to anybody whose e-mail address you know. After starting a new message, you can specify the recipient's address either by typing it directly into the To field or by selecting it from your list of contacts in the Contacts app.

You can send an e-mail message to a single person or to multiple people. You can send copies to Cc, or carbon-copy, recipients or send hidden copies to Bcc, or blind carbon-copy, recipients.

Send an E-Mail Message

1 In Mail, click **New Message** (✐).

Note: You can also press ⌘+N or click **File** on the menu bar, and then click **New** to start a new message.

Note: If your MacBook has the Touch Bar, you can tap **Compose** (✐) to create a new message.

A new message window opens.

2 Click **Add Contact** (⊕).

The Contacts panel opens.

3 Click the contact.

4 Click the e-mail address.

Note: In the Contacts panel, a name in lighter gray has no e-mail address in the contact record.

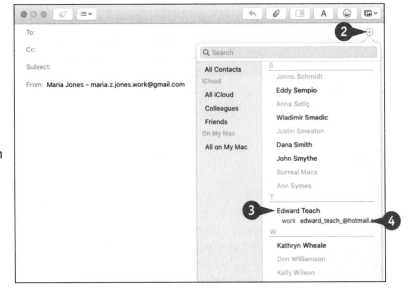

The contact name appears as a button in the To field.

Note: You can add other addresses to the To field as needed.

5 To add a Cc recipient, click the Cc field.

6 Start typing a name or e-mail address.

Mail displays matches from Contacts.

7 Click the appropriate match or finish typing.

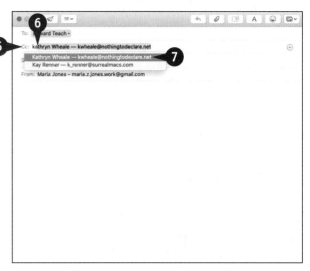

The name or address appears in the Cc box.

8 Type the subject for the message.

9 Type the body text of the message.

A You can click **Show Format Bar** (A) to display the Format bar, which contains controls for setting the font family, font size, and font color, and applying boldface, italics, or underline. For more formatting choices, press ⌘+T to open the Fonts window.

Note: You can switch a message between plain text and rich text by clicking **Format** on the menu bar, and then clicking **Make Rich Text** or **Make Plain Text**.

10 Click **Send** (✐).

Mail sends the message and stores a copy in your Sent folder.

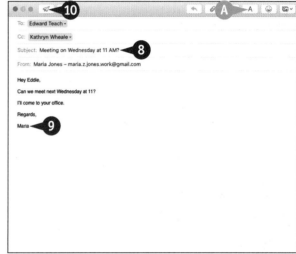

TIP

How can I send Bcc (blind carbon-copy) messages?
Mail hides the Bcc field in the New Message window by default. To display the Bcc field, click **Customize** (☰) on the toolbar of a message window, and then click **Bcc Address Field** on the pop-up menu. The Bcc field appears below the Cc field, and you can add recipients either by clicking **Add Contact** (⊕) or by typing their names or e-mail addresses.

Each Bcc recipient sees only his own address, not the addresses of other Bcc recipients. The To recipients and Cc recipients see none of the Bcc recipients' names and addresses.

Receive and Read Your Messages

Mail enables you to receive your incoming messages easily and read them in whatever order you prefer. A message sent to you goes to your mail provider's e-mail server. To receive the message, you cause Mail to connect to the e-mail server and download the message to your MacBook.

When working with e-mail, it often helps to display the mailbox list on the left side of the Mail window. You can use this list to navigate among mailboxes and to see which activities Mail is currently performing.

Receive and Read Your Messages

Display the Mailboxes List and Receive Messages

1 In Mail, click **Mailboxes** (📖).

A The Mailboxes list appears.

2 Click the mailbox you want to view.

3 Click **Get Mail** (✉).

Mail connects to the e-mail server and downloads any messages.

B Depending on how you have configured notifications, a notification banner or alert may appear as a message arrives.

C The new messages appear in your inbox.

D A blue dot (🔵) indicates an unread message.

E A gray star (⭐) indicates an unread message from someone you have designated a VIP.

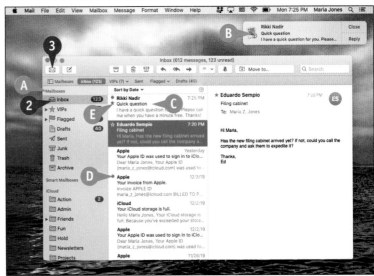

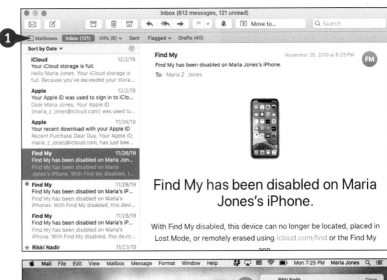

Read Your Messages

1 Click a message in the message list.

F The message appears in the reading pane.

2 Double-click a message in the message list.

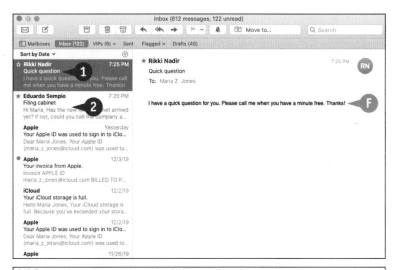

The message's text and contents appear in a separate window.

3 Read the message.

4 Click **Close** (🔴).

The message window closes.

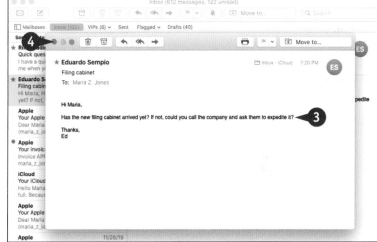

Reply to a Message

Mail enables you to reply to any e-mail message you receive. When you reply, you can include either the whole of the original message or just the part of it that you select.

If you are one of multiple recipients of the message, you can choose between replying only to the sender and replying to both the sender and all the other recipients other than Bcc recipients. You can also adjust the list of recipients manually if necessary, removing existing recipients and adding other recipients.

Reply to a Message

1 In the inbox, click the message to which you want to reply.

Note: You can also double-click the message to open it in a message window, and then start the reply from there.

2 Click **Reply** (↩).

Note: If the message has multiple recipients, you can click **Reply All** (↩↩) to reply to the sender and to all the other recipients except Bcc recipients.

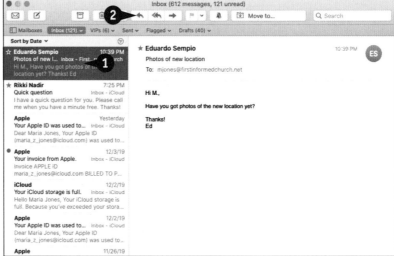

Mail creates the reply and opens it in a window.

A The recipient's name appears as a button.

B You can position the pointer over the contact's name, click the pop-up button (▾) that appears, and then click a different address if necessary.

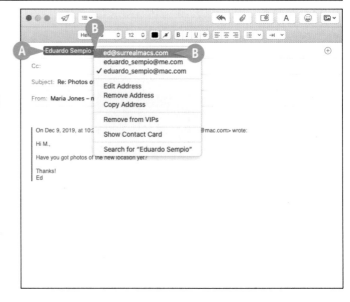

3 Type the text of your reply.

It is usually best to type your text at the beginning of the reply rather than after the message you are replying to.

Note: You can also add other recipients to the message as needed. If you have chosen to reply to all recipients, you can remove any recipients as necessary.

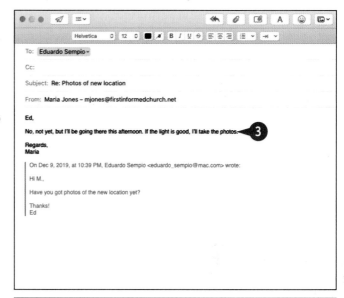

4 Click **Send** (✈).

Mail sends the reply and saves a copy in your Sent folder.

Note: Click **Message** and then click **Send Again** to send the same message again — for example, because the recipient has deleted it by accident. You can change recipients or the message contents as needed.

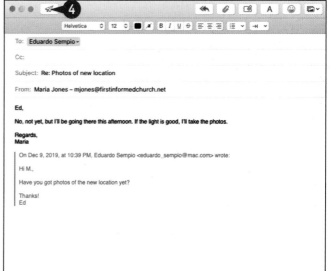

TIP

How do I reply to only part of a message rather than send the whole of it?

Select the part you want to include, and then click **Reply** (↩) or **Reply All** (↩), as appropriate. Mail creates a reply containing only the part you selected. If Mail still includes all of the message, click **Mail**, click **Preferences**, click **Composing** (✏), and then click **Include selected text, if any; otherwise include all text** (○ changes to ●) instead of **Include all of the original message text**.

Forward a Message

Mail enables you to forward to other people a message that you receive. You can either forward the entire message or forward only a selected part of it.

When you forward a message, you can add your own comments to the message. For example, you might want to explain to the recipient which person or organization sent you the original message, why you are forwarding it, and what action — if any — you expect him to take.

Forward a Message

1 If necessary, click **Mailboxes** (▦) and then click the mailbox that contains the message you want to forward.

A The Replied arrow (↰) indicates you have replied to a message.

B The Forwarded arrow (→) indicates you have forwarded a message.

2 Click the message.

The message's content appears in the reading pane.

Note: You can also forward a message that you have opened in a message window.

3 Click **Forward** (→).

Note: You can click **Message** and then click **Redirect** to redirect a message to someone else without the Fwd: indicator appearing.

A window opens showing the forwarded message.

The subject line shows Fwd: and the message's original subject, so the recipient can see it was forwarded.

4 Enter the recipient's name or address. You can either type the address or click **Add Contact** (⊕) and then select the address from the Contacts panel.

5 Edit the subject line of the message if necessary.

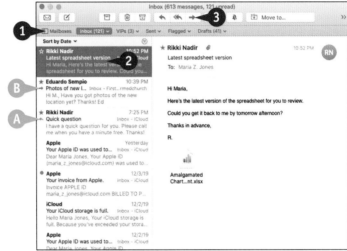

6 Optionally, edit the forwarded message to shorten it or make it clearer to the recipient.

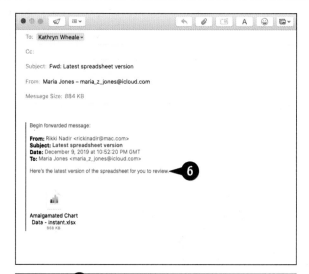

7 Type any message you want to include to the recipient.

8 Click **Send** (✈).

Mail sends the forwarded message to the recipient.

What does the Forward as Attachment command on the Message menu do?

The Forward as Attachment command enables you to send a copy of a message as an attachment to a message instead of in the message itself. This command is useful when you want to send a forwarded message that includes formatting in a plain text message.

How do I forward only part of a message rather than all of it?

Select the part you want to forward, and then click **Forward** (➡). Mail includes only the part you selected.

Send a File via E-Mail

As well as enabling you to communicate via e-mail messages, Mail gives you an easy way to transfer files to other people. You can attach one or more files to an e-mail message so that the files travel as part of the message. The recipient can then save the file on her computer and open it.

Mail's Send Large Attachments with Mail Drop feature enables you to transfer large files without running up against the size constraints that some mail servers impose.

Send a File via E-Mail

1 In Mail, click **Compose New Message** (☑).

Note: If you have multiple accounts, Mail creates the new message as being sent by the account that is currently active. To use a different account, click that account in the Mailboxes pane.

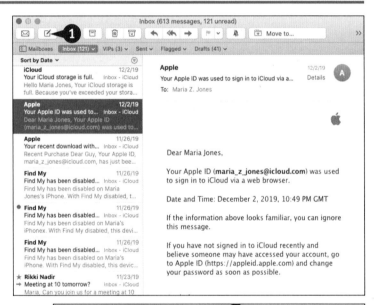

A new message window opens.

2 Add the recipient's name or address. You can either type the address or click **Add Contact** (⊕) and then select the address from the Contacts panel.

3 Type the subject for the message.

4 Type any message body text that is needed.

5 Click **Attach** (📎).

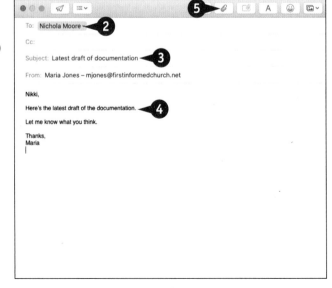

A dialog opens.

6 Click the file you want to attach to the message.

7 Click **Choose File**.

Note: Ask yourself whether the recipient will have an app that can open the file you are sending. The Portable Document Format, PDF, is usually a safe choice, because many people have a PDF reader installed; if not, they can download a free one.

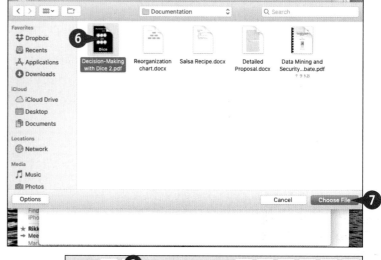

The dialog closes.

A Mail attaches the file to the message.

Note: Depending on the file type, the attachment may appear as an icon in the message or as a picture.

B The Message Size readout appears below the Subject line.

8 Click **Send** (✈).

Mail sends the message with the file attached.

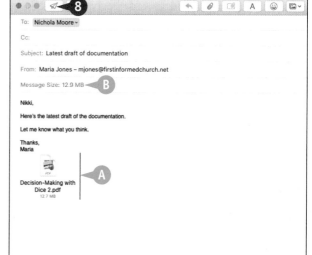

TIP

What does Send Large Attachments with Mail Drop do?

Send Large Attachments with Mail Drop uploads large attachments to Apple's Internet storage instead of including them in the message. If the message's recipient is using an iCloud account, she receives the attachments in the e-mail message via automatic download; if the recipient is using another type of account, she receives a link to download the file manually.

To enable Send Large Attachments with Mail Drop, click **Mail** on the menu bar, and then click **Preferences**. Click **Accounts** (@) to display the Accounts pane, click the account in the left pane, and then click **Account Information**. Click **Send large attachments with Mail Drop** (☐ changes to ☑), and then click **Close** (⬤).

Receive a File via E-Mail

A file you receive via e-mail appears as an attachment to a message in your inbox. You can use the Quick Look feature to examine the file and decide whether to keep it or delete it. Quick Look can display the contents of many types of files well enough for you to determine what they contain.

To keep an attached file, you can save it to your MacBook's drive. You can then remove the attached file from the e-mail message to help keep down the size of your mail folder.

Receive a File via E-Mail

1 In your inbox, click the message.

The message appears in the reading pane.

2 Press Control +click the attachment.

The contextual menu opens.

3 Click **Quick Look Attachment**.

A Quick Look window opens showing the attachment's contents.

A You can click **Full Screen** (⊙) if you want to view the document full screen.

B You can click **Open with** to open the file in a suitable app — for example, click **Open with Preview** to open a text file in the Preview app.

4 When you finish previewing the file, click **Close** (⊗).

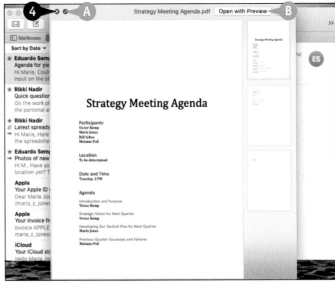

The Quick Look window closes.

5 Press **Control** +click the attachment.

The contextual menu opens.

6 Click **Save Attachment**.

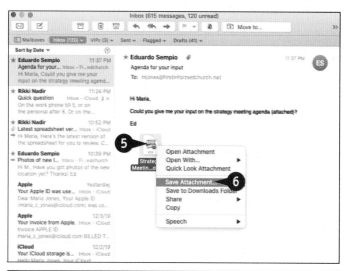

The Save As dialog opens.

Note: If the Save As dialog opens at its small size, click **Expand Dialog** (▶) to expand it.

7 Navigate to the folder in which you want to save the file.

8 Optionally, click the **Tags** box and click each tag you want to assign to the file.

9 Click **Save**.

Mail saves the file.

Note: If you want to remove the attachment from the message, click **Message**, and then click **Remove Attachments**.

TIPS

Should I check incoming files for viruses and malevolent software?
Yes, you should always check incoming files with antivirus software. Most antivirus and security apps scan incoming files automatically, but they also enable you to scan individual files manually. Even though Macs generally have fewer problems with viruses and malevolent software than Windows PCs, it is possible for a file to cause damage, steal data, or threaten your privacy.

Is there a quick way to see what messages have attachments?
In the inbox, click the **Sort by** pop-up menu (▾), and then click **Attachments**. Mail sorts the inbox so that the messages with attachments appear first.

View E-Mail Messages by Conversations

Mail enables you to view an exchange of e-mail messages as a conversation instead of viewing each message as a separate item. Conversations, also called *threads*, let you browse and sort messages on the same subject more easily by separating them from other messages in your mailboxes.

If you decide to organize your messages by conversations, you can expand or collapse all conversations to see the messages you want.

View E-Mail Messages by Conversations

1 In Mail, click the mailbox that contains the messages you want to view.

A The messages in the folder appear.

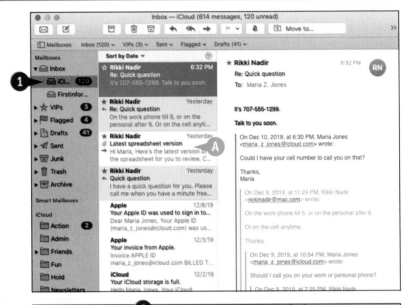

2 Click **View**.

The View menu opens.

3 Click **Organize by Conversation**.

Note: To change the order in which the conversation's messages appear, click **Mail** on the menu bar, and then click **Preferences**. Click **Viewing** (👓) to display the Viewing pane, go to the View Conversations area, and then click **Show most recent message at the top** (☐ changes to ☑ or ☑ changes to ☐). Click **Close** (⬤) to close the Preferences window.

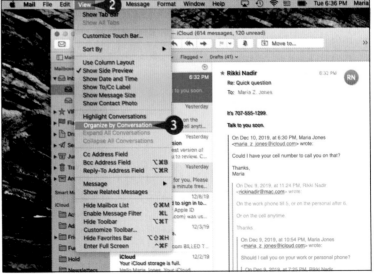

204

Mail organizes the messages into conversations, so that each exchange appears as a single item rather than as separate messages.

Ⓑ The number to the right of a conversation indicates how many messages it contains.

④ Click the conversation.

Note: You can expand all conversations in the folder by clicking **View** and clicking **Expand All Conversations**. Click **View** and click **Collapse All Conversations** to collapse them again.

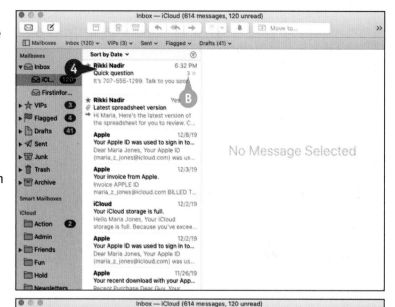

Ⓒ All the messages in the conversation appear in summary.

⑤ Click the number to the right of the conversation.

Ⓓ Mail expands the conversation so that you can see each of the messages it contains.

Ⓔ You can click a message to display it in the reading pane.

Note: You can mute a thread by Control +clicking it, and then clicking **Mute** on the contextual menu.

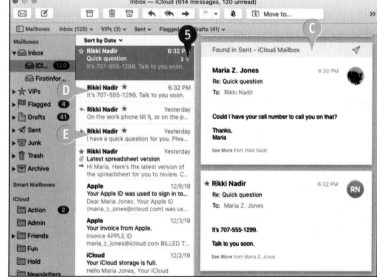

TIP

Are there other advantages to viewing an exchange as a conversation?

When you view an exchange as a conversation, you can manipulate all the messages in a single move instead of having to manipulate each message individually. For example, click the conversation and drag it to a folder to file all its messages in that folder, or click the conversation and press ⌘ + Delete to delete the entire conversation.

Block and Unblock Contacts

If you receive unwanted e-mail messages from a contact, you may want to block that contact. You can choose whether the blocking simply marks the message as blocked, with the message still appearing in your inbox, or whether Mail puts the message in your Trash folder.

You can unblock a contact quickly either by starting from a message from that contact or by opening Junk Mail preferences and working on the Blocked tab.

Block and Unblock Contacts

Block a Contact

1 In Mail, click the message.

The message appears in the reader pane.

2 Press <kbd>Control</kbd>+click the contact's name.

The pop-up menu opens.

3 Click **Block Contact**.

A The Blocked icon (👋) appears in the preview pane.

B A blue bar saying *This message is from a blocked sender* appears across the top of the reader pane.

C You can click **Preferences** to display the Blocked tab in the Junk Mail preferences pane.

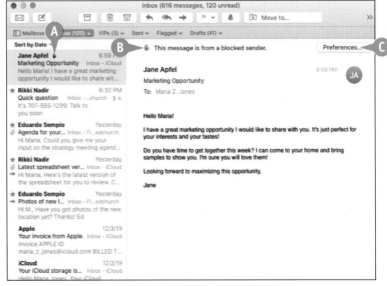

Unblock One or More Contacts

1 In Mail, click a message from the blocked contact.

The message appears in the reader pane.

2 Press `Control`+click the contact's name.

The pop-up menu opens.

3 Click **Unblock Contact**.

4 To unblock multiple contacts, click **Preferences** if the button appears. Otherwise, click **Mail** on the menu bar, click **Preferences**, click **Junk Mail** (🔲), and then click **Blocked**.

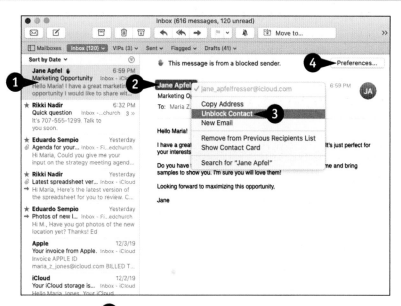

The Blocked tab of the Junk Mail preferences pane appears.

5 Click the contact or contacts you want to unblock.

6 Click **Remove** (⊟).

Mail removes the contact from the block list.

ⓓ In the When Email from Blocked Address Arrives area, click **Mark as blocked mail, but leave it in my Inbox** (◉) or **Move it to the Trash** (◉), as appropriate.

7 Click **Close** (●).

The Preferences window closes.

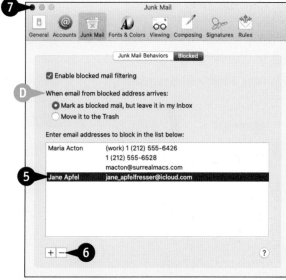

TIP

Why does the Block Contact command not appear for some of my contacts?
The Block Contact command does not appear if the contact is a VIP. Press `Control`+click the contact's name in a message header to display the pop-up window, and then click **Remove from VIPs**. You can then press `Control`+click the name again and click **Block Contact** to block the now-demoted contact.

Reduce the Amount of Spam You Receive

*S*pam is unwanted e-mail messages, also called *junk mail*. Spam ranges from messages offering specialized products, such as pharmaceuticals, to attempts to steal your financial details, passwords, or personal information.

Mail includes features that enable you to reduce the amount of spam that reaches your inbox. You can configure Mail to identify junk mail automatically, and you can learn to spot identifying features of spam messages. Unfortunately, it is not yet possible to avoid spam completely.

Reduce the Amount of Spam You Receive

Set Mail to Identify Junk Mail Automatically

1. With the Mail app active, click **Mail**.

   The Mail menu opens.

2. Click **Preferences**.

   The Preferences window opens.

3. Click **Junk Mail** (🗑).

4. Click **Junk Mail Behaviors**.

   The Junk Mail Behaviors tab appears.

5. Click **Enable junk mail filtering** (☐ changes to ☑).

6. Click **Mark as junk mail, but leave it in my Inbox** (◯ changes to ◉) to review junk mail in your inbox.

7. Click each of the three check boxes (☐ changes to ☑).

8. Click **Trust junk mail headers in messages** (☐ changes to ☑).

9. Click **Close** (●).

   The Preferences window closes.

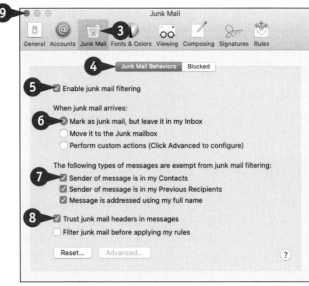

Review Your Junk Mail

1 Click **Inbox** or the inbox of a particular account, such as **Google**.

2 Click a message.

3 See whether Mail has identified the message as junk mail.

4 See if the message is addressed to you.

5 Check whether the message greets you by name or with a generic greeting.

6 Look for typos, odd phrasing, or odd grammar.

7 Read the message's content for veracity.

8 If a message appears to be spam, and Mail has not identified it as junk, click **Junk** (⊠).

9 Click **Delete** (🗑) to delete the message.

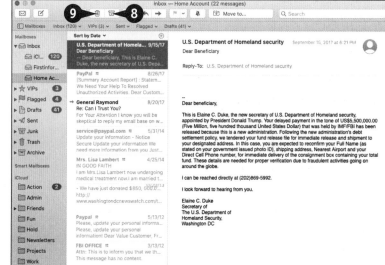

TIP

How can I tell whether a message is genuine or spam?

If a message does not show your e-mail address and your name, it is most likely spam. If the message does show your e-mail address and name, read the content carefully to establish whether the message is genuine. If the message calls for action, such as reactivating an online account that you have, do not click a link in the message. Instead, open Safari and type the address of the website, making sure it is correct — if in doubt, use a search engine to search for it. Log in to the website as usual, and see if an alert is waiting for you.

CHAPTER 8

Chatting and Calling

macOS includes Messages for instant messaging and FaceTime for video chat with users of Macs and iOS devices. You can also configure Handoff with your iPhone so that you can phone and send SMS messages using your MacBook.

Set Up Messages and Choose Preferences

The Messages app enables you to chat with your contacts via instant messaging. Using Messages, you can connect via Apple's iMessage service to contacts on Macs, iOS devices, and iPads. If you have messaging accounts on the Jabber service, you can add those to Messages, too.

If you have set up iCloud on your MacBook, Messages should already be configured for your iCloud account, and you can add any other messaging accounts as needed. If you have not set up iCloud, you must add an account to Messages before you can use the app.

Set Up Messages and Choose Preferences

1 Click **Messages** (🗨) on the Dock.

The iMessage window opens.

Note: If the Messages window opens instead of the iMessage window, go to step **5**.

2 Type your Apple ID.

3 Click **Next**.

A You can click **Create new Apple ID** to create an Apple ID if you do not have one.

4 Type your password.

5 Click **Next**.

The Messages window opens.

6 Click **Messages**.

The Messages menu opens.

7 Click **Preferences**.

The Preferences window opens.

8 Click **General** (🔲).

The General tab appears.

9 Click **Keep messages** (🔽) and click the length of time to keep messages: **30 Days**, **One Year**, or **Forever**.

10 Click **Save history when conversations are closed** (☐ changes to ☑) if you want to save history.

11 Click **Notify me about messages from unknown contacts** (☑ changes to ☐) if you want to suppress notifications about messages from unknown people.

12 Click **Notify me when my name is mentioned** (☐ changes to ☑) to have Messages tell you when your first name or full name appears in a message. This can be useful in group chats.

13 Select (☑) **Play sound effects** if you want to hear sound effects. Click **Message received sound** (⬥) and select the sound for incoming messages.

14 Click **Save received files to** (⬥), click **Other**, click the appropriate folder, and then click **Select**.

15 Drag the **Text size** slider as needed to set the text size for Messages.

16 Click **iMessage** (@) to display the iMessage tab.

Ⓑ You can click **Enable this account** (☑ changes to ☐) to disable an account without removing it.

17 Click **Enable Messages in iCloud** (☐ changes to ☑) if you want to sync your messages via iCloud so that all your devices can show the same conversations.

18 In the You Can Be Reached for Messages At list, click (☑ changes to ☐) any phone number or address at which you do not want to be contacted.

19 Click **Send read receipts** (☐ changes to ☑) if you want to send read receipts for messages in all conversations.

20 Click **Start new conversations from** (⬥) and then click the phone number or e-mail address from which to start conversations.

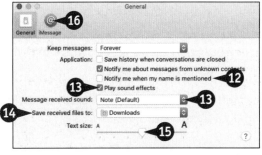

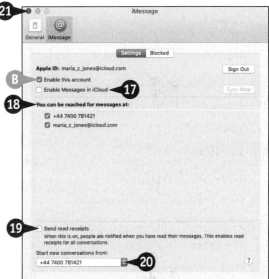

21 Click **Close** (⬤).

The Preferences window closes.

Chat with a Buddy

Messages enables you to chat with your contacts, or *buddies*, via instant messaging. The easiest way to start using Messages is by sending text messages. Depending on the messaging services and the computers or devices your buddies are using, you may be able to chat via audio or video as well.

To start chatting, you send your buddy an invitation. If your buddy accepts the invitation, the reply appears in the Messages window. You can conduct multiple chats simultaneously, switching from chat to chat as needed.

Chat with a Buddy

1 Click **Messages** ( ) on the Dock.

The Messages window opens.

2 Click **Compose New Message** ( ).

A New Message entry appears in the left pane.

3 Click **Add Contact** ( ).

The Contacts panel opens.

4 Click the buddy with whom you want to chat.

The buddy's addresses appear.

5 Click the appropriate address.

Ⓐ The buddy's name appears as a button in the To area.

Note: If the buddy's button appears red, it means that the buddy is not registered with iMessage. You may need to use a different address to contact the buddy.

6 Type the text you want to send, and then press Return.

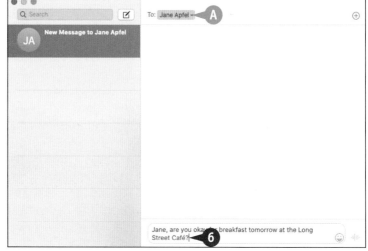

B Your message appears in a bubble on the right side of the right pane.

Note: You can make messages display buddy pictures by clicking **View** on the menu bar and then clicking **Show All Buddy Pictures in Conversations**.

C A reply from your buddy appears on the left side of the right pane.

7 Type a reply to your buddy's reply.

8 Click **Special Characters** (☺).

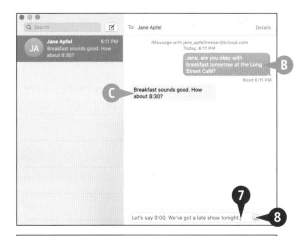

The **Special Characters** panel opens.

9 Click the category of special characters you want: **Recents and Favorites** (🕐), **Smileys & People** (☺), **Animals & Nature** (🐻), **Food & Drink** (🍴), **Activity** (⚽), **Objects** (💡), **Symbols** (🔣), or **Flags** (🏳).

10 Click the special character you want to use.

The special character appears in the message.

11 Press Return.

Messages sends the message.

TIP

How can I turn off notifications for a conversation?
In the left pane, press Control +click the conversation you want to affect, and then click **Do Not Disturb** on the contextual menu.

From the contextual menu, you can also give other commands, such as clicking **Open Conversation in Separate Window** to move this conversation to a separate window or **Delete Conversation** to delete this conversation.

Send and Receive Files with Messages

As well as chat, Messages enables you to send files easily to your buddies and receive files they send to you. During a chat, you can send a file either by using the Send File command or by dragging a file from a Finder window into Messages.

When a buddy sends you a file, you can decide whether to receive it. Messages automatically stores the files you receive in the Downloads folder in your user account, but you can change the destination to another folder if you so choose.

Send and Receive Files with Messages

Send a File

1 Start a text chat with the buddy to whom you want to send a file, or accept a chat invitation from that buddy.

2 Click **Buddies**.

The Buddies menu opens.

3 Click **Send File**.

The Send File dialog opens.

4 Click the file you want to send.

5 Click **Send**.

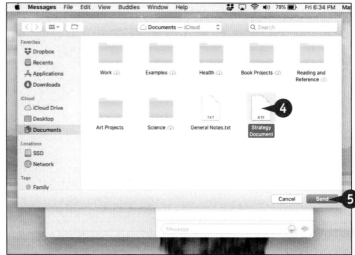

Ⓐ A button for the file appears in the text box.

⑥ Type any message needed.

⑦ Press Return.

Messages sends the message, including a button for transferring the file.

If your buddy accepts the file, Messages transfers it.

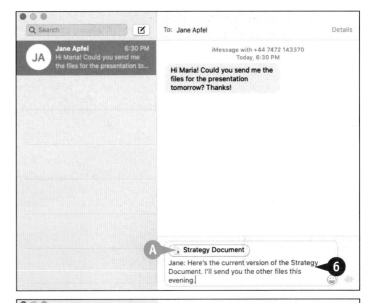

Receive a File

Ⓑ When your buddy sends you a file, it appears as a button in the Chat window.

① Press Control + click the file's button.

The contextual menu opens.

② Click **Save to Downloads**.

Messages saves the file to the Downloads folder.

You can then open the Downloads folder — for example, click **Finder** (🙂) on the Dock, and then click **Downloads** in the sidebar — and double-click the file to open it in its default app.

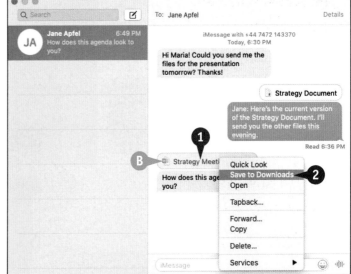

TIP

Can I change the folder in which Messages puts files I download?
Yes, you can change the folder from its default location, the Downloads folder in your user account. To change the folder, click **Messages**, and then click **Preferences**. The Preferences window opens. Click **General** (🔲) in the upper-left corner. The General preferences pane opens. Click **Save Received Files To** (⬦), and then click **Other**. A dialog opens. Click the folder you want to put your downloaded files in, and then click **Select**. Click **Close** (⚫) to close the Preferences window.

Sign In to FaceTime and Set Preferences

A pple's FaceTime technology enables you to make audio and video calls easily across the Internet. FaceTime works with all recent Macs and with current and recent models of the iPhone, iPod touch, and iPad.

Your MacBook includes a built-in video camera and microphone, so it is ready to use FaceTime right out of the box. Before you can make calls, you may need to sign in to FaceTime. You may also want to choose preferences for FaceTime.

Sign In to FaceTime and Set Preferences

Open and Set Up FaceTime

1 Click **FaceTime** (🎥) on the Dock.

Note: If the FaceTime icon does not appear on the Dock, click **Launchpad** (🚀) on the Dock, and then click **FaceTime** (🎥) on the Launchpad screen.

> The FaceTime window opens.
>
> The FaceTime app signs you in to the FaceTime service.

Note: If FaceTime prompts you to sign in, type your Apple ID and password, and then click **Sign In**.

2 Click **FaceTime** on the menu bar.

> The FaceTime menu opens.

3 Click **Preferences**.

The Preferences window for FaceTime opens.

4 Click **Settings**.

The Settings tab appears.

5 In the You Can Be Reached for FaceTime At list, select (☑) or deselect (☐) each phone number or Apple ID, as needed.

6 Select (☑) or deselect (☐) **Calls From iPhone** to control whether FaceTime on your MacBook can make FaceTime audio calls over your iPhone's cellular connection.

7 Click **Start new calls from** (🔽) and click the phone number or Apple ID to use for new calls.

8 Click **Ringtone** (🔽) and choose the ringtone you want to use.

9 Verify that the **Location** pop-up menu (🔽) shows your correct location. If not, click **Location** (🔽) and click your location.

10 Click **Blocked**.

The Blocked tab appears.

Ⓐ To remove a phone number or an Apple ID from the blocked list, click the appropriate line, and then click **Remove** (−).

Ⓑ To block a phone number or an Apple ID, click **Add** (+), and then click the contact you want to block. The contact's addresses appear in the list.

11 Click **Close** (⬤).

The Preferences window closes.

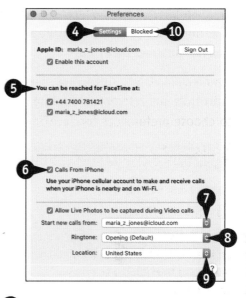

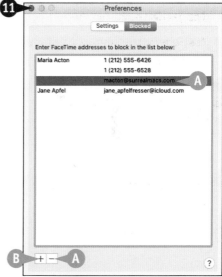

TIP

What does the Allow Live Photos to Be Captured During Video Calls setting do?
Unlike "live" photos in the Photos app, which include several seconds of video around a still image captured on an iPhone or iPad, "live" photos in FaceTime refers to taking still shots by tapping **Take Photo** (◯) during a FaceTime video call. If you deselect (☐) this check box, no participant in the call can take still photos in the FaceTime call. Instead, the Live Photos Is Disabled message box appears, prompting you to tap **Enable** to enable Live Photos for future calls. Any participant can still take screenshots of the call — for example, by pressing ⌘+Shift+3 to capture the full screen on a Mac.

Make and Receive FaceTime Calls

When you have set up FaceTime with your Apple ID, you can make and receive FaceTime calls from your MacBook. You can call any iPhone user or any user of a Mac, iPhone, iPad, or iPod touch who has enabled FaceTime.

To make a call, you open FaceTime, click the contact, and then select the e-mail address or phone number to use for contacting him. To receive a call, you simply answer when FaceTime alerts you to the incoming call.

Make and Receive FaceTime Calls

Make a FaceTime Call

1 Click **FaceTime** (▣) on the Dock.

Note: If no FaceTime icon appears on the Dock, click **Launchpad** (🚀), and then click **FaceTime** (▣).

2 Click **Enter a name, email, or number** at the top of the left pane.

3 Start typing the contact's name, and then click the contact.

4 Click **Video**.

FaceTime places the call.

5 When your contact answers, begin chatting.

Ⓐ Your video preview appears as a thumbnail.

Ⓑ You can tap **Take Photo** (◎) to take a photo of the chat.

6 When you are ready to finish the call, move the mouse to display the pop-up controls, and then click **End** (⊗).

Receive a FaceTime Call

When you receive a FaceTime call, a FaceTime window appears.

1 Click **Accept**.

Note: In the Contacts app, you can assign a specific ringtone and a specific text tone to a contact. These tones can help you identify which contact is calling or messaging you.

The call begins.

C You can move the mouse to display the pop-up controls and then click **Mute** (🔇) to mute the audio.

2 Chat with your caller.

3 When you are ready to finish the call, click **End** (❌) on the pop-up controls.

Configure and Use Handoff with Your iPhone

If you have an iPhone, iPad, or iPod touch, you can enjoy the impressive integration that Apple has built into the iOS, iPadOS, and macOS operating systems. Apple calls this integration Continuity. Continuity involves several features including Handoff, which enables you to pick up your work or play seamlessly on one device exactly where you have left it on another device. For example, you can start writing an e-mail message on your Mac and then complete it on your iOS device. This section shows you Continuity and Handoff using an iPhone, which offers more extensive features than an iPad or an iPod touch.

Understand Which iPhone Models and Mac Models Can Use Continuity

All current and recent iPhone models and Mac models can use Continuity. Your Mac must have Bluetooth 4.0 hardware. In practice, this includes a Mac mini or MacBook Air from 2011 or later, a MacBook Pro or iMac from 2012 or later, a Mac Pro from 2013 or later, or a MacBook from 2015 or later.

Enable Handoff on Your iPhone

To enable your iPhone to communicate with your Mac, you need to enable the Handoff feature. From the Home screen, tap **Settings** (⚙) to open the Settings app, tap **General** (⚙) to display the General screen, and then tap **AirPlay & Handoff**. On the AirPlay & Handoff screen, set the **Handoff** switch to On (⚪).

Enable Handoff on Your Mac

You also need to enable Handoff on your Mac. To do so, click **Apple** (🍎) on the menu bar and then click **System Preferences** to open the System Preferences window. Click **General** (▦) to display the General pane. Click **Allow Handoff between this Mac and your iCloud devices** (☐ changes to ☑). You can then click **System Preferences** on the menu bar and click **Quit System Preferences** to quit System Preferences.

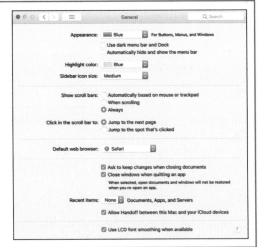

Make and Take Phone Calls on Your Mac

When you are using your Mac within Bluetooth range of your iPhone, Continuity enables you to make and take phone calls on your Mac instead of your iPhone. For example, when someone calls you on your iPhone, your Mac displays a call window automatically, and you can pick up the call on your Mac.

Send and Receive Text Messages from Your Mac

Your Mac can already send and receive messages via Apple's iMessage service, but when your iPhone's connection is available, your Mac can send and receive messages directly via Short Message Service (SMS) and Multimedia Messaging Service (MMS). This capability enables you to manage your messaging smoothly and tightly from your Mac.

Your SMS conversations appear in green bubbles, whereas iMessage conversations appear in blue bubbles, enabling you to distinguish SMS conversations easily from iMessage conversations and to know that you cannot use iMessage features, such as file exchange, in SMS conversations.

CHAPTER 9

Organizing Your Life

To help you keep your daily life organized, your MacBook includes the Calendar, Contacts, Reminders, and Maps apps.

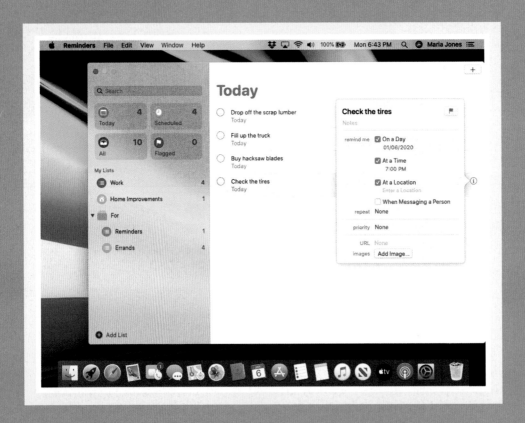

Manage Your Apple ID and iCloud Account

Your Apple ID is your personal account for accessing Apple's services, from iCloud to the iTunes store and from FaceTime to iMessage. Your MacBook uses your Apple ID for authentication, authorization, and payments on Apple's services, so you should make sure that your Apple ID information is accurate. You can do so by working in the Apple ID pane in the System Preferences app.

Display the Apple ID Pane in System Preferences

Press **Control**+click **System Preferences** (⚙) on the Dock to open the contextual menu, and then click **Apple ID** to display the Apple ID preferences pane in the System Preferences window.

Your picture — if you have assigned one — appears at the top of the sidebar on the left of the Apple ID pane, with the e-mail address used for your Apple ID under it. Below the e-mail address appear four buttons for navigating the categories of Apple ID settings: Overview (⬛); Name, Phone, Email (📞); Password & Security (🔒); and Payment & Shipping (📧).

In the next section of the sidebar are buttons for iCloud (☁) and Media & Purchases (🅰). The iCloud category is selected by default, and you can use the controls to specify which apps use iCloud, to set options for iCloud Drive, to optimize storage on your MacBook, and to manage your iCloud storage.

Configure Overview Settings and "Name, Phone, Email" Settings

Click **Overview** (⬛) to display the Overview category of Apple ID settings. The Overview pane is mostly empty, but you can click **Sign Out** if you need to sign out of your iCloud account — normally, you would stay signed in — or click **About Apple ID & Privacy** to display information on these topics.

Click **Name, Phone, Email** (📞) to display the "Name, Phone, Email" category of settings. In the upper part of this pane, you can edit your display name; edit your official birthdate; and manage the phone numbers and e-mail addresses at which you are reachable on iMessage, FaceTime, Game Center, and other Apple Services.

In the lower half of this pane, you can edit the Hide My Email settings, which enable you to avoid giving your real e-mail address to developers you do not trust. You can also choose which announcements, news updates, and promotional information you receive from Apple's services.

Configure Password & Security Settings

Click **Password & Security** (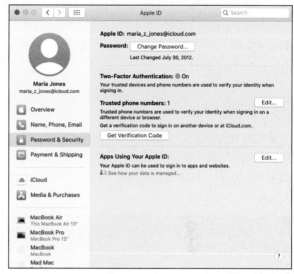) to display the Password & Security category of Apple ID settings. At the top of this pane, you can click **Change Password** to change the password for your Apple ID. Further down, verify that the Two-Factor Authentication readout shows On to make sure that your trusted devices — such as your iPhone and iPad — are being used to verify your identity when you sign in on untrusted devices.

Also in this pane, you can click **Edit** in the Trusted Phone Numbers section to edit the trusted phone numbers used to verify your identity. You can click **Get Verification Code** to have Apple's ID services send you a verification code for signing in on another device.

In the Apps Using Your Apple ID section, you can click **Edit** to display the list of apps and websites using your Apple ID as your sign-in credential. From the Apps Using Your Apple ID dialog that opens, you can change your Hide My Email settings or click **Stop Using Apple ID** to cease using your Apple ID for that app or website.

Configure Payment & Shipping Settings

Click **Payment & Shipping** () to display the Payment & Shipping category of Apple ID settings. At the top of this pane, the Payment Method section shows the payment method or methods you have set up for use with your Apple ID.

Further down the pane, the Family Sharing section shows the services you are sharing via Family Sharing — such as iTunes, Apple Books, App Store, and iCloud storage purchases — and the payment method or methods you are using.

The Apple Cash Balance section shows the available balance of Apple Cash for use on Apple Pay.

Last, the Shipping Address section shows your shipping name and address. If you have not yet added shipping information, click **Add a shipping address** to do so.

Navigate the Calendar App

The Calendar app enables you to input your appointments and events and track them easily. After launching the app, you can navigate to the dates with which you need to work. You can sync your calendar data with your iPhone, iPad, or iPod touch.

Calendar has a streamlined user interface that makes it easy to move among days, weeks, months, and years. You can click the **Today** button to display the current day, or use the Go to Date dialog to jump directly to a specific date.

Navigate the Calendar App

Open Calendar and Navigate by Days

1 Click **Calendar** (▦) on the Dock.

Calendar opens.

2 Click **Day**.

Calendar displays the current day, including a schedule of the day's events.

3 Click **Next** (>) to move to the next day or **Previous** (<) to move to the previous day.

Calendar displays the day you chose.

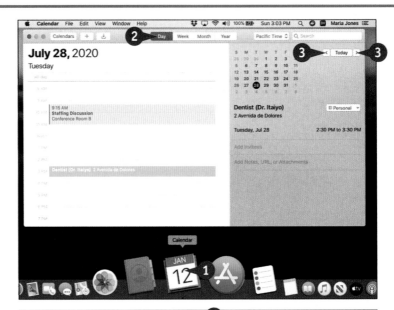

View and Navigate by Weeks

1 Click **Week**.

Calendar displays the week for the date you were previously viewing.

2 Click **Next** (>) to move to the next week or **Previous** (<) to move to the previous week.

Calendar displays the week you chose.

View and Navigate by Months

1 Click **Month**.

Calendar displays the current month.

2 Click **Next** (**>**) to move to the next month or **Previous** (**<**) to move to the previous month.

Calendar displays the month you chose.

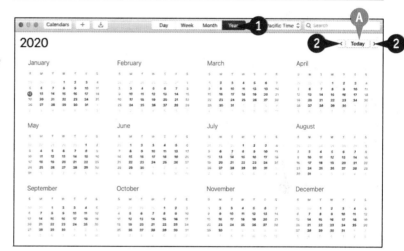

View and Navigate by Years

1 Click **Year**.

Calendar displays the year for the date you were last viewing.

2 Click **Next** (**>**) to move to the next year or **Previous** (**<**) to move to the previous year.

Calendar displays the year you chose.

Note: In Week view, Month view, or Year view, double-click a day to display it in Day view.

A You can click **Today** to display today's date.

TIP

Which keyboard shortcuts can I use to navigate in Calendar?

Press ⌘+**1** to display the calendar by day, ⌘+**2** by week, ⌘+**3** by month, or ⌘+**4** by year. Press ⌘+**→** to move to the next day, week, month, or year, or ⌘+**←** to move to the previous one. Press ⌘+**Shift**+**T** to open the Go to Date dialog, which enables you to jump to a specific date. Press ⌘+**T** to jump to today's date.

Create a New Calendar

Calendar enables you to create as many calendars as you need to separate your events into logical categories. Calendar comes with three iCloud calendars already created for you: the Home calendar, the Family calendar, and the Work calendar. Any calendars in other online accounts you have set up on your MacBook and enabled calendars on appear automatically as well. You can create new calendars as needed alongside these calendars.

After creating a new calendar, you can create events in it. You can also change existing events from another calendar to the new calendar.

Create a New Calendar

1 Click **Calendar** (📅) on the Dock.

Calendar opens.

2 Click **File** on the menu bar.

The File menu opens.

3 Click **New Calendar**.

Note: If, when you click **New Calendar**, the New Calendar submenu opens, click the calendar service, such as iCloud, in which to create the new calendar.

Note: If the Calendars pane is open, you can create a new calendar by pressing `Control` + clicking in open space in the Calendars pane and then clicking **New Calendar** on the contextual menu.

Calendar displays the Calendars pane if it was hidden.

Calendar creates a new calendar and displays an edit box around its default name, Untitled.

4 Type the name for the calendar and press `Return`.

Calendar applies the name to the calendar.

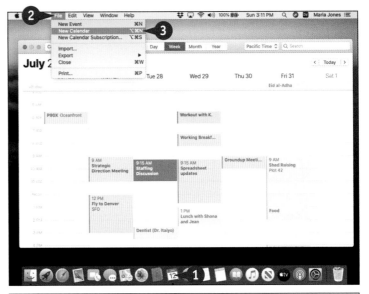

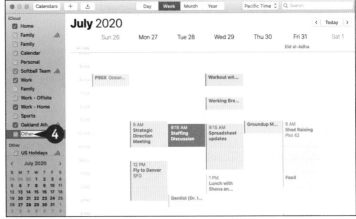

5 Press **Control** +click the calendar's name.

The contextual menu opens.

6 Click **Get Info**.

A dialog opens showing information for the calendar.

7 Click **Color** (◆) and then select the color you want the calendar to use.

8 Type a description for the calendar.

Ⓐ Click **Ignore alerts** (☐ changes to ✓) if you want to suppress alerts for the calendar.

9 Click **OK**.

The dialog closes.

You can now add events to the calendar.

TIPS

What do the check boxes in the Calendars pane do?

The check boxes control what calendars Calendar displays. Click a check box (✓ changes to ☐) to remove a calendar's events from display.

What does the Merge command on the pop-up menu for a calendar do?

The Merge command enables you to merge the contents of one calendar into another calendar. For example, if you have two calendars whose content areas overlap, you might merge them into a single calendar. After merging the calendars, the Calendar app deletes the calendar from which you start the merge operation.

Create an Event

Calendar makes it easy to organize your time commitments by creating an event for each appointment, meeting, trip, or special occasion. Calendar displays each event as an item on its grid, so you can see what is supposed to happen when.

You can create an event either for a specific length of time, such as 1 or 2 hours, or for an entire day. And you can create either an event that occurs only once or an event that repeats one or more times, as needed.

Create an Event

1 Click **Calendar** (🗓) on the Dock.

Calendar opens.

2 Navigate by days, weeks, months, or years to reach the day on which you want to create the event.

3 Click **Day**.

Calendar switches to Day view.

4 Click the event's start time and drag to its end time.

Calendar creates an event where you clicked and applies a default name, New Event.

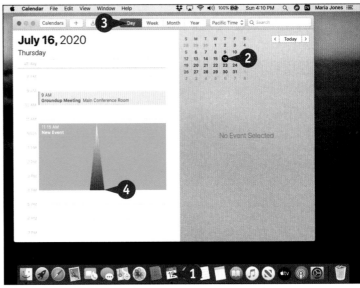

When you release the trackpad button, the event's details appear in the right pane.

5 Type the name for the event and then press Return.

6 Click **Add Location** and enter the location.

7 Click **Calendar** (🔽) and then click the calendar to which you want to assign the event.

8 Click **Add Alert, Repeat, or Travel Time**.

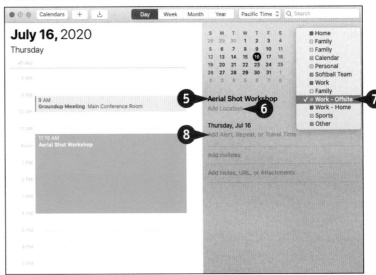

Controls for setting the alert, repeat, and travel time appear.

Ⓐ You can click **all-day** (☐ changes to ☑) to make the event an all-day event.

Ⓑ You can click **travel time** and specify the travel time required.

⑨ If you want a reminder, click **alert** and specify the details of the alert, such as **10 minutes before**. Choose **Time to Leave** to have macOS calculate the travel time to the address you have specified.

⑩ Click **Add Invitees** and specify anybody to invite to the event.

⑪ To add more information, click **Add Notes, URL, or Attachments**.

⑫ Click **Add Note** and type any notes needed.

⑬ Click **Add URL** and type or paste the URL for the event.

⑭ Click **Add Attachment**, click the file in the Open dialog, and then click **Open**.

⑮ When you finish entering details, click outside the details pane.

The details pane closes.

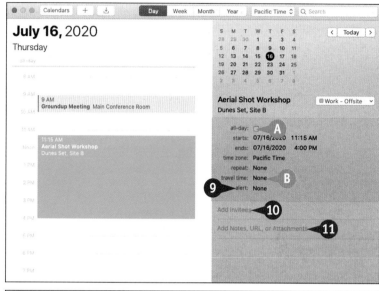

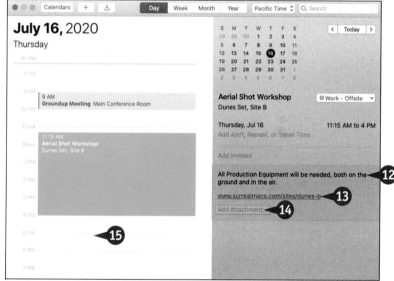

TIP

How do I create a repeating event?

In the details pane, click **repeat** and click **Every Day**, **Every Week**, **Every Month**, or **Every Year**. Use the controls that appear for setting the details of the repetition — for example, click **end repeat**, click **After**, and then specify **8 times**. For other options, click **Custom** to open the Custom dialog. You can then click **Frequency** (▣) and select **Daily**, **Weekly**, **Monthly**, or **Yearly**, and then specify the repetition patterns, such as **Every 2 Weeks**.

Share an iCloud Calendar with Other People

Calendar enables you to share any calendar stored on iCloud with other people so that they know when you are busy. You can share an iCloud calendar either as a private calendar, available only to the people whose names or e-mail addresses you specify, or as a public calendar, available to everyone.

If you store your calendars on your MacBook rather than in iCloud, you can publish any calendar to a calendar server on the Internet to share it with others.

Share an iCloud Calendar with Other People

Open the Dialog for Sharing a Calendar

1. Click **Calendar** (📅) on the Dock.

   Calendar opens.

2. Click **Calendars**.

   The Calendars pane opens.

3. Press Control+click the calendar you want to share.

   The contextual menu opens.

4. Click **Share Calendar**.

   The Share dialog opens.

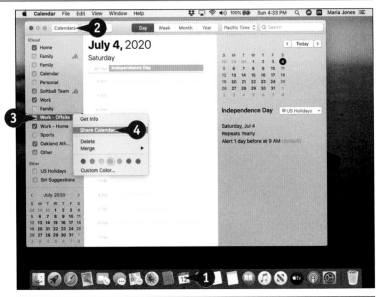

Share a Calendar with Specific People

1. In the Share dialog, start typing a name or e-mail address.

2. Click the e-mail address for the contact.

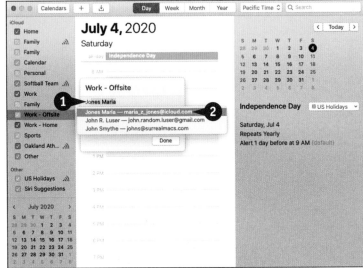

The contact's name appears as a button in the Shared With list.

③ Click the pop-up button (⌄) on the contact's button.

The pop-up menu opens.

④ Click **View & Edit** to enable the contact to edit the calendar. Click **View Only** to enable the contact to only view the calendar.

Ⓐ You can add other contacts as needed by clicking **Share With** (⊕).

⑤ Click **Done**.

Calendar shares the calendar with the people you specified.

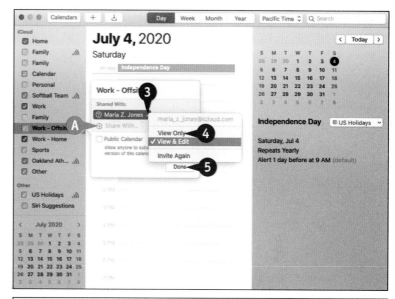

Make a Calendar Public

① In the Share dialog, click **Public Calendar** (☐ changes to ☑).

The URL field appears, showing the web address for the shared calendar.

Ⓑ You can click **Share** (↥) to share the URL.

② Click **Done**.

The Share dialog closes, and the Calendar app makes the calendar public.

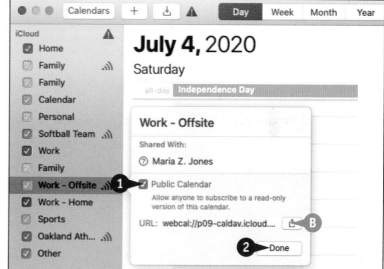

TIP

How do I publish a calendar stored on my MacBook?

Click **Calendars** to display the Calendars pane, then click the calendar. Click **Edit** on the menu bar, and then click **Publish** to open the Publish Calendar dialog. In the **Publish calendar as** box, type the name under which to share the calendar. Click **Base URL** and type or paste the URL for the calendar server, click **Login** and type your login name, and then click **Password** and type your password. Choose options, such as clicking **Publish changes automatically** (☐ changes to ☑), at the bottom of the Publish Calendar dialog, and then click **Publish** to publish the calendar.

Subscribe to a Shared Calendar

Calendar enables you to subscribe to calendars that others have shared on iCloud or published on the Internet. By subscribing to a calendar, you add it to Calendar so that you can view the events in the calendar along with those in your calendars.

You can subscribe to a calendar either by typing or pasting its URL into Calendar or by clicking a link in a message that you have received.

Subscribe to a Shared Calendar

1 Click **Calendar** (📅) on the Dock.

Calendar opens.

2 Click **File**.

The File menu opens.

3 Click **New Calendar Subscription**.

Note: Many organizations, sports teams, and artists make their calendars available on their websites. You can either copy the calendar's URL or download the calendar.

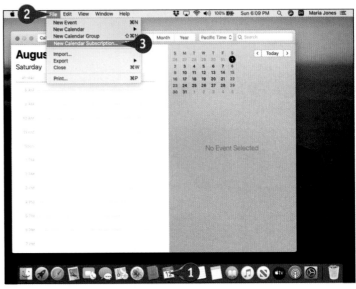

The Enter the URL of the Calendar You Want to Subscribe To dialog opens.

4 Type or paste in the calendar's URL.

Note: If you receive a link to a published calendar, click the link in Mail. Calendar opens and displays the Enter the URL of the Calendar You Want to Subscribe To dialog with the URL inserted.

5 Click **Subscribe**.

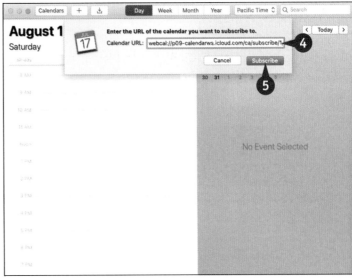

A dialog opens showing the details of the calendar.

6 If necessary, edit the default name to display for the calendar.

7 Click **Color** (⬦) and select the color to use for the calendar.

8 Click **Location** (⬦) and choose where to store the calendar. Your choices are **iCloud** or **On My Mac**.

9 Click **Alerts** (☐ changes to ☑) if you want to remove alerts.

10 Click **Attachments** (☐ changes to ☑) if you want to remove attachments.

11 Click **Auto-refresh** (⬦) and select your preferred option for automatically refreshing the calendar, such as **Every day** or **Every week**.

12 Click **Ignore alerts** (☐ changes to ☑) if you want to ignore alerts set in the calendar.

13 Click **OK**.

Calendar adds the calendar, and its events appear.

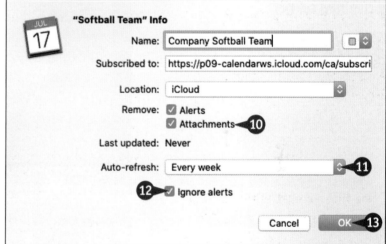

TIPS

How do I update a published calendar?
You can update all your published calendars at the same time by clicking **View** on the menu bar and then clicking **Refresh Calendars**. You can also give the Refresh Calendars command by pressing ⌘+R.

How do I unsubscribe from a published calendar?
Click **Calendars** to display the Calendars pane, press Control+click the calendar, and then click **Unsubscribe** on the contextual menu.

Add Someone to Your Contacts

The Contacts app enables you to track and manage your contacts. Contacts stores the data for each contact on a separate virtual address card that contains storage slots for many different items of information, from the person's name and phone numbers to the e-mail addresses and photo.

To add a contact, you create a new contact card and enter the person's data on it. You can also add contact information quickly from vCard address card files that you receive.

Add Someone to Your Contacts

1 Click **Contacts** (⬛) on the Dock.

The Contacts app opens.

2 Click **Add** (+).

The Add pop-up menu opens.

3 Click **New Contact**.

Note: You can also create a new contact card by clicking **File** on the menu bar and then clicking **New Card** on the File menu.

Contacts creates a new card and selects the First placeholder.

4 Type the contact's first name.

Note: Press Tab to move the focus from the current field to the next.

5 Type the contact's last name.

6 If the contact works for a company, type the company name.

Ⓐ You can click **Company** (☐ changes to ☑) when creating a card for a company or organization rather than for an individual. Contacts then uses the company name for sorting.

⑦ Click the pop-up menu (◌) next to the first Phone field and select the type of phone number, such as **work** or **mobile**.

⑧ Type the phone number.

⑨ Add other phone numbers as needed.

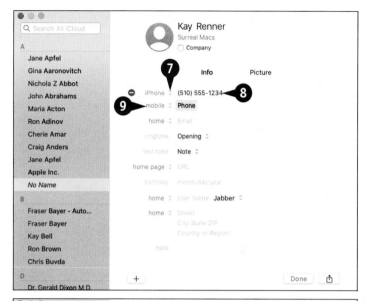

⑩ Click the pop-up menu (◌) next to the first Email field and then click the type of e-mail address, such as **work** or **home**.

⑪ Type the e-mail address.

⑫ Add the physical address and other information.

⑬ Click **Done**.

Contacts closes the card for editing.

The card appears in the contacts list.

Note: Only the fields that contain data appear in the card.

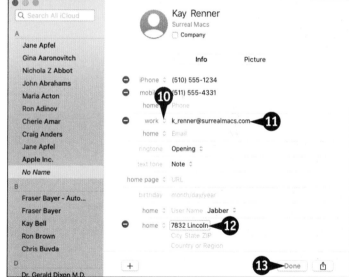

How do I add a vCard to Contacts?
If you receive a vCard file, which has the .vcf file extension and contains a virtual address card, in Mail, press Control +click the card, highlight **Open With** on the contextual menu, and then select **Contacts**. A dialog opens prompting you to confirm that you want to import the card into Contacts. Click **Import**.

How do I delete a contact from Contacts?
To delete a contact, click the card, click **Edit**, and then select **Delete Card** or press Delete. A confirmation dialog opens. Click **Delete**.

Change a Contact's Information

Contacts makes it easy to change the information for a contact. So when you learn that a contact's details have changed, or you need to add extra information, you can open the contact record and make the changes needed.

Contacts enables you to add a wide variety of different fields to a contact record to store the information about a contact. You can also add a photo to a contact record.

Change a Contact's Information

1 Click **Contacts** (📘) on the Dock.

The Contacts app opens.

2 In the left pane, click the contact whose information you want to change.

3 Click **Edit**.

Contacts opens the contact's card for editing.

4 To change an existing field, click it, and then type the updated information.

A You can add a field by clicking **Add** (+) and then clicking the field on the contextual menu or the More Fields submenu.

5 To remove an existing field, click **Remove** (➖) next to it.

6 To add a photo for the contact, click **Picture**.

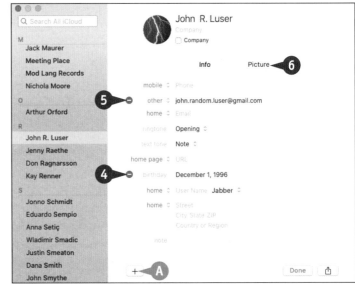

The Picture tab appears.

7 Click **Add** (⊕) or the existing picture, if there is one.

A dialog for choosing a picture appears.

8 Click the photo source, such as **Photo Booth**.

Note: Click **Defaults** to assign one of macOS's user account pictures. Click **Camera** to take a photo with your MacBook's camera. Click **Photos** to use a picture from the Photos app. Click **Photo Booth** to use a picture from the Photo Booth app.

9 Click the photo you want to use.

The photo opens for editing.

10 Drag the slider to zoom in or out.

11 Drag the photo to change the part that appears.

12 Click **Save**.

Contacts adds the photo to the contact record.

13 Click **Done**.

Contacts closes the contact record for editing.

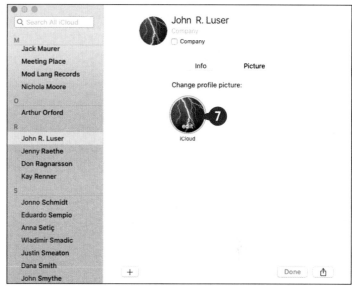

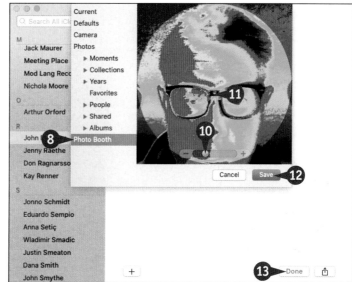

TIPS

How can I add information that does not fit in any of Contacts' fields?

You can use the Notes field for any information, but you can also create custom fields. Click the pop-up menu (↕) next to an empty field, and then click **Custom** to open the Add Custom Label dialog. Type the name for the field and click **OK.** You can then type the data for the field.

Are there other ways of adding photos to contact records?

Yes. You can drag a photo from the Photos app, a Finder window, an e-mail message, or a web page to the photo placeholder.

Organize Contacts into Groups

Contacts enables you to organize your contacts into separate groups, making it easier to find the contacts you need. Groups are useful if you have several different categories of contacts, such as family, friends, and colleagues. You can assign any contact to as many groups as needed.

After creating groups, you can view a single group at a time or search within a group. You can also send an e-mail message to all the members of a group.

Organize Contacts into Groups

Create a Group of Contacts

1 Click **Contacts** (■) on the Dock.

The Contacts app opens.

2 Click **View**.

The View menu opens.

3 Click **Show Groups**.

Note: You can also press ⌘+Shift+1 to display or hide the Groups pane.

The Groups pane opens on the left side of the Contacts window.

4 Position the pointer over the account in which you want to create the group, such as **iCloud**.

The Add button (●) appears.

5 Click **Add** (●).

Contacts adds a group and displays an edit box around the default name, Untitled Group.

6 Type the name and press Return.

The name appears.

Note: Your contact groups appear on any iOS device you sync with the same iCloud account. iOS devices enable you to create and edit contacts, but not to manipulate groups.

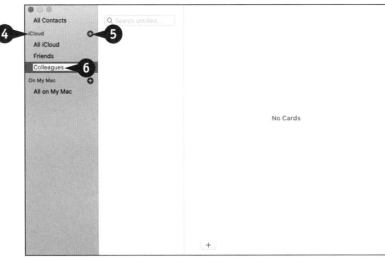

Add Contacts to a Group

1 Click **All Contacts**.

Contacts displays all your contacts.

2 Drag one or more contacts to the new group.

Note: To add multiple contacts to the group, click the first, and then press ⌘ + click each of the others. Drag the selected contacts to the group.

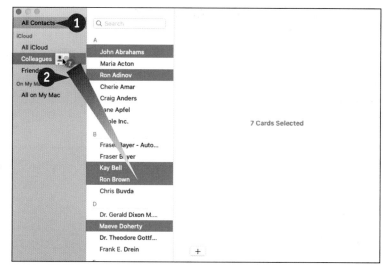

View a Group or Search Within It

1 Click the group.

Contacts displays the contacts in the group.

2 To search within the group, click in the Search box and type a search term.

Contacts displays matching contacts.

3 Click the contact you want to view.

A The contact's details appear.

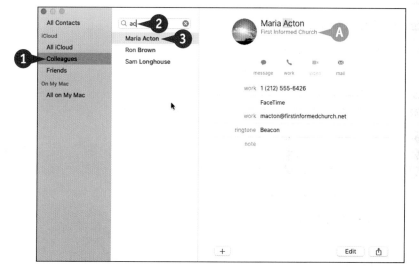

TIPS

How do I remove a contact from a group?

Click the group and then click the contact. Click **Edit** and select **Remove from Group**. Contacts removes the contact from the group but does not delete the contact record.

How do I delete a group?

Click the group in the Groups pane, so that the group is selected in blue. Click **Edit**, and then select **Delete Group**. Contacts displays a confirmation message. Click **Delete**. Deleting a group does not affect the contacts it contains; the contacts remain available through the All Contacts group or any other groups to which they belong.

Create Notes

The Notes app enables you to create notes stored in an online account, such as your iCloud account, and sync them across your devices. Alternatively, you can store notes on your MacBook itself, which is useful for private notes you do not want to sync in online accounts.

The Notes app automatically saves your notes when you make changes. You can create straightforward notes in plain text, but you can also add formatting, check boxes, photos, and other items.

Create Notes

Open the Notes App and View an Existing Note

1 Click **Notes** (⬜) on the Dock.

Note: If Notes (⬜) does not appear on the Dock, click **Launchpad** (🚀), and then click **Notes** (⬜) on the Launchpad screen.

The Notes window opens.

2 Click an existing note.

Ⓐ The contents of the note appear in the right pane.

Work with Folders

1 Click **Show Folders** (▥).

Note: You can also toggle the display of the Folders pane by clicking **View** on the menu bar and then clicking **Show Folders**.

Ⓑ The Folders pane appears.

2 Click **New Folder** (➕).

Notes creates a new folder and displays an edit box around the default name, Untitled.

3 Type the name for the folder.

4 Click elsewhere or press Return to apply the name.

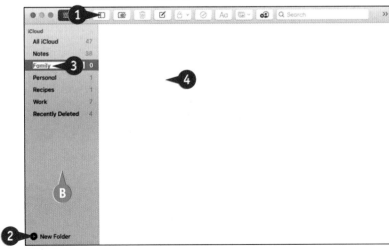

Create a New Note and Apply Formatting

1 In the Folders pane, click the folder in which you want to create the new note.

Note: If you do not have the Folders pane displayed, you cannot control which folder Notes creates the new note in. You can move the note to another folder later if necessary.

2 Click **Create a Note** (✎).

Notes creates a new blank note.

3 Type the title of the note and press Return.

Note: To set the style Notes uses for the first paragraph of a note, click **Notes** on the menu bar, and then click **Preferences**. In the Preferences window, click **New Notes Start With** (🔁), and then click **Title**, **Heading**, or **Body**, as needed. Click **Close** (⬤).

4 Start typing the text of the note.

5 When you need to change the style for a paragraph, click **Styles** (Aa).

The Styles pop-up panel opens.

6 Click the style you want to apply: **Title**, **Heading**, **Subheading**, **Body**, **Monospaced**, **Bulleted List**, **Dashed List**, or **Numbered List**.

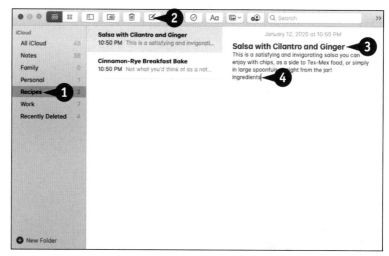

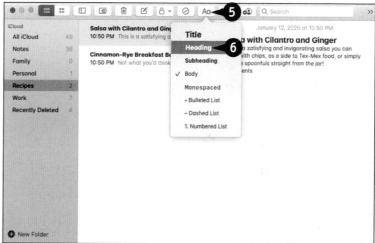

Note: Notes automatically switches to the Body style for the paragraph after a Title paragraph or a Heading or Subheading paragraph. Notes continues the Body, Monospaced, Bulleted List, Dashed List, and Numbered List styles until you change styles manually.

TIPS

Can I use styles and formatting in all my notes?
Styles are available only in notes you store in iCloud or in the On My Mac account. Basic formatting — boldface, italic, and underline — works for notes in Google, Exchange, and IMAP accounts as well as for notes in iCloud.

How do I store notes on my MacBook itself?
Click **Notes** and click **Preferences**. In the Preferences window, click **Enable the On My Mac account** (☐ changes to ☑). Click **Close** (⬤) to close the Preferences window.

continued ▶

Create Notes (continued)

The Notes app includes eight built-in styles that enable you to format your notes with a title, headings, body text, monospaced text, bulleted lists, dashed lists, and numbered lists. By using these styles to format notes instead of using direct formatting, such as bold and italic, you can create structured notes that you can easily use in a word processing app.

You can also create checklists, lists from which you can check off completed items, and create tables with as many columns and rows as you need.

Create Notes (continued)

The Styles pop-up panel closes.

Notes applies the style to the paragraph.

7 To create a checklist, drag to select the paragraphs for the list.

8 Click **Make a checklist** (⊘).

A round check box (◯) appears before each paragraph.

C You can click a check box to select it (◯ changes to ⊘).

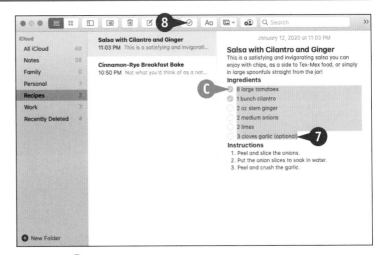

9 When you want to apply other formatting, drag to select the text you want to affect.

10 Click **Format**.

The Format menu opens.

11 Click or highlight **Font**, **Text**, or **Indentation**. This example uses **Font**.

The submenu opens.

12 Click the formatting you want to apply. For example, click **Italic**.

Notes applies that formatting to the text.

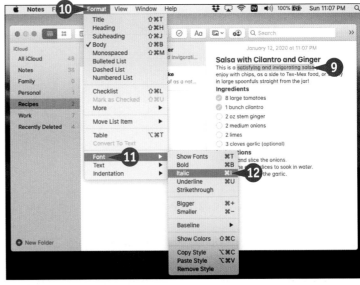

Insert a Table

1 Position the insertion point where you want the table to appear.

2 Click **Add Table** (⊞).

Notes inserts a table with two columns and two rows.

The insertion point appears in the first cell.

3 Type the content for the first cell.

4 Press Tab.

The focus moves to the next cell.

5 Type the content for the next cell.

6 Press Control+click **Select Column** (⬚).

The pop-up menu appears.

7 Click **Add Column After**.

Notes adds a new column.

8 Continue typing the cell entries, pressing Tab to move to the next cell.

Note: If the current cell is the last cell in the table, pressing Tab automatically adds a row to the table.

ⓓ You can add a new row below the current row by pressing Control+ clicking **Select Row** (⬚) and then clicking **Add Row Below** on the pop-up menu.

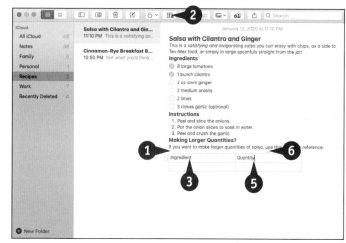

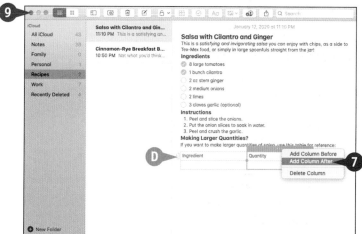

9 When you finish working with Notes, click **Close** (●).

The Notes app closes.

TIPS

How do I move a note from one folder or account to another?
Click **Show Folders** (⬚) to display the Folders pane. Click the current folder, then click the note and drag it to the destination folder.

How do I delete a note?
Either click the note in the Notes list and then click **Delete** (🗑) on the toolbar, or press Control+click the note, and then click **Delete** on the contextual menu.

Notes moves the note to the Recently Deleted folder, from which you can recover it if necessary. After 30 days, Notes permanently deletes the note.

Track Your Commitments with Reminders

The Reminders app gives you an easy way to track what you have to do and your progress on your tasks. Reminders enables you to link a reminder to a specific time, a specific location, or both. Linking a reminder to a location is useful when you sync your reminders from your MacBook with an iPhone, iPad, or iPod touch that you carry from location to location. You can assign your reminders to different reminders lists for easy management.

Track Your Commitments with Reminders

Open Reminders and Manage Your Reminders Lists

1 Click **Reminders** (📖) on the Dock.

Note: If the Reminders icon (📖) does not appear on the Dock, click **Launchpad** (🚀), and then click **Reminders** (📖).

The Reminders app opens.

Ⓐ The sidebar on the left shows your various lists of reminders.

Note: If the sidebar does not appear, click **View** on the menu bar, and then click **Show Sidebar** to display it.

Ⓑ The main pane shows the reminders in the selected list.

2 Click **Add List** (➕).

Ⓒ A new reminders list appears, provisionally titled New List.

3 Type the name for the list, and then press `Return`.

Note: You can drag your lists of reminders into a different order if you want.

Note: To delete a list of reminders, press `Control` + click the list, click **Delete**, and then click **Delete** in the confirmation dialog.

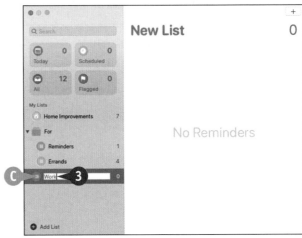

248

Create a Reminder

1 In the sidebar, click the list in which to create the new reminder.

2 Click **Add** (+).

A new reminder appears in the list.

3 Type the text of the reminder.

The Info button (ⓘ) appears to the right of the reminder.

4 Click **Add Date** (▭).

A pop-up panel opens.

D You can click a suggested date, such as **Today** or **Tomorrow**.

5 To choose a custom date, click **Custom**.

The calendar panel opens.

6 Double-click the date for the task.

E You can click **Add Location** (✈) to quickly add a location at which you want to receive a reminder for a task. Clicking this button produces a short list of suggested locations. To choose other locations, see the tip.

F You can click **Flag** (⚑ changes to ⚑) to flag the task. The task then appears in the Flagged list in the sidebar.

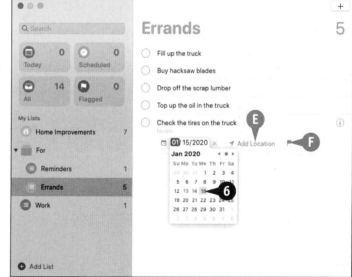

TIP

How do I link a reminder to a location?

In the pop-up panel containing the reminder's details, click **At a Location** (☐ changes to ☑). A new section appears under At a Location. Click **Enter a Location** to display the Suggestions list; if a suggestion is suitable, click it. If not, type a contact's name or an address, and then click the correct location in the Suggestions list that appears. Click either **Arriving** (◯ changes to ◉) or **Leaving** (◯ changes to ◉).

continued ▶

To find the reminders you need to work with, you can search through your reminders.

When you have completed the task for a reminder, you select the reminder's check box to mark it as complete. The reminder then disappears from your reminder lists, but you can view your completed reminders at any time by displaying the Completed list.

Track Your Commitments with Reminders (continued)

The date appears on the date button.

G You can click **Add Time** (⊙) to add a time to the task. The pop-up menu provides a list of suggested times. To choose another time, use the Info panel for the task.

7 Click **Info** (ⓘ).

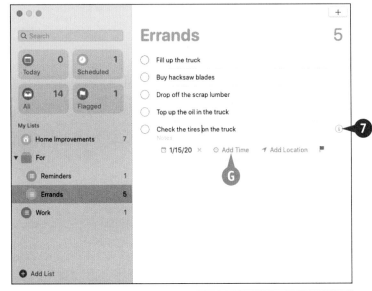

The Info panel appears.

The date and time controls appear.

8 Click **Notes** and type any notes needed for the reminder.

9 Click **At a Time** (☐ changes to ☑) and then set the time for the reminder.

H You can click **When Messaging a Person** (☐ changes to ☑) and then specify the appropriate contact.

10 If you want the reminder to repeat, click **repeat** and specify the frequency, such as **Every Week**.

11 Click **priority** (✦) and then click the priority: **None**, **Low**, **Medium**, or **High**.

12 Click outside the Info panel.

The Info panel closes.

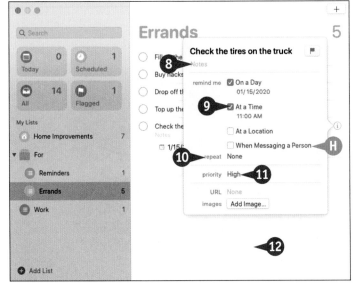

Search for a Reminder

1 Click in the Search box.

Note: You do not need to select a particular list before searching, because Reminders searches across all your reminder lists.

2 Start typing your search term or terms.

I A list of matches appears.

J You can click **Clear** (⊗) to clear the search, restoring the view to the reminders list you were viewing before.

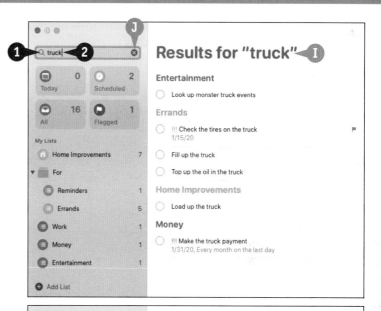

Mark a Reminder as Completed

1 Click the check circle to the left of the reminder (○ changes to ◉).

Reminders slides the completed reminder to the top of the list and then removes it.

K To see the reminders you have completed, click **Show** on the Completed line. If the Completed line is hidden, scroll to the top of the reminder list to display it.

Note: To delete a reminder, press `Control`+click it, and then click **Delete** on the contextual menu.

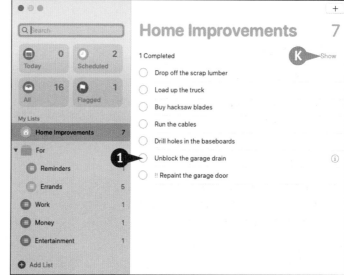

TIPS

How can I look at multiple reminder lists at the same time?

Press `Control`+click a list, and then click **Open List in New Window** on the contextual menu to open a new window showing that list.

How do I change the color of a reminder list?

Press `Control`+click the list to display the contextual menu, and then click the desired color at the bottom of the menu.

Get Directions

The Maps app enables you to pinpoint your MacBook's location by using known wireless networks. You can view your location on a road map, display a satellite picture, or view transit information for some areas. You can easily switch among map types to find the most useful one for your current needs, and you can use Maps to get directions to where you want to go.

Get Directions

Open Maps and Find Your Location

1 Click **Maps** (🧭) on the Dock or Launchpad.

The Maps window opens.

2 Click **Show Your Current Location** (➤).

Ⓐ A blue dot shows your current location.

Ⓑ You can display the scale temporarily by placing two fingers on the trackpad and pinching together or apart a short way.

Change the Map Type and Zoom In or Out

1 Click **Satellite** to switch to Satellite view.

2 Click **Zoom Out** (—) or **Zoom In** (+) to zoom in or out, as needed.

Note: You can rotate the map by placing two fingers on the trackpad and turning them. To return the map to its default northward orientation, click the orange triangle on the 3D icon ( ).

3 Click **Show** (▾).

4 Click **Show Labels** to display place names.

Ⓒ You can click **Show Traffic** to show traffic.

Ⓓ You can click **Show 3D Map** to toggle the 3D map.

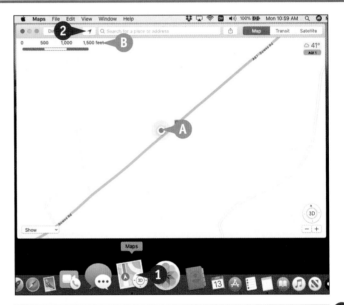

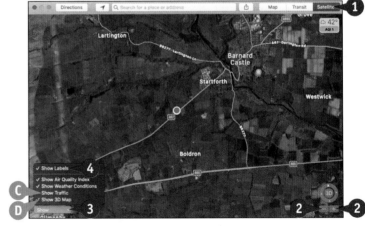

Get Directions

1 Click **Directions**.

The Directions pane opens, suggesting Current Location as your starting point.

2 Click **Start** and type your start point.

The Suggestions panel appears.

3 Click the best suggestion.

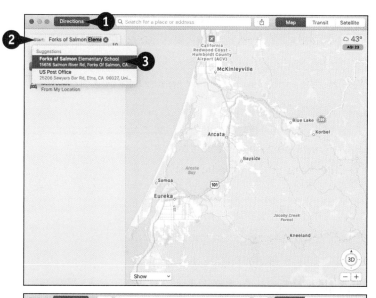

4 Click **End** and type your end point.

Maps displays suggested routes.

5 Click **Details** for the route you want to view.

E The current route's details appear in the Directions pane.

F The green pin marks the start.

G The red pin marks the end.

H The current route appears in darker blue.

I You can click another route or its time box to display its details.

6 Click a direction to display that part of the route.

TIPS

How do I get directions for walking?
Click **Walk** in the Directions pane to display the distance and time for walking the route. Be aware that walking directions may be inaccurate or optimistic. Before walking the route, verify that it does not send you across pedestrian-free bridges or through rail tunnels.

How can I send directions to my iPhone?
Click **Share** (⬆) to display the Share pop-up menu, and then click **Send to iPhone**; if you have an iPad, you can click **Send to iPad** instead. Unlock your iPhone if it is locked, and then tap the banner that appears. The Maps app on the iPhone displays the directions.

Explore with 3D Flyovers in Maps

The Maps app enables you not only to find out where you are and get directions to places, but also to explore with 3D flyovers of the places on the map.

To use 3D flyovers, you navigate to the place you want to explore, and then switch on the 3D feature. You can then zoom in and out on the map, pan around, and move backward to forward.

Explore with Maps

1 Click **Maps** ( ) on the Dock.

Note: If Maps ( ) does not appear on the Dock, click **Launchpad** ( ) on the Dock, and then click **Maps** ( ) on the Launchpad screen.

The Maps window opens.

2 Display the area of interest in the middle of the screen by browsing or searching.

3 Click **3D** ( ).

The map switches to Flyover view.

4 Click **Zoom In** (+) to zoom in.

5 Drag to scroll the map.

Note: You can also scroll the map by placing two fingers on the trackpad and dragging.

6 Place two fingers on the trackpad and turn them clockwise or counterclockwise.

Note: You can also rotate the view by pressing `Control`+clicking and dragging clockwise or counterclockwise.

The view rotates, and you can explore.

Note: Pan and zoom as needed to explore the area.

A The white arrow on the 2D icon (![2D icon]) indicates north. You can click this icon to restore the direction to north.

7 Click **2D** (![2D icon]).

The map returns to normal view.

TIP

What does 3D do with the Standard map?

When you tap **3D** (![3D icon]) to switch on Flyover with the Standard map displayed, Maps tilts the map at an angle, as you might do with a paper map, and displays outlines of buildings if they are available. For most purposes, Flyover is more useful with the Satellite map.

CHAPTER 10

Enjoying Music, Video, and Books

Your MacBook comes equipped with apps for enjoying music, podcasts, video, and books. The Music app enables you to copy songs from CDs, play them back, and create playlists. The TV app enables you to watch movies, TV shows, and videos. The Podcast app lets you enjoy podcasts. The Books app enables you to build an e-book library on your MacBook and read books anywhere.

Add Your Music to the Music App

The Music app enables you to build your music library quickly by adding your existing songs to it. You can copy songs from your CDs by using a SuperDrive or other optical drive connected to your MacBook. You can also import songs that you already have as digital files on your MacBook.

When importing songs from CDs, you can choose among different settings to create files using different formats and higher or lower audio quality. The highest-quality files give the best sound but require the most space on your MacBook's disk.

Add Your Music to the Music App

1 Click **Music** (🎵) on the Dock.

The Music app opens.

2 Insert a CD in the optical drive.

A The Devices section of the sidebar displays an entry for the CD. Occasionally, a phantom second entry appears as well.

Music looks up the CD's details online and opens a dialog asking if you want to import the CD.

Note: If you want to prevent Music from prompting you to import each audio CD you insert, click **Do not ask me again** (☐ changes to ☑) before clicking **No**.

3 Click **No** to close the dialog.

4 Click **CD Info**.

The CD Info dialog opens.

5 Verify that the information is correct. If it is not, correct it.

Note: Many entries for CDs in the online database that Music uses contain misspelled or inaccurate information.

6 Click **Album is a compilation of songs by various artists** (☐ changes to ☑) if the CD is a compilation by various artists.

7 Click **OK**.

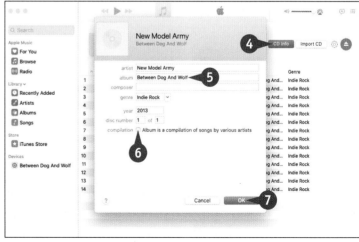

The CD Info dialog closes.

8 Click **Import CD**.

The Import Settings dialog opens.

Note: AAC Encoder is the best general-purpose choice for encoding files; the iTunes Plus setting produces high-quality audio with a modest file size. The Apple Lossless encoder produces full-quality audio, but the file size is substantially larger.

9 Click **Import Using** () and select the encoder to use.

10 Click **Setting** (⬦) and select the setting.

11 Click **Use error correction when reading Audio CDs** (☐ changes to ✓).

Note: Using error correction for reading CDs is almost always a good idea. Importing may be a little slower, but not enough to matter.

12 Click **OK**.

The Import Settings dialog closes.

Music imports the songs.

13 When Music finishes importing, click **Eject** (⏏).

The optical drive ejects the CD.

TIPS

How can I create MP3 files rather than AAC files?
In the Import Settings dialog, click **Import Using** (⬦) and select **MP3 Encoder**. Click **Setting** (⬦) and select the quality you want: **Higher Quality** gives reasonable quality, but for top quality, select **Custom**, click **Stereo Bit Rate** (⬦), and then click the **320 kbps** bit rate.

How do I import music from digital files on my MacBook?
Click **File** on the menu bar to open the File menu, and then click **Add to Library**. In the dialog that opens, navigate to the digital files, select them, and then click **Open**.

Set Up Home Sharing

macOS, iOS, and iPadOS include a feature called *Home Sharing* that enables you to share songs and videos among your and your family's Macs, PCs, iPads, and iOS devices. Home Sharing saves time and effort over copying song files manually between computers. Each family member who uses Home Sharing must have an Apple ID, such as the one created when setting up an account on Apple's iTunes Store. Anyone without an Apple ID can create one in a couple of minutes.

Set Up Home Sharing

1 Press Control+click **System Preferences** (⚙) on the Dock.

The contextual menu opens.

2 Click **Sharing**.

System Preferences opens and displays the Sharing pane.

3 Click **Media Sharing**.

The Media Sharing controls appear.

Ⓐ You can change the default name under which your library appears when shared.

4 Click **Home Sharing** (☐).

The Enter the Apple ID Used to Create Your Home Share dialog opens.

5 Type your Apple ID.

6 Type your password.

7 Click **Turn On Home Sharing**.

The Verify Your Identity dialog opens.

Note: If you have not enabled two-step verification for your Apple ID, go to step **10**.

8 Click the device (○ changes to ●) on which you want to receive the verification code.

9 Click **Continue**.

The Home Sharing Is Now On dialog opens.

10 Click **OK**.

The Home Sharing Is Now On dialog closes.

11 Click **Source** (⌄).

The Source pop-up menu opens.

12 Click the appropriate shared library.

The shared content appears.

13 Select the items you want to import.

14 Click **Import**.

The Music app imports the items.

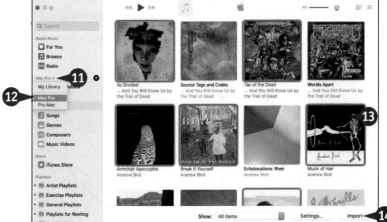

TIP

Can I prevent a family member from accessing shared libraries?

Yes. Have the family member log in to her account, and then take the keyboard yourself. Open the Music app, and then click **Music** and **Preferences** to open the Preferences window. Click **Restrictions** (🔞) to display the Restrictions tab, and then click **Shared Libraries** (☐ changes to ☑) in the Disable section. To lock the preferences against change, click the lock icon (🔓 changes to 🔒), and then enter your administrator name and password in the Music Wants to Make Changes dialog that opens.

Buy Songs Online

The Music app enables you to buy songs and other content from the iTunes Store, Apple's online store for music and media. To buy items from the iTunes Store, you must set up an account including either your credit card details or another means of payment, such as an iTunes Gift Card, PayPal, or an allowance account. If you do not already have an account, Music prompts you to set one up when you first attempt to buy an item.

Buy Songs Online

1 Click **Music** (🎵) on the Dock.

Music opens.

2 Click **iTunes Store** (⭐).

Music displays the home page of the iTunes Store.

3 Click **Genre** (⌄).

The Genre pop-up menu opens.

4 Click the type of music you want to browse.

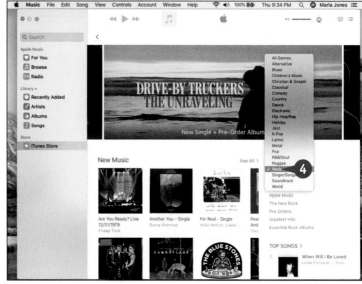

The Music app displays the kind of music you clicked.

5 Click an item to display information on it.

6 Highlight a song and then click **Play** (▶) to play a sample.

7 Click the price button.

A You can click **Buy** to buy the whole album or **Pre-Order** to pre-order it.

Note: If the Sign In to the iTunes Store dialog opens, type your password, and then click **Buy**.

Music downloads the song.

Note: To locate the song, click **Library** (◇) and click **My Library**. Then click **Recently Added** to see songs you have added recently.

What other online stores sell songs I can play in Music?
Many online stores sell songs in the widely used MP3 format, which you can play in Music and on iOS and iPadOS devices. Explore stores such as Amazon.com (www.amazon.com), eMusic (www.emusic.com), and 7digital (www.7digital.com). Other stores, such as HDtracks (www.hdtracks.com), sell high-resolution files in various formats. To add the songs to Music, click **File** on the menu bar, click **Import**, select the file or files, and then click **Open**.

How can I restart a download that fails?
Click **Account** on the menu bar and then click **Check for Available Downloads**. Sign in if Music prompts you to do so. Music then automatically restarts any downloads that were not completed.

Play Songs

Music makes it easy to play back your songs. You can view your music listed by songs, albums, artists, composers, or genres, which enables you to quickly locate the songs you want to hear. You can also search for songs using artist names, album or song names, or keywords.

After locating the music you want to hear, you can start a song playing by simply double-clicking it. You can then control playback by using the straightforward controls at the top of the Music window.

Play Songs

Play a Song in Songs View

1 In Music, click **Source** (◌) and then click the appropriate source, such as **My Library** or a shared library.

Music displays the available music.

2 Click **Songs** (♫).

Music switches to Songs view.

The column browser appears.

Note: If the column browser does not appear, click **View**, click **Column Browser**, and then click **Show Column Browser**.

3 Click the genre.

4 Click the artist.

5 Click the album.

6 Double-click the song.

The song starts playing.

Play a Song in Albums View

1 Click **Albums** (◎).

Music switches to Albums view.

2 Click the album you want to open.

The album's contents appear.

3 Double-click the song.

The song starts playing.

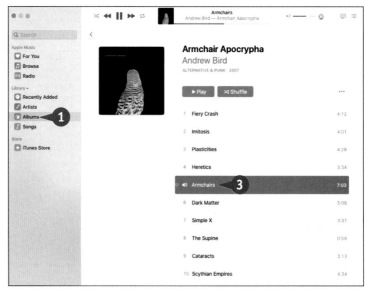

Play a Song in Artists View

1 Click **Artists** ().

Music switches to Artists view.

2 Click the artist whose music you want to see.

Note: If necessary, scroll up or down to locate the appropriate album.

3 Double-click a song to start it playing.

Play a Song in Genres View

1 Click **Genres**.

Note: If Genres does not appear, hold the pointer over the Source heading to make the Edit button appear, and then click **Edit**. Click **Genres** (☐ changes to ☑), and then click **Done**.

Music switches to Genres view.

2 Click the genre you want to browse.

Note: If necessary, scroll up or down to locate the album.

3 Double-click a song to start it playing.

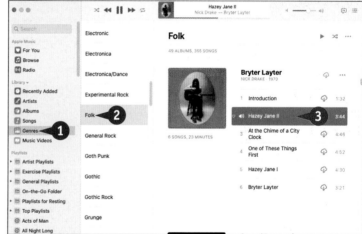

TIP

How can I search for songs?

Click in the Search box at the top of the sidebar and start typing your search term. Click **Apple Music** to search Apple Music, **Your Library** to search your library, or click **iTunes Store** to search the iTunes Store. Music shows suggestions as you type. Click an item to go to it in your current view. On Apple Music or in your library, double-click the item to start it playing. For other actions, click the item, click **More** (⋯), and then click the appropriate item on the menu that opens.

Create Playlists

The Music app enables you to create playlists that contain the songs you want in your preferred order. Playlists are a great way of getting more enjoyment out of your music. You can listen to a playlist, share it with others, or burn it to a CD for listening on a CD player.

The easiest way to create a playlist is by selecting some suitable songs and then giving the New Playlist from Selection command. You can then change the songs' order and add other songs as needed.

Create Playlists

1 Click **Music** (🎵) on the Dock.

The Music app opens.

2 Select one or more songs you want to put into a new playlist.

Note: Click the first song you want to select, and then press ⌘+click each other song.

3 Click **File**.

The File menu opens.

4 Click **New**.

The New submenu opens.

5 Click **Playlist from Selection**.

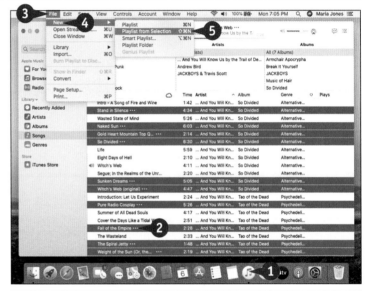

The Playlists screen appears, showing the playlist with a default name, Playlist, which is selected so you can type over it.

6 Type the name for the playlist and then press (Return).

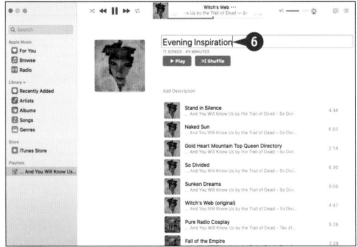

The playlist appears.

7 Drag the songs in the playlist into the order you want.

8 Click **Add Description**.

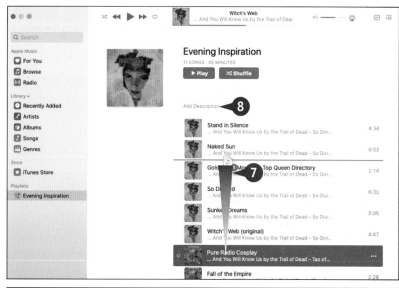

9 Type a description for the playlist to help you identify it, and then press Return.

You can now play the playlist by clicking the first song in the playlist.

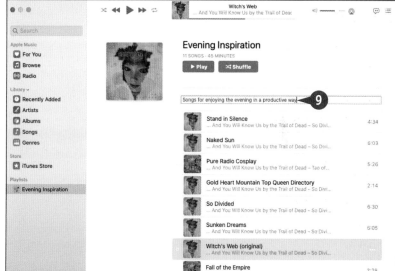

TIP

How can I keep my playlists organized?

You can organize your playlists into playlist folders. Click **File**, click **New**, and then click **Playlist Folder**. Music creates a folder and displays an edit box around the name. Type the name for the folder and press Return to apply it. You can then drag playlists to the folder. Click **Expand** (▶) to expand a folder and reveal its playlists; click **Collapse** (▼) to collapse the folder and hide its playlists.

Create Smart Playlists

Instead of creating playlists manually by adding songs to them, you can have the Music app's Smart Playlists feature create playlists automatically for you. A *Smart Playlist* is a playlist Music builds based on criteria you specify. You can set Music to update a Smart Playlist automatically as well.

To create a Smart Playlist, you set up the criteria, also called *rules*, and name the playlist. Music then adds content to the playlist for you.

Create Smart Playlists

1 Click **Music** (♫) on the Dock.

The Music app opens.

2 Click **File**.

The File menu opens.

3 Click **New**.

The New submenu opens.

4 Click **Smart Playlist**.

Note: You can also start a Smart Playlist by pressing ⌘ + Option + N.

The Smart Playlist dialog opens.

5 Click **Source** (◉) and then click **music**.

6 Click the first pop-up menu (◌) and select the item for the first condition — for example, **Genre**.

7 Click the second pop-up menu (◌) and select the comparison for the first condition — for example, **contains**.

8 Click the text field and type the text for the comparison — for example, **Alternative** — making the condition "Genre contains Alternative."

9 To add another condition, click **Add** (+).

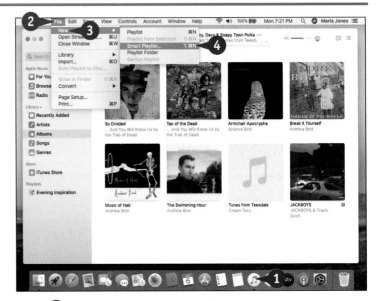

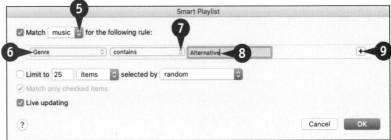

10 Click **all/any** (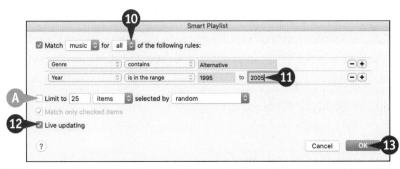) and select **any** to match any of the rules or **all** to match all the rules.

11 Set up the second condition by repeating steps **6** to **8**.

Note: You can add as many conditions as you need to define the playlist.

A You can limit the playlist by clicking **Limit to** (☐ changes to ✓) and specifying the limit.

12 Click **Live updating** (☐ changes to ✓).

13 Click **OK**.

Music creates the Smart Playlist and adds it to the Playlists section of the Source list.

B An edit box appears around the suggested name.

14 Type the name for the Smart Playlist, and then press Return.

Music applies the name to the playlist.

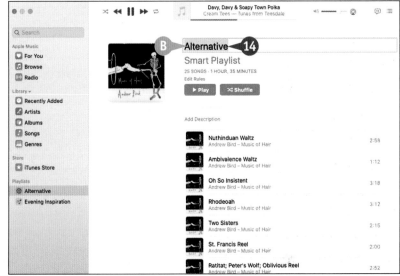

How do I produce a Smart Playlist the right length for a CD?

In the Smart Playlist dialog, click **Limit to** (☐ changes to ✓). Click the left pop-up menu (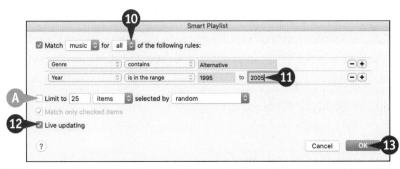) and select **minutes**, and then set the number before it to **74** or **80**, depending on the capacity of the CD.

What does Match Only Checked Items do?

Click **Match only checked items** (☐ changes to ✓) to restrict your Smart Playlist to songs whose check boxes are selected. This means you can uncheck the check box for a song to prevent it from appearing in your Smart Playlists. If the check boxes do not appear, click **Music**, click **Preferences**, and click **General** (▣) to display the General Preferences pane. Click **List view checkboxes** (☐ changes to ✓), and then click **OK**.

Listen to Apple Radio and Internet Radio

The Music app enables you to listen to online radio stations. The Apple Radio feature comes set to access a selection of stations on demand, which means you can pause the radio stream and resume it from the same place. You can skip some songs if you do not want to listen to them, and you can create custom stations. To listen to Apple Radio, you must sign in to the Apple Music service.

You can also use Music to access radio stations that broadcast across the Internet in real time. When listening to such stations, you cannot pause the content or skip songs.

Listen to Apple Radio and Internet Radio

Listen to a Radio Station

① Click **Music** (♫) on the Dock.

The Music app opens.

② Click **Radio**.

The Radio screen appears.

③ Position the pointer over the station you want to listen to.

The Play button (⊙) appears.

④ Click **Play** (⊙).

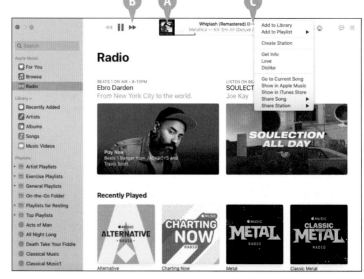

The station starts playing.

Ⓐ Details of the current song appear.

Ⓑ You can click **Skip** (▶▶) to skip to the next track.

Ⓒ You can click **More** (⋯) to display a menu of other actions, such as starting a new station from the artist or sharing the song.

5 To explore the selection of genres available, scroll down to the bottom of the screen.

The Radio by Genre section appears.

6 Click the genre you want to explore.

The genre appears.

7 Position the pointer over the station you want to listen to.

The Play button (▶) appears.

8 Click **Play** (▶).

The station starts playing.

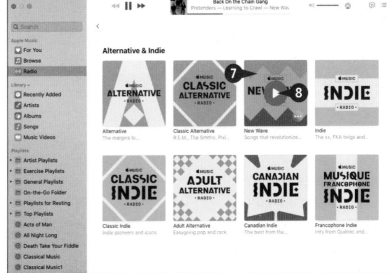

TIP

How can I listen to an Internet radio station that does not appear on Music's list?
Find out the URL of the station's audio stream by consulting the station's website. In Music, click **File** and select **Open Stream URL** to display the Open Stream dialog. Type or paste the URL into the dialog and then click **OK**. Music starts playing the radio station's audio stream.

Enjoy Podcasts

A *podcast* is an audio or video file that you can download from the Internet and play on your MacBook or a digital player like the iPhone, iPad, or iPod. The Podcasts app enables you to access the Apple Podcasts service. Apple Podcasts makes a wide variety of podcasts available. You can either download a single podcast episode or subscribe to a podcast so that Podcasts automatically downloads new episodes for you.

Enjoy Podcasts

1 Click **Podcasts** (⊚) on the Dock.

Podcasts opens.

2 Click **Browse** (⊚).

3 Scroll down.

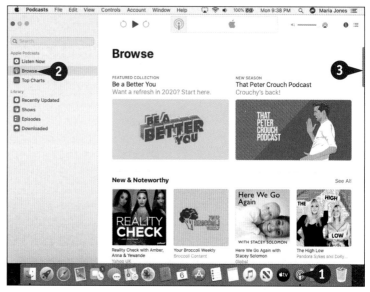

The Categories section appears.

Ⓐ You can click **See All** to see all the categories.

4 Click the category of podcasts you want to browse.

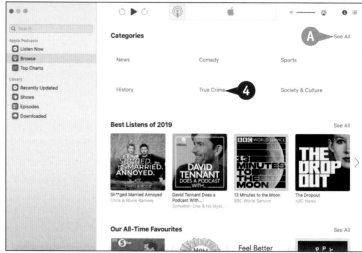

Podcasts shows the category you clicked.

5 Click the podcast you want to view.

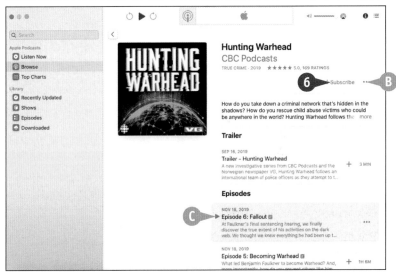

B Click **More** (⋯) to display other actions, such as reporting a concern and sharing the podcast.

C To start an episode playing immediately, move the pointer over the episode, and then click **Play** (▶).

6 Click **Subscribe** if you want to subscribe to the podcast.

Podcasts subscribes you to the podcast and downloads the most recent episode.

TIP

How do I listen to or watch the podcasts I have subscribed to?

The Podcasts app stores the podcasts you have subscribed to in your library. The Library section of the sidebar enables you to view the library's contents in different ways. For example, click **Downloaded** (▣) to see the episodes you have downloaded; click **Recently Updated** (▣) to see the podcasts that have been updated recently; or click **Shows** (▣) to browse the shows you have subscribed to. Click an episode to display it, and then click **Play Episode**.

Play Videos with the TV App

The TV app enables you to play videos, TV shows, and movies. You can buy and watch TV shows and movies from Apple's services or export files of your own movies from iMovie or other applications. After adding videos to the TV app, you access them by using the tabs at the top of the application window. You can download files and watch them offline.

You can watch video content full screen or as a picture-in-picture floating window. You can also play videos from your MacBook to a TV connected to an Apple TV.

Play Videos with the TV App

1 Click **TV** (◉tv) on the Dock.

The TV app opens.

2 Click **Library**.

The Library tab appears.

Note: To browse movies, click **Movies**. To browse TV shows, click **TV Shows**. To browse children's content, click **Kids**.

3 Click the item you want to view.

The item's screen appears.

4 Click the thumbnail for the item you want to play.

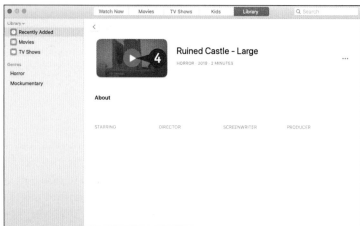

The TV app starts playing the movie full screen.

5 Move the pointer over the video.

The pop-up controls appear.

6 Use the controls on the pop-up bar to control playback.

A You can click **Picture-in-Picture** (⬚) to switch the video to a small floating window.

Note: From the picture-in-picture window, click **Expand** (⬚) to expand the video to a larger window. You can then click **View** and click **Enter Full Screen** or press ⌘+Control+F to switch to full screen.

7 Click **Close** (⊗) to stop viewing the video.

TIP

How do I play a video from the Music app on the TV connected to my Apple TV?
First, make sure your MacBook is connected to the same network as the Apple TV via either a wireless network or a wired network. You can then click **AirPlay** (◉) to the right of the volume control in the TV app to display the AirPlay menu. Click the Apple TV's name on the menu. The TV app sends the video output to the Apple TV, which displays it on the TV's screen.

Read Books

macOS includes the Books app, which enables you to enjoy electronic books, or *e-books*, on your MacBook. Using Books, you can read e-books that you already have on your MacBook, download free or paid-for e-books from online stores, or read PDF files stored on your MacBook.

Before you can read e-books that you have on your MacBook, you must add them to Books. You can then open a book and start reading it.

Read Books

Add Your E-Books to Books

Note: This method shows you how to add e-books not purchased from Apple. Any books you have bought via Books appear automatically in the Books app when you sign in using your Apple ID.

1 Click **Books** (📖) on the Dock.

Note: If Books (📖) does not appear on the Dock, click **Launchpad** (🚀) on the Dock and then click **Books** (📖) on the Launchpad screen.

The Books window opens.

2 Click **File**.

The File menu opens.

3 Click **Add to Library**.

The Add to Library dialog opens.

4 Navigate to the folder that contains the books.

5 Select the books you want to add to Books.

6 Click **Add**.

The Add to Library dialog closes.

The books appear in Books.

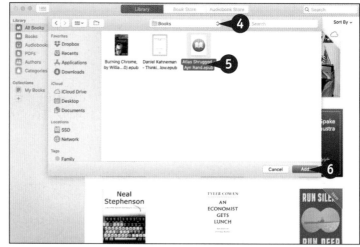

Read E-Books

1 Click **Books** (📖) on the Dock.

The Books window opens.

2 Click the button for the view by which you want to browse. For example, click **Library** to view the books in your library.

Ⓐ You can search for a book by clicking in the Search box and typing keywords.

3 Double-click the book you want to open.

The book opens.

4 Press ➡ to display the next page or ⬅ to display the previous page.

Note: You can also swipe left or right on the trackpad to change pages.

Ⓑ You can click **Appearance** (ᴀA) to adjust the appearance of the page and the text.

Ⓒ You can click **Library** (📖) to display your library, leaving the book open.

5 When you finish reading, click **Close** (●).

The book closes, and your library appears.

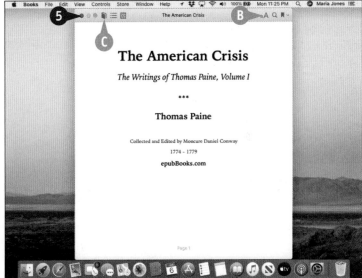

TIP

How can I add my Kindle e-books to Books?

As of this writing, Books cannot display books in Amazon's proprietary Kindle format. To read Kindle books on your Mac, download the free Kindle app from the App Store and log in to the Kindle service using the e-mail address and password you have registered with Amazon.

CHAPTER 11

Making the Most of Your Photos

Each new MacBook comes with Photos, a powerful but easy-to-use application for managing, improving, and enjoying your photos. You can import photos from your digital camera, phone, or tablet; crop them, straighten them, and improve their colors; and use them in albums, slide shows, or e-mail messages.

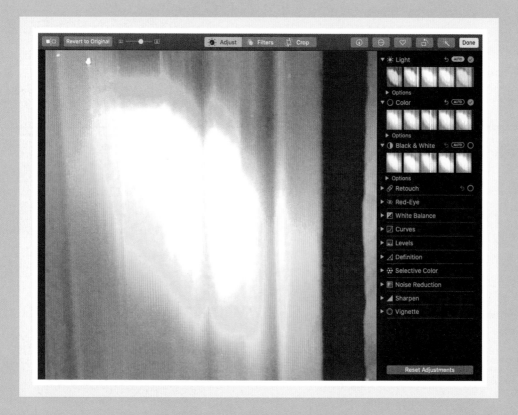

Import Photos

hotos enables you to import photos directly from a wide range of digital cameras, phones, and tablets, including the iPhone, iPad, and iPod touch. Photos normally recognizes a camera automatically when you connect it to your MacBook and switch it on.

If you do not have a suitable cable to connect your digital camera directly to your MacBook, you can remove the digital camera's memory card and insert it in a memory card reader connected to the MacBook. Another possibility for some cameras and phones is to import photos via Bluetooth File Exchange.

Import Photos

1 Connect your digital camera or device to your MacBook via USB.

2 Turn on the digital camera or device.

Note: Some digital cameras turn on automatically when you connect them to a powered USB port, but most cameras need to be turned on manually. Phones and tablets usually remain on and wake from sleep.

Photos opens and displays the contents of the digital camera or device.

A If Photos does not open automatically, click **Photos** ( ) on the Dock, click the device — such as **iPhone** — in the Devices list, and then click **Open Photos** (changes to).

B You can drag the **Zoom** slider to enlarge the thumbnails.

Note: Scroll up and down as needed by swiping or dragging two fingers on the trackpad.

3 Click each photo you want to import, placing a check mark ( ) on it. You can drag across multiple photos to select them.

Note: To select a range of photos, click the first photo, and then press Shift+click the last photo.

Note: If you want to import all the new photos, you need not select any.

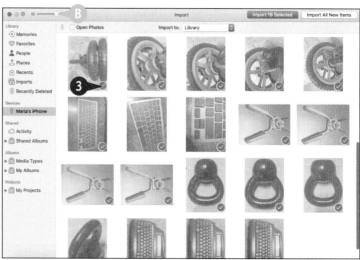

④ Click **Import to** (⊞) and then click the destination. Your choices are **Library**, **New Album**, or an album in the My Albums list.

⑤ Click **Import Selected** to import the photos you selected. Click **Import All New Items** to import all the new photos.

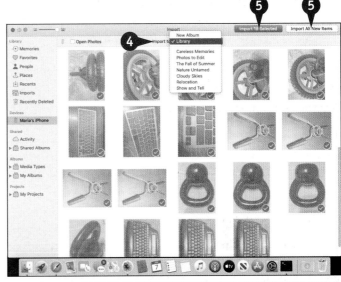

Photos copies the photos from the digital camera or device to your MacBook.

ⓒ Photos displays the Imports screen, showing the photos you have just imported.

ⓓ An individual photo appears as a thumbnail.

ⓔ Photos in a burst appear as a stack.

Note: For a digital camera, click **Eject** (⏏) next to the camera's name in the Devices list to eject the camera before you disconnect it.

⑥ Disconnect the camera or device from your MacBook.

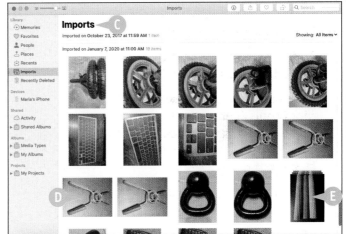

TIP

What is the Showing pop-up menu for?

The Showing pop-up menu enables you to switch between displaying all items — click **All Items** on the menu — and displaying only specific types of items. For example, you can click **Photos** (▣) to display only photos, click **Videos** (◉) to display only videos, click **Edited** (☰) to display only items you have edited, or click **Favorites** (♥) to display only items you have marked as favorites.

Browse Your Photos

To locate the photos you want to view and work with, you browse your photos. Photos enables you to browse your photos easily: You first select a category in the sidebar on the left side of the Photos window, and then use the main part of the window to view the photos in the source.

If you have just imported photos, the best way to begin browsing is by viewing the Imports category, which contains the photos you have imported.

Browse Your Photos

Open the Photos App and Browse by Albums

1. Click **Photos** (✳) on the Dock.

   Photos opens.

   Ⓐ You can click **Imports** in the Library section of the sidebar to see photos you have imported.

   Note: If the Albums list is hidden, move the pointer over the Albums heading, making the Show button appear, and then click **Show**.

2. Click **Expand** (▶ changes to ▼) next to My Albums.

   The Albums list appears.

3. Click the album you want to view.

   Note: Scroll up and down as needed by swiping or dragging two fingers on the trackpad.

   Ⓑ You can move the pointer over a photo and click **Add to Favorites** (♥ changes to ♡) to add the photo to your Favorites.

4. Double-click the photo you want to view.

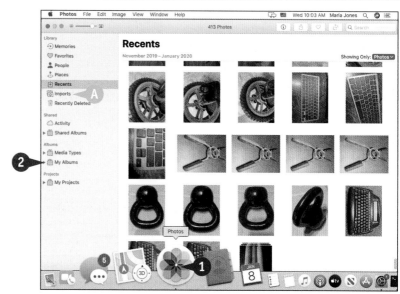

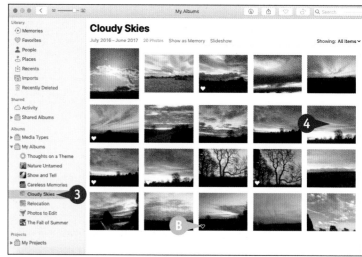

Photos displays the photo.

Ⓒ You can press **Control**+click the photo to display the contextual menu.

Ⓓ You can click **Share** to display options for sharing the photo.

Ⓔ You can click **Remove 1 Photo from Album** to remove this photo from the album.

⑤ Swipe left with two fingers on the trackpad to display the next photo, or swipe right with two fingers to display the previous photo.

The next photo or the previous photo appears, depending on which way you swiped.

Note: You can also press ⬅ to display the previous photo or ➡ to display the next photo.

Ⓕ You can also switch photos by moving the pointer to the left side of the photo and clicking **Previous** (‹) or moving the pointer to the right side and clicking **Next** (›).

⑥ Drag the **Zoom** slider to zoom in.

TIP

Is there another way to navigate the Photos app?
When viewing a photo, you can click **View** on the menu bar and click **Show Thumbnails** to display a bar of thumbnails across the bottom of the window. You can then click a thumbnail to display that photo. This can be a quick way to navigate large collections of photos.

continued ▶

The Photos app automatically organizes your photos into groups called Years, Months, and Days. To access these groups, you select the Photos category in the Library section of the sidebar. You can then click the Years button, the Months button, or the Days button on the bar across the top of the Photos window to display the groups you want to see, and then double-click a group to open it.

Browse Your Photos (continued)

Photos zooms in on the middle of the photo.

Note: You can also zoom in by placing two fingers, or your finger and thumb, together on the trackpad and then moving them apart. To zoom out, place two fingers, or your finger and thumb, apart and then pinch inward.

7 Drag with two fingers as needed to pan around the photo after zooming in.

8 Click **Back** (‹).

The album appears again.

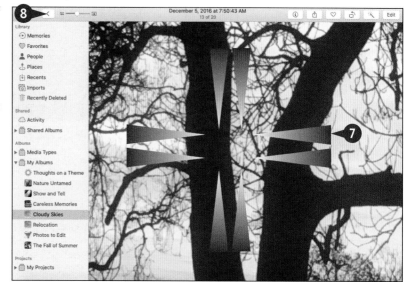

Browse Photos by Years, Months, and Days

1 In the Library section of the sidebar, click **Photos** (📷).

The Photos pane appears.

2 Click **Years**.

The Years pane appears.

3 Double-click the photo thumbnail for the Year you want to view.

The Months pane for the Year appears, showing larger thumbnails that represent the Months.

④ Double-click the thumbnail for the Month you want to view.

The Days pane for the Month appears.

⑤ Double-click the thumbnail for the photo you want to view.

What is the People item in the Library category?

The People album contains photos of people that you have identified to Photos. Photos analyzes the faces and attempts to use facial recognition on other photos. You can double-click a person to view all the photos in which the Photos app has identified him or her.

What is the Memories item in the Library category?

The Memories album contains Memories, groups of photos that Photos automatically selects based on locations and dates.

continued ▶

The Photos app enables you to browse your photos by the places in which you took them or the places with which you tagged them. Browsing by places is helpful when you need to find photos taken at a particular place without having to search by dates. Photos shows only the main places when the map is zoomed out, but displays more places the further you zoom in.

Browse Your Photos (continued)

The photo opens.

G You can click **Back** (<) to return to the Days screen.

Note: You can swipe left or right with two fingers to display the next photo or the previous photo.

Browse Your Photos by Places

Note: If the Library list is hidden, move the pointer over the Library heading, making the Show button appear, and then click **Show**.

1 In the Library section of the sidebar, click **Places** (⚓).

The Photos app displays a map showing the places in which your photos were taken.

2 Click **Zoom In** (+) one or more times to zoom in.

H You can click **Zoom Out** (—) to zoom out.

Note: You can also zoom in by pinching apart on the trackpad or zoom out by pinching together.

I You can click **Satellite** to switch to the photographic Satellite View.

J You can click **Grid** to display the available places as a list that shows place names, dates, and photo thumbnails.

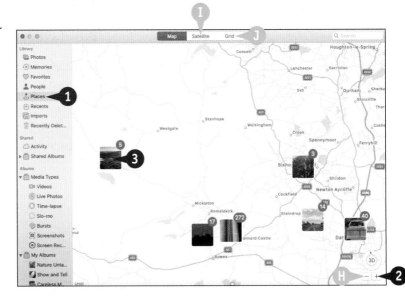

3 Click the thumbnail for the photo or group of photos you want to see.

286

The photos taken in that place appear.

4 Double-click the photo you want to view.

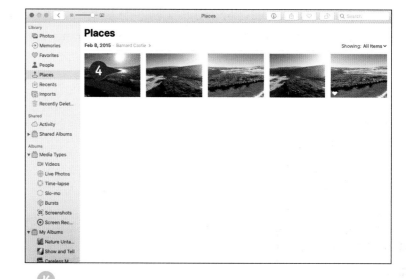

The photo opens.

K You can click **Zoom** (⬤) to expand the Photos window to full screen so that you can examine the photo more closely.

5 Click **Back** (⟨).

The photos in the place appear again.

6 Click **Back** (⟨) again.

The map appears again.

How do I add location information to a photo that lacks it?

Open the photo and click **Info** (ⓘ) to display the Info pane. Click **Assign a Location** and start typing the address or other identifying information. In the pop-up menu of results, click the correct information. A map appears with a pin showing the location. If necessary, press Shift +drag the pin to adjust the location. Click **Close** (⬤) to close the Info pane.

To hide a photo's location, open the photo, click **Image** on the menu bar, click or highlight **Location**, and then click **Hide Location**. From the Location submenu, you can also click **Revert to Original Location** to revert the photo to its original location.

Select Photos from Bursts

Many digital cameras and devices, including most models of iPhone, can take bursts of photos. Bursts are great when you are trying to capture facial expressions, live action, or other unrepeatable moments.

The Photos app enables you to browse the photos you have taken in bursts. From a burst, you can choose which photos to keep as individual photos; you can also choose whether to keep the rest of the burst photos or delete them.

Select Photos from Bursts

1 In Photos, navigate to the burst. For example, if you have added the burst recently, click **Recents** (⬇).

The Recents pane appears.

Note: Scroll up and down as needed by swiping or dragging two fingers on the trackpad.

A Each burst appears as a stack of photos.

2 Double-click the burst you want to open.

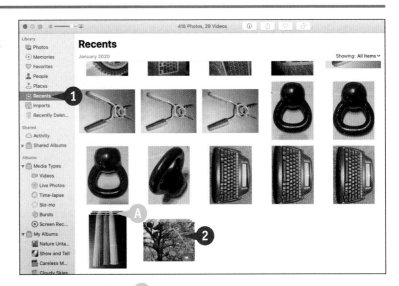

Photos displays the photo at the top of the stack in the burst.

B The Burst indicator shows you how many photos the burst contains.

3 Click **Make a Selection**.

Note: The Make a Selection prompt appears on a burst of photos, not on individual photos.

The Make a Selection pane appears.

Ⓒ You can swipe left or right with two fingers, or press ➡ or ⬅ to display the next photo or previous photo.

Ⓓ The inverted triangle indicates the thumbnail for the current photo.

④ Click the thumbnail for the photo you want to view.

The photo appears.

⑤ Click the selection circle (⚫ changes to ✅) if you want to keep the photo.

Ⓔ A check mark appears on the thumbnail for each photo you select.

⑥ When you finish selecting photos from the burst, click **Done**.

The Would You Like to Keep the Other Photos in This Burst? dialog opens.

⑦ Click **Keep Only Selection** or **Keep Everything**, as needed. Click **Cancel** to return to the Make a Selection pane.

TIP

How can I quickly access and review the bursts in my Photos library?
In the Albums section of the sidebar, click **Expand** (▶ changes to ▼) next to Media Types, and then click **Bursts** (📷) to open the Bursts album. You can then either browse the bursts or double-click the burst you want to open.

Crop a Photo

To improve a photo's composition and emphasize its subject, you can crop off the parts you do not want to keep. Photos enables you to crop to any rectangular area within a photo, so you can choose exactly the part of the photo that you need. You can either constrain the crop area to a specific aspect ratio or crop freely. Constraining an area to specific dimensions is useful for producing an image with a specific aspect ratio, such as 3 × 5 or the ratio of your MacBook's display.

Crop a Photo

1. In Photos, open the photo you want to edit.

2. Click **Edit**.

Photos opens the photo for editing and displays the editing tools.

3. Click **Crop** (⬚).

Photos displays the cropping tools.

④ If you want to crop to specific proportions or dimensions, click **Aspect** (▨).

The Aspect pop-up menu opens.

Note: For non-square aspects, click **Crop as Landscape** (▬ changes to ☑) or **Crop as Portrait** (▮ changes to ☑) to set the orientation.

⑤ Click the aspect ratio you want to use, such as **Square**.

ⓐ You can click **Flip** (▨) to flip the photo horizontally. Press Option (▨ changes to ▶) and then click **Flip** (▶) to flip the photo vertically.

The crop box changes to show the aspect ratio you chose.

⑥ Drag the corner handles to crop to the area you want.

⑦ If necessary, click inside the cropping rectangle and drag the picture to change the part shown.

ⓑ You can click **Revert to Original** at any point to undo all the changes you have made to the photo.

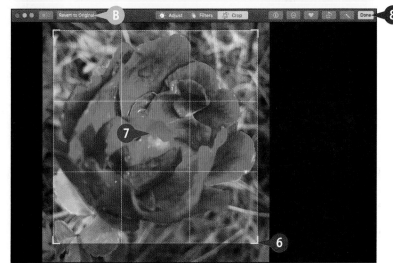

⑧ Click **Done**.

Photos crops the picture to the area you chose.

Photos hides the editing tools again.

I cropped off the wrong part of the photo. How can I get back the missing part? Open the photo, click **Edit**, and then click **Revert to Original**.	**How can I crop a photo evenly around its center?** Hold Option as you drag the cropping handles. Holding Option makes Photos adjust the crop box around the center of the photo.

Rotate or Straighten a Photo

ith digital cameras, and especially with phones and tablets, you can easily take photos with the device sideways or the wrong way up. Photos enables you to rotate a photo easily by 90, 180, or 270 degrees to the correct orientation.

Photos also enables you to straighten a photo by rotating it a few degrees clockwise or counterclockwise. To keep the straightened picture in its current aspect ratio, Photos automatically crops off the parts that no longer fit.

Rotate or Straighten a Photo

Rotate a Photo

1 In Photos, press **Control**+click the photo you want to rotate.

The contextual menu opens.

2 Click **Rotate Clockwise**.

Note: Press **Option** and then click **Rotate Counterclockwise** to rotate the photo counterclockwise.

Photos rotates the photo 90 degrees clockwise.

Note: If you need to rotate the photo further, repeat the move.

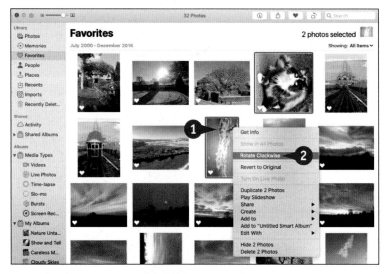

Straighten a Photo

1 In Photos, open the photo you want to straighten.

2 Click **Edit**.

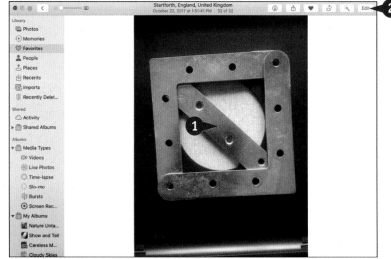

Photos opens the photo for editing and displays the editing tools.

③ Click **Crop** (⊞).

Ⓐ You can click **Rotate** (↻) to rotate the photo 90 degrees counterclockwise. To rotate the photo 90 degrees clockwise, press `Option` (↻ changes to ↺) and then click **Rotate** (↺).

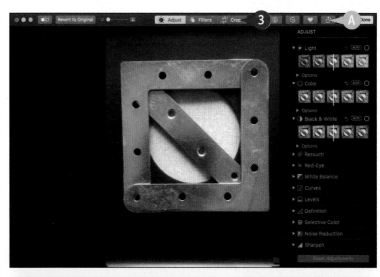

Photos displays the cropping and straightening tools.

④ Drag the **Angle** dial to straighten the photo.

Note: Use the lines in the straightening grid to judge when lines in the picture have reached the horizontal position or the vertical position.

⑤ Click **Done**.

Photos applies the straightening.

Photos hides the editing tools again.

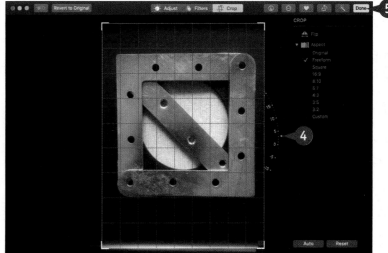

TIP

What does the Auto button in the Crop pane do?
Click the Auto button to apply automatic straightening to the photo you are editing. This feature analyzes the horizontal and vertical lines in the photo and attempts to apply straightening based on what it finds. For photos that have obvious orientation problems, this feature can work well. For other photos, such as those where you need to use the background rather than a foreground object to determine what should be horizontal and what should be vertical, you may do better to apply straightening manually.

Remove Red-Eye

A camera's flash can make all the difference when you are taking photos in dark or dull conditions, but flash often gives people *red-eye* — glaring red spots in the eyes. Photos' Fix Red-Eye tool enables you to remove red-eye from your photos, making your subjects' eyes look normal again.

To use Fix Red-Eye, you open the photo and switch to Edit mode. You can then either have Photos detect and fix the red-eye automatically or fix it manually by clicking the eyes.

Remove Red-Eye

1 In Photos, open the photo from which you want to remove red-eye.

2 Click **Edit**.

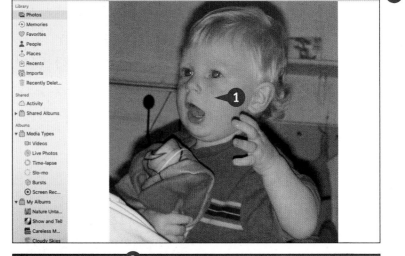

Photos opens the photo for editing and displays the editing tools.

3 Click **Adjust**.

Photos displays the Adjust tools.

4 Click **Expand** (▶) next to Red-Eye.

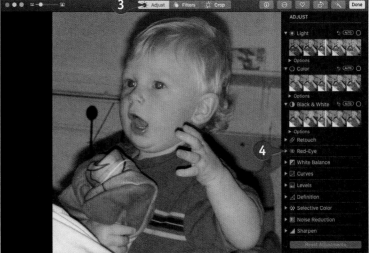

Photos displays the red-eye tools.

5 Drag the **Zoom** slider to zoom in, as needed.

A You can click **Auto** to have Photos attempt to remove any red-eye in the photo automatically. See the tip for more information.

6 Drag the **Size** slider to set the size of the circle for removing red-eye.

7 Click the first eye afflicted with red-eye.

B Photos removes the red-eye from the eye.

8 Click the other afflicted eye.

9 Click **Done**.

Photos applies the changes to the photo.

Photos hides the editing tools again.

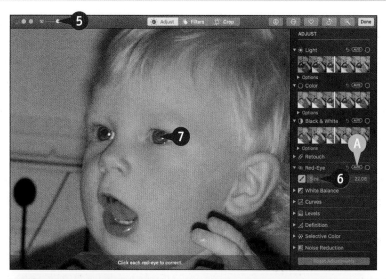

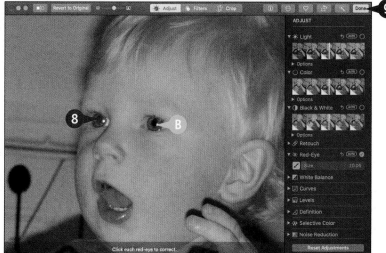

Should I use the Auto button or fix red-eye manually?
This is up to you. The Auto button should be the quickest way to remove red-eye from a photo, and in many photos it successfully identifies and removes red-eye. But where the tool cannot remove red-eye automatically, drag the **Size** slider to the right size for the red-eye you need to remove, and then click each affected eye in turn.

Improve a Photo's Colors

Photos includes powerful tools for improving the colors in your photos. If a photo is too light, too dark, or the colors look wrong, you can use these tools to make it look better.

Usually, the best way to start is to use the Auto Enhance tool, which boosts flat colors while muting overly bright ones. If Auto Enhance does not give you the results you need, you can use the Adjust tools to edit settings such as exposure, contrast, and saturation.

Improve a Photo's Colors

Quickly Enhance the Colors in a Photo

1 In Photos, open the photo you want to enhance.

2 Click **Auto Enhance** (✺ changes to ✺).

Photos adjusts the exposure and enhances the colors.

Note: If the Auto Enhance tool does not improve the photo, click **Auto Enhance** again (✺ changes to ✺) to remove the enhancement, and then use the Adjust tools instead.

Use the Adjust Tools

1 Open the photo you want to adjust.

2 Click **Edit**.

Photos opens the photo for editing and displays the editing tools.

③ Click **Adjust** (⬚).

The Adjustments tools appear.

Note: If the set of tools you want to appear is collapsed, move the pointer over its heading and click **Expand** (▶) to expand it.

Ⓐ You can click **Auto** to have Photos adjust the group of settings automatically.

④ Drag the group's slider to adjust all the settings using preset balances.

⑤ Drag an individual slider to adjust that setting alone.

Ⓑ You can click **Reset Adjustments** to undo your adjustments.

Note: If you need to make the same adjustments to other photos, press Control+click the photo and click **Copy Adjustments**. You can then open each other photo for editing, press Control+click the photo, and click **Paste Adjustments** to apply the copied adjustments.

⑥ When you finish working on the colors, click **Done**.

Photos applies the changes to the photo.

Photos hides the editing tools again.

TIP

What other adjustments can I make using Photos?

You can make a wide range of adjustments by using the tools in the lower section of the Adjust pane. The tools include Retouch for removing blemishes; White Balance for adjusting misrepresented white tones; Levels for changing red-green-blue levels, white point, and black point; Curves for adjusting tonal range; Selective Color for adjusting only the color of your choice; Noise Reduction for reducing *noise* or graininess in low-light photos; Sharpen for increasing definition; and Vignette for fading out the corners of the photo to emphasize the subject.

Add Filters to Photos

Photos includes ten preset filters that you can quickly apply to change a photo's look and add life and interest to it. For example, you can change a color photo to black-and-white, boost or fade the color, or apply an instant-camera filter.

To add filters, you open the photo for editing and display the Filters panel. You can then experiment with the available filters to see which filter works best.

Add Filters to Photos

1 In Photos, open the photo to which you want to apply a filter.

2 Click **Edit**.

Photos opens the photo for editing and displays the editing tools.

3 Click **Filters** (●).

The Filters pane appears.

4 Click the filter you want to apply. This example uses the Vivid Warm filter.

Note: The Photo Booth app provides a similar but more extensive collection of filters.

The photo takes on the filter.

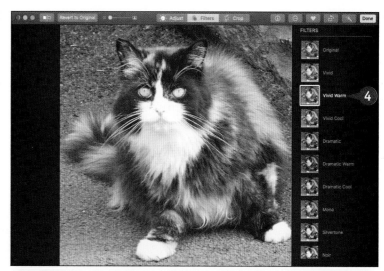

5 When you are satisfied with the filter, click **Done**.

Photos applies the filter to the photo.

Photos hides the editing tools again.

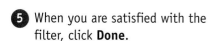

How can I remove the filter from a photo?
To remove the filter you have applied to a photo, open the photo for editing, click **Filters** (◉), and then click **Original** at the top of the Filters pane.

Create Photo Albums

When you want to assemble a custom collection of photos, you create a new album. You can then add to it exactly the photos you want from any of the sources available in Photos. After assembling the collection of photos, you can arrange them in your preferred order.

Photos can also create *Smart Albums* that automatically include all photos that meet the criteria you choose. Photos updates Smart Albums automatically when you download photos that match the criteria.

Create Photo Albums

1 In Photos, move the pointer over the My Albums item in the Albums section of the sidebar.

The Add (⊕) button appears.

2 Click **Add** (⊕).

The Add pop-up menu opens.

3 Click **Album**.

Note: To add photos to an existing album, select the photos, click **Image** on the menu bar, highlight **Add to** without clicking, and then click the album on the Add To submenu.

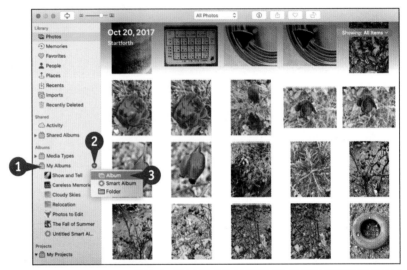

Ⓐ Photos creates a new album, provisionally naming it Untitled Album and placing an edit box around its name in the sidebar.

4 Type the name for the new album and press Return.

5 In the sidebar, click the photo collection from which you will add photos to the new album. This example uses the **Photos** (🖼) category.

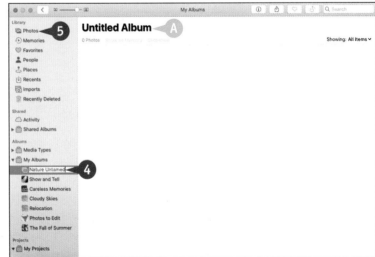

The photo collection you clicked appears.

6 Click the first photo you want to add.

A blue outline appears around the photo.

7 Press ⌘+click each other photo you want to add.

A blue outline appears around each photo you click.

8 Drag the photos to the new album in the sidebar.

9 Click the new album.

The photos in the album appear.

10 To change the order of the photos, click a photo and drag it to where you want it.

Photos arranges the photos.

11 Click **Back** (⟨) when you want to return to the Albums pane.

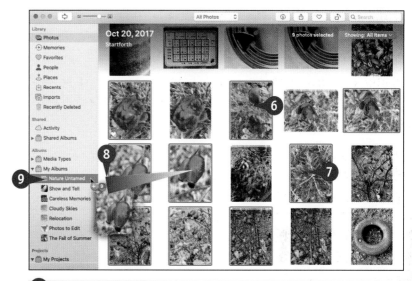

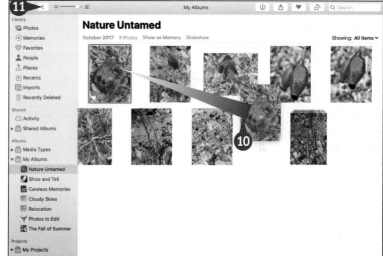

TIP

What is a Smart Album, and how do I create one?

A Smart Album is an album based on criteria you choose. For example, you can create a Smart Album of photos with the keyword "family" and a rating of four stars or better. Photos then automatically adds each photo that matches those criteria to the Smart Album. To create a new Smart Album, click **File** and select **New Smart Album**, and then set your criteria in the New Smart Album dialog. Click **Add** (⊕) to add another row of criteria to the Smart Album.

Create and Play Slide Shows

One of the best ways to enjoy your photos and share them with others is to play a slide show. Photos enables you to create two types of slide shows: instant slide shows and saved slide shows. For an instant slide show, you simply select the collection of photos you want to view and then start the slide show playing, as explained in the tip in this section. For a saved slide show, you select photos, create the slide show, arrange the photos into your preferred order, and save the show so that you can run it when needed.

Create and Play Slide Shows

1 In Photos, click the photo collection from which you first want to select photos for the slide show.

2 Click the first photo you want to use.

A blue outline appears around the photo.

3 Press ⌘+click each other photo you want to use.

A blue outline appears around each photo you click.

4 Click **File**.

The File menu opens.

5 Highlight **Create** without clicking.

The Create submenu opens.

6 Click **Slideshow**.

The Slideshow submenu opens.

7 Click **Photos**.

The Add Photos to Slideshow dialog opens. The dialog's name shows the number of photos you selected.

8 Type the slide show name in the Slideshow Name box.

9 Click **OK**.

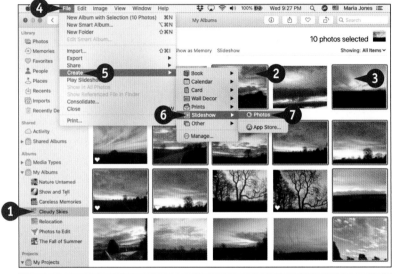

The photos in the slide show appear.

Ⓐ The slide show appears in the My Projects list in the Projects section of the sidebar.

Ⓑ The slide show's first slide and title appear.

Ⓒ You can click **Preview** to preview the slide show with its current settings.

Ⓓ You can click **Add** (⊕) to add other photos to the slide show.

Ⓔ You can click **Loop Slideshow** (⊡ changes to ⊡) to turn off looping.

⑩ Drag the photos into the order in which you want them to appear in the slide show.

⑪ Click **Themes** (⬚).

TIP

How do I play an instant slide show?

Click the photo collection you want to use for the slide show, click **File** on the menu bar, and then click **Play Slideshow** on the File menu.

To play a slide show of an album, click the album in the My Albums list, and then click the **Slideshow** button at the top of the album's pane.

continued ▶

To make a slide show look the way you want it to, you can give the slide show one of Photos' themes. The themes include animated transitions between slides that give your slide show a particular look.

During the slide show, you can play a particular song or an existing playlist, or you can create a custom playlist to accompany the slide show. You can also choose whether to play each slide for a minimum length of time or to fit the slide show to the music you provide for it.

Create and Play Slide Shows (continued)

The Themes pane appears.

12 Click the theme you want to use. This example uses **Ken Burns**, an effect that gradually pans and zooms over a photo.

The Preview pane shows a preview of the theme.

F For Ken Burns, click **Ken Burns Effect** (▣) in the lower-left corner of the preview. Click **Ken Burns In-Point** (◄) to display the In-Point controls, drag the slider to zoom the photo, and then drag the photo to display the area at which to start the effect. Click **Ken Burns Out-Point** (►) to display the Out-Point controls, and then zoom and drag to set the out-point.

13 Click **Music** (♫).

The Music pane appears.

G The Selected Music section shows the default music for the theme at first.

Note: If the Music Library section is hidden, click **Show** (⌄) on the Music Library heading to display it.

14 Click **Music** (⬗), and then click **Theme Songs** or **Music** to specify the source of the music.

15 In the list of music that appears, click the song or playlist to use.

16 Click **Duration Settings** (⏱).

304

The Duration panel appears.

17 Click **Fit to Music** (○ changes to ●) or **Custom** (○ changes to ●), as needed.

Note: If you click **Custom**, drag the slider to set the time.

18 Click **Scale photos to fit screen** (□ changes to ☑) to scale the photos to fit the screen size.

Note: Scale Photos to Fit Screen appears only for some themes.

19 Click **Play** (▶).

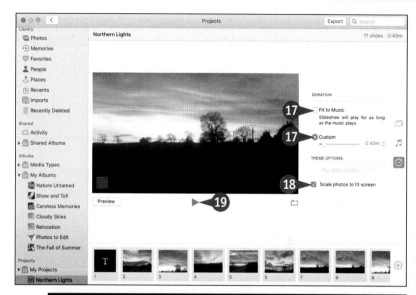

Photos starts playing the slide show.

20 Move the pointer to display the control bar.

Ⓗ You can drag **Volume** to set the playback volume.

Ⓘ You can click **Previous** (◄) to display the previous slide.

Ⓙ You can click **Pause** (❚❚) to pause the slide show.

Ⓚ You can click **Next** (▶❘) to display the next slide.

Ⓛ You can click **Close** (⊗) to end the slide show.

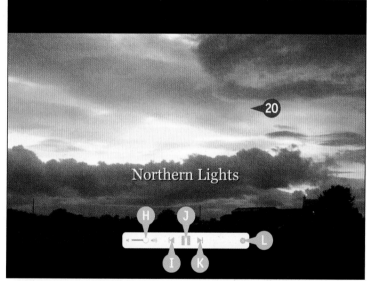

TIP

How do I delete the text from the title slide?
Press `Control`+click the title slide in the thumbnail bar at the bottom of the screen, and then click **Delete Text** on the contextual menu.

E-Mail a Photo

From Photos, you can quickly create an e-mail message containing one or more photos you want to send to a contact or multiple contacts. You can specify the subject line for the message, add any text needed to explain what you are sending, and choose between including the full version of the photo and creating a smaller version of it that will transfer more quickly.

E-Mail a Photo

1 In Photos, click the photo you want to send via e-mail.

2 Click **Share** (⬆) on the toolbar.

The Share pop-up menu opens.

3 Click **Mail** (✉).

Note: The first time you give the Mail command, you may need to follow through a procedure to set up Photos with your e-mail account.

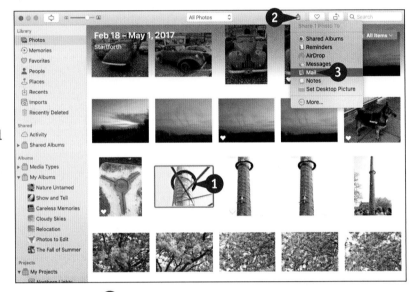

Photos creates a message containing the photo.

4 Type the recipient's address.

Ⓐ If Photos displays a pop-up menu of matching contacts, click the correct address.

5 Click **Subject** and type the subject for the message.

6 Click in the message box and type any message text needed to explain why you are sending the photo.

7 Click **Image Size** (⬍).

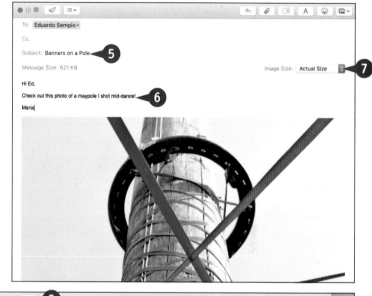

The Image Size pop-up menu opens.

Ⓑ The tooltip shows the resolution of the photo at this size.

8 Click the size of photo to send — for example, **Large**. See the tip for recommendations.

9 Click **Send** (✐).

Photos sends the message.

TIP

Which size should I use for sending a photo?
In the Image Size pop-up menu, choose **Small** if the recipient needs only to view the photos at a small size in the message. Choose **Medium** to let the recipient view more detail in the photos in the message. Choose **Large** to send versions of the photos that the recipient can save and use in albums or web pages. Choose **Actual Size** to send the photos unchanged, so that the recipient can enjoy, edit, and use them at full resolution.

Take Photos or Movies of Yourself

Your MacBook includes a built-in FaceTime HD camera that is great not only for video chats with Messages and FaceTime but also for taking photos and movies of yourself using the Photo Booth application. You can use Photo Booth's special effects to enliven the photos or movies. The special effects include distorted views, color changes such as Thermal Camera and X-Ray, and preset backgrounds that you can use to replace your real-world background.

Take Photos or Movies of Yourself

1 Click **Launchpad** (🚀) on the Dock.

The Launchpad screen appears.

2 Click **Photo Booth** (📷).

Note: You can use some macOS-compatible external cameras with Photo Booth. To change cameras, click **Camera** on the menu bar, and then click the appropriate camera on the menu.

Photo Booth opens.

A The photo well shows photos taken earlier in Photo Booth.

3 If your face appears off center, either rotate or tilt your MacBook's screen or move yourself so that your face is correctly positioned.

4 Choose the type of picture to take:

B For four pictures, click **Take four quick pictures** (⊞).

C For a single still, click **Take a still picture** (☐).

D For a movie, click **Record a movie clip** (🎞).

5 To add effects to the photo or movie, click **Effects**.

The Photo Booth window shows various effects applied to the preview.

E To see more effects, click **Previous** (◀) or **Next** (▶) or click a different dot in the bar. The center effect on each screen is Normal. Use this effect to remove any other effect.

6 Click the effect you want to use. This example uses **Thermal Camera**.

7 Click **Take Photo** (📷) or **Take Movie** (📹).

Photo Booth counts down from 3 and then takes the photo or photos, or starts recording the movie.

8 If you are taking a movie, click **Stop Recording** (⏹) when you are ready to stop.

Photo Booth adds the photo or movie to the photo well.

TIP

How can I use the photos and movies I take in Photo Booth?
After taking a photo or movie, click it in the photo well, and then click **Share** (⬆). Photo Booth displays a panel with buttons for sharing the photo or movie. Click **Mail** to send it in a message. Click **Add to Photos** to add it to Photos. Click **Change Profile Picture** to use it as your account picture. Click **Messages** to make it your picture in Messages.

CHAPTER 12

Networking and Protecting Your MacBook

macOS enables you to share files, printers, scanners, and optical drives across networks. macOS includes many security features for protecting your MacBook against network and Internet threats.

Transfer Files Using AirDrop

macOS's AirDrop feature enables you to transfer files easily via wireless between your MacBook and nearby Macs, iPads, or iOS devices via drag and drop. Activating AirDrop in a Finder window shows you available Macs and iOS devices, and you can drag a file to the Mac or iOS device to which you want to send it. Similarly, nearby Macs and iOS devices can send files to your MacBook via AirDrop, and you can decide whether to accept or reject each file.

Transfer Files Using AirDrop

Send a File via AirDrop

1 Click **Finder** ( ) on the Dock.

A Finder window opens.

Note: If AirDrop does not appear in the sidebar, click **Go** on the menu bar, and then click **AirDrop**. If AirDrop does not appear on the Go menu either, your Mac is not compatible with AirDrop.

2 Click **AirDrop** ( ).

The AirDrop screen appears.

3 Click **Allow me to be discovered by**.

The pop-up menu opens.

4 Click **No One**, **Contacts Only**, or **Everyone** to specify which people's Macs, iOS devices, and iPads can see your MacBook via AirDrop.

5 Press ⌘+N.

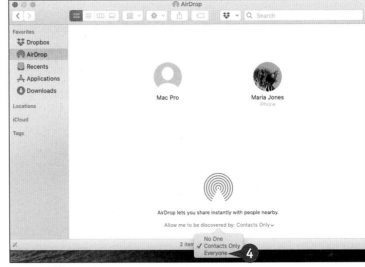

A second Finder window opens.

6 Arrange the Finder windows so you can see both.

7 Drag the file to the icon for the Mac, iOS device, or iPad you want to send it to.

The Mac or iOS device prompts the user to accept the file.

If the user accepts the file, the Finder sends the file to the recipient.

Note: If the Mac iOS device declines the file, the Finder displays a dialog telling you so.

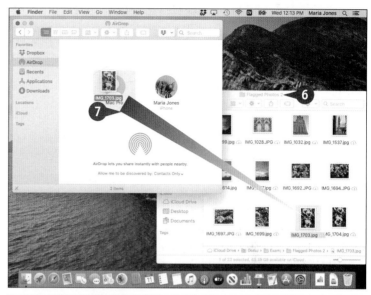

Receive a File via AirDrop

When someone sends you a file via AirDrop, a dialog appears on-screen.

1 Click **Open** if you want to open the item in the default application for that file type, if it has a default application.

Note: If the AirDrop folder is open in a Finder window, AirDrop may receive the file without notifying you.

Note: To locate an item received via AirDrop, go to the Downloads folder. Click **Finder** ( ) on the Dock to open a Finder window, and then click **Downloads** in the sidebar.

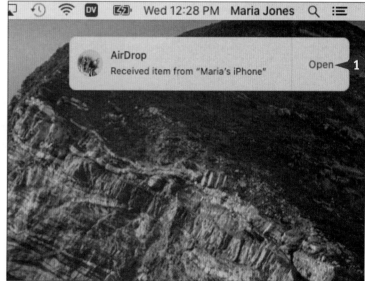

TIP

Should I use AirDrop or a shared folder on the network to transfer files?

If your MacBook connects to a network with shared folders, use those folders instead of AirDrop. By storing a file in a shared folder, you and your colleagues can work on it directly without transferring copies back and forth. AirDrop is useful for sharing on networks that do not have shared folders or for sharing files with Macs, iOS devices, or iPads to which your MacBook does not normally connect. As an alternative, you can use Messages or Mail to transfer files.

Connect to a Shared Folder

macOS enables each Mac to share folders with other computers on the same network. You can connect your MacBook to other Macs and work with the files in their shared folders.

The user who sets up the sharing can assign other users different levels of access to the folder. Depending on the permissions set for the folder, you may be able to view files in the folder but not alter them, or you may be able to create, change, and delete files in the folder.

Connect to a Shared Folder

1 Click **Finder** (🙂) on the Dock.

A Finder window opens.

2 If the Locations category is collapsed, position the pointer over it, and then click **Show** to expand it.

3 Click **Network** (🌐).

The list of devices on the network appears.

4 Click the computer that is sharing the folder.

5 Click **Connect As**.

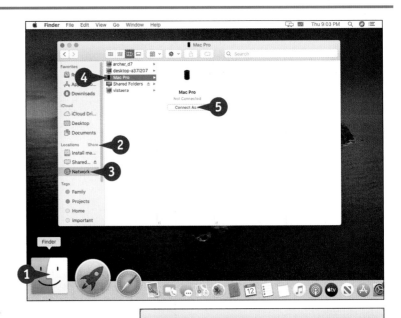

The You Are Attempting to Connect to the Server dialog opens.

6 Click **Connect**.

The Connect As dialog opens.

7 Click **Registered User** (○ changes to ◉) if you have a user account on the Mac. Click **Using an Apple ID** to use your Apple ID as your credential. Otherwise, click **Guest** (○ changes to ◉) and go to step **8**.

8 Type your username.

9 Type your password.

A You can click **Remember this password in my keychain** (☐ changes to ☑) if you want to store your password for future use.

10 Click **Connect**.

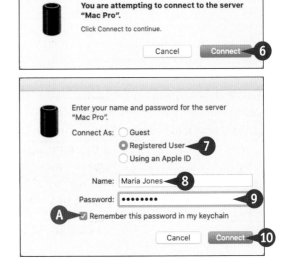

The Connect As dialog closes.

B The shared folders appear.

Note: The shared folders you see are the folders you have permission to access. Other users may be able to access different folders.

11 Click the folder whose contents you want to see.

12 Work with files as usual. For example, open a file to work on it, or copy it to your MacBook.

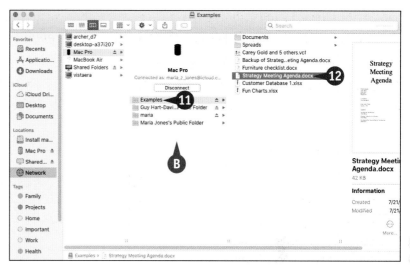

13 When you finish using the shared folder, click **Eject** (⏏) next to the computer's name in the Locations list.

Your MacBook disconnects from the computer sharing the files.

C You can also click **Disconnect** to disconnect from the sharing computer.

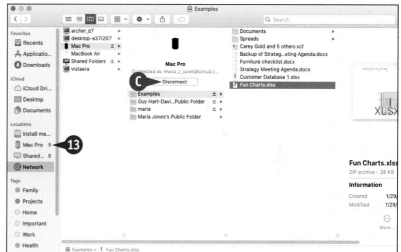

TIP

How can I connect to a shared folder that does not appear in the Shared list in the Finder window?
If the shared folder does not appear in the Shared list, find out the name or IP address of the computer sharing the folder. Click **Go** on the menu bar and click **Connect to Server**. The Connect to Server dialog opens. In the Server Address field, type or paste the computer's name or IP address; for a Windows computer, type **smb://** and then the IP address, such as 192.168.1.55. Click **Connect**, and then provide your username and password if prompted. To reconnect to a server you have used before, click the server in the Favorite Servers list box, and then click **Connect**.

Share a Folder

macOS enables you to share folders on your MacBook with other users on the network. You can set different permissions for different users, such as allowing some users to change files, allowing other users to view files but not change them, and allowing other users no access at all.

To share a folder, you enable and configure the File Sharing service in Sharing preferences. System Preferences sets up sharing for Macs automatically. You can configure sharing for Windows users manually.

Share a Folder

1 Press **Control**+click **System Preferences** (⚙) on the Dock.

The contextual menu opens.

2 Click **Sharing**.

System Preferences opens and displays the Sharing pane.

3 Click **File Sharing** (☐ changes to ☑).

System Preferences turns on file sharing.

4 Click **Add** (+) under the Shared Folders box.

A dialog for choosing a folder opens.

5 Click the folder you want to share.

6 Click **Add**.

Note: Each user account includes a drop box folder into which other people can place files and folders but whose contents only you can see. To access this folder, click **Finder** (😊) on the Dock, click **Go** on the menu bar, and then click **Home**. Click or double-click **Public**, depending on the Finder view, and then click or double-click **Drop Box**.

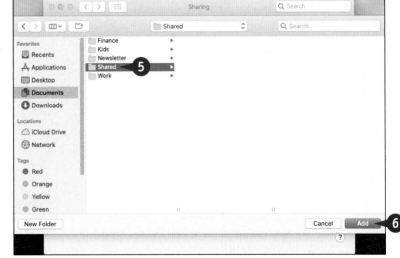

The dialog closes, and the folder appears in the Shared Folders list.

7 Click the folder.

8 Click **Everyone**.

9 Click the pop-up menu (⬙) and select the appropriate permission. See the tip for details.

10 If you need to configure sharing for Windows users, click **Options**. Otherwise, go to step **16**.

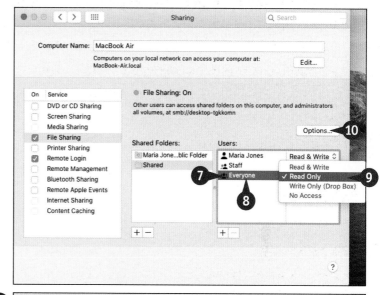

The Options dialog opens.

11 Click **Share files and folders using SMB** (☐ changes to ☑).

12 Click **On** for a user (☐ changes to ☑).

The Authenticate dialog opens.

13 Type the user's password.

14 Click **OK**.

The Authenticate dialog closes.

15 Click **Done**.

The Options dialog closes.

16 Click **Close** (⬤).

System Preferences closes.

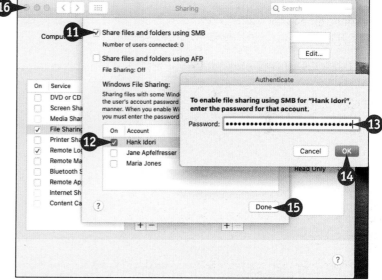

TIP

What permissions should I assign to a folder I share?
Assign **Read Only** permission if you want other people to be able only to open or copy files in the folder. If you want other people to be able to create and change files in the folder, including renaming and deleting them, click **Read & Write**. If you need to create a drop box folder that people cannot view but can add files to, click **Write Only (Drop Box)**.

Connect to a Shared or Network Printer

m acOS enables you to connect to shared printers and network printers and print documents to them. By sharing printers, you can not only enable each computer to print different types of documents as needed, but also reduce the costs of printing.

To use a shared printer or network printer, you first set it up on your MacBook using Printers & Scanners preferences. After you set up the printer, you can access it from the Print dialog just like a printer connected directly to your MacBook.

Connect to a Shared or Network Printer

1 Press **Control** + click **System Preferences** (⚙) on the Dock.

The contextual menu opens.

2 Click **Printers & Scanners**.

System Preferences opens and displays the Printers & Scanners pane.

3 Click **Add** (+).

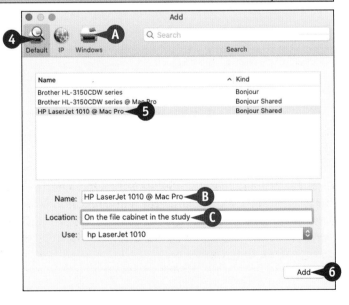

The Add dialog opens.

4 Click **Default** (🔍).

Ⓐ Click **Windows** (🖨) to see printers shared by Windows PCs on the network.

The Default pane appears.

5 Click the printer.

Ⓑ You can change the name shown in the Name box.

Ⓒ You can change the location shown in the Location box.

6 Click **Add**.

If the printer requires software that is not yet installed on your MacBook, the Some of the Software for the Printer Is Missing dialog opens.

7 Click **Download & Install**.

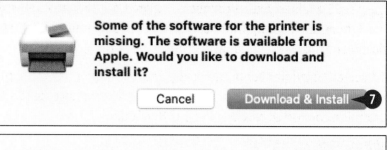

A dialog opens showing the progress as macOS downloads and installs the software.

The dialog then closes automatically.

The Add dialog closes.

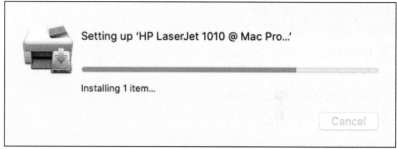

The printer appears in the Printers & Scanners pane.

8 Click **Default printer** (⬍) and click the printer to use as the default. Your options are Last Printer Used or one of the printers you have added.

9 Click **Default paper size** (⬍) and click the default paper size, such as US Letter.

10 Click **Close** (●).

System Preferences closes.

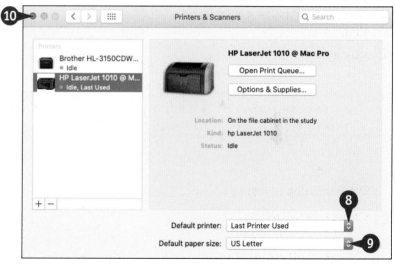

TIPS

What should I do when the Use pop-up menu says "Choose a Driver or Printer Model"?
Click **Use** (⬍) and then click **Select Software**. The Printer Software dialog opens. Type a distinctive part of the name in the Search box to see a list of matching items, and then click the driver for the printer model. Click **OK**.

Can I print without connecting to a printer?
You can create a PDF file — an image of the document — that you can print elsewhere. Click **File** and then click **Print** to open the Print dialog. Click **PDF** (⬍) and then click **Save as PDF**. In the dialog that opens, specify the filename and location, and then click **Save**.

Share Your MacBook's Printer

m acOS's Printer Sharing feature enables you to share a printer connected to your MacBook with other computers on your network. You can choose what users can print on the printer and block other users from accessing the printer.

To share the printer, you turn on the Printer Sharing feature in Sharing preferences, specify the printer, and set permissions for using it. Permitted users can access the printer from the Print dialog on their computers any time your MacBook is running.

Share Your MacBook's Printer

1 Click **System Preferences** (⚙) on the Dock.

Note: If System Preferences (⚙) does not appear on the Dock, click **Apple** () to open the Apple menu, and then click **System Preferences**.

The System Preferences window opens.

2 Click **Sharing** (☀).

The Sharing pane opens.

3 Click **Printer Sharing** (☐ changes to ✅).

macOS turns on Printer Sharing and displays the Printer Sharing preferences.

4 Click each printer you want to share (☐ changes to ✅).

A macOS makes the printer available to everyone by default.

5 To control who can use the printer, click **Add** (+).

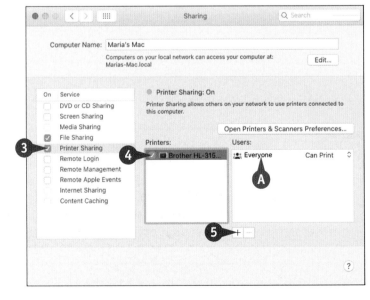

A dialog for selecting users opens.

6 Click the user you want to add.

Note: To select multiple users, click the first, and then press ⌘+click each of the others.

7 Click **Select**.

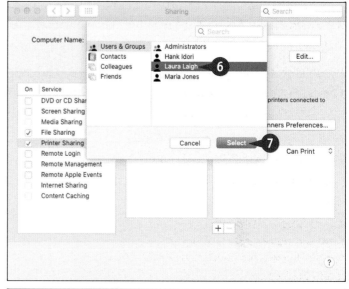

B Each user appears in the Users list.

C macOS automatically changes the Everyone item from Can Print to No Access when you add specific users.

8 Click **Close** (●).

System Preferences closes.

TIP

How can I print from my iPad or iPhone to my MacBook's printer?

First, see whether the printer is AirPrint-capable. If so, you can print by selecting the printer on your iPad or iOS device, usually from an app's Share menu. If not, either add Printer Pro to your iPad or iOS device or install handyPrint (www.netputing.com/applications/handyprint-v5) on your MacBook.

Turn Off Automatic Login

macOS enables you to set your MacBook to log in one user account automatically, bypassing the login screen. Automatic login is convenient if you are the only person who can access your MacBook, but it is more secure to disable automatic login so each user must log in.

To enable or disable automatic login, you use the Login Options pane in Users & Groups preferences. You must have an administrator account or provide administrator credentials to change these options.

Turn Off Automatic Login

① Press **Control**+click **System Preferences** (⚙) on the Dock.

The contextual menu opens.

② Click **Security & Privacy**.

System Preferences opens and displays the Security & Privacy pane.

③ Click **General**.

The General pane appears.

④ Click the **lock** icon (🔒).

The authentication dialog opens.

⑤ Type your password.

⑥ Click **Unlock**.

System Preferences unlocks the preferences (🔓 changes to 🔓).

⑦ Click **Disable automatic login** (☐ changes to ✅).

⑧ For greater security, click **Require password** *timing* **after sleep or screen saver begins** (☐ changes to ✅).

⑨ Click the pop-up menu (⬍) and click **immediately** or a short time: 5 seconds, 1 minute, or 5 minutes.

⑩ Click **Advanced**.

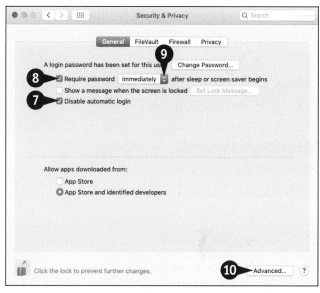

The Advanced dialog opens.

⑪ Click **Log out after *N* minutes of inactivity** (☐ changes to ✅).

⑫ Click the text box and enter the period of inactivity.

⑬ Click **OK**.

The Advanced dialog closes.

⑭ Click **Close** (⬤).

System Preferences closes.

TIP

What other options can I set to tighten my MacBook's security?
In Users & Groups preferences, click **Login Options**. You can then click **Name and password** (◯ changes to ⦿) to hide the list of usernames so that anyone logging on must type a username as well as a password. Click **Show the Sleep, Restart, and Shut Down buttons** (✅ changes to ☐) to remove these buttons from the login screen, so that nobody can shut down the MacBook without logging in unless he turns off the MacBook's power. Click **Show password hints** (✅ changes to ☐) if you want to prevent password hints from appearing.

Enable and Configure the Firewall

macOS includes a firewall that protects your MacBook from unauthorized access by other computers on your network or on the Internet. macOS enables you to configure the firewall to suit your needs. To configure the firewall, you use the Firewall pane in Security & Privacy preferences.

Even if your Internet router includes a firewall configured to prevent Internet threats from reaching your network, you should use the macOS firewall to protect against threats from other computers on your network.

Enable and Configure the Firewall

1 Press **Control** +click **System Preferences** (⚙) on the Dock.

The contextual menu opens.

2 Click **Security & Privacy**.

System Preferences opens and displays the Security & Privacy pane.

3 Click the **lock** icon (🔒).

The authentication dialog opens.

4 Type your password.

5 Click **Unlock**.

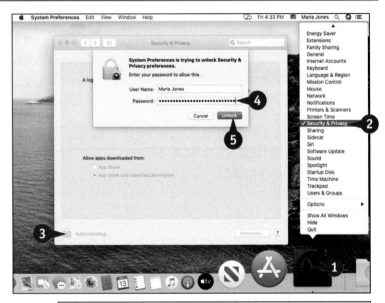

System Preferences unlocks the preferences (🔒 changes to 🔓).

6 Click **Firewall**.

The Firewall pane appears.

7 If Firewall: Off appears, click **Turn On Firewall**.

The firewall starts, and Firewall: On appears.

8 Click **Firewall Options**.

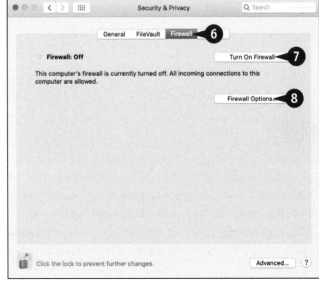

The Firewall Options dialog opens.

9 Click **Automatically allow built-in software to receive incoming connections** (☐ changes to ☑) if you want to allow your MacBook's built-in software to receive incoming connections.

10 Click **Automatically allow downloaded signed software to receive incoming connections** (☑ changes to ☐) if you want to prevent apps you have installed from accepting connections automatically across the network.

11 Click **Enable stealth mode** (☐ changes to ☑) if you want to prevent your MacBook from responding to network test applications.

12 To allow incoming connections to a particular application, click **Add** (+).

The Add dialog opens.

13 Click the app.

14 Click **Add**.

The Add dialog closes.

System Preferences adds the app to the list.

15 Click **OK**.

The Firewall Options dialog closes.

16 Click **Close** (●).

System Preferences closes.

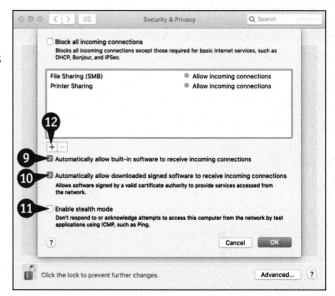

TIPS

When should I use the Block All Incoming Connections option?
Click **Block all incoming connections** when you need to tighten security as much as possible. The usual reason for blocking all connections is connecting your MacBook to a network that you cannot trust, such as a public wireless network.

How do I block incoming connections only to a specific application?
Add that application to the list in the Advanced dialog. Then click the application's **Allow incoming connections** button in the list and click **Block incoming connections**.

Choose Privacy Settings

The settings in the Privacy pane in Security & Privacy preferences enable you to control which apps can request access to potentially sensitive information, such as the MacBook's location, and files, such as contacts and photos. You can also specify whether to send diagnostic data and usage data to Apple to help it improve macOS and its apps, and whether to share app crash data with the developers of the apps in question.

Choose Privacy Settings

1 Press **Control** + click **System Preferences** (⚙) on the Dock.

The contextual menu opens.

2 Click **Security & Privacy**.

System Preferences opens and displays the Security & Privacy pane.

3 Click the **lock** icon (🔒).

The authentication dialog opens.

4 Type your password.

5 Click **Unlock**.

The controls in the Security & Privacy pane become enabled.

6 Click **Privacy**.

The Privacy pane appears.

7 Click **Location Services**.

The Location Services preferences appear.

8 Click **Enable Location Services** to enable (☑) or disable (☐) the feature.

9 If you enable Location Services, click each app or service in the list to enable (☑) or disable (☐) its use of Location Services.

10 Click **Details**.

The Allow System Services to Determine Your Location dialog opens.

11 In the upper section, click each item to enable (☑) or disable (☐) it from determining your location.

12 Click **Show location icon in menu bar when System Services request your location** to enable (☑) or disable (☐) the icon from appearing in the menu bar.

13 Click **Done**.

14 Click **Contacts** (📇) and choose which apps can access contacts. Similarly, choose settings for other apps and features, such as **Calendars** (📅), **Reminders** (📋), and **Accessibility** (♿).

15 Click **Analytics & Improvements** (📊) at the bottom of the left pane.

16 Click **Share Mac Analytics** to enable (☑) or disable (☐) sharing diagnostic and usage data.

17 Click **Improve Siri & Dictation** to enable (☑) or disable (☐) sharing your Siri and Dictation recordings with Apple.

18 Click **Share with App Developers** to enable (☑) or disable (☐) sharing data with third-party developers.

19 Click **Share iCloud Analytics** to enable (☑) or disable (☐) sharing iCloud usage data.

20 Click **Close** (⬤).

System Preferences closes.

TIP

What does the Advanced button in Privacy preferences do?

The Advanced button is shared among all four Security & Privacy preferences panes — the General pane, the FileVault pane, the Firewall pane, and the Privacy pane — rather than being specific to any pane. See the section "Turn Off Automatic Login," earlier in this chapter, for coverage of the options in the Advanced dialog, which appears when you click this button.

Install and Use Antivirus Software

macOS includes a built-in antimalware app called XProtect that helps protect your MacBook against *malware* — malevolent software — hidden in incoming files, such as files you download or that others send you. It is a good idea to augment this protection by installing and running antivirus software. You can buy and download antivirus software from the App Store, buy it on a disc from a physical store or by mail order, or download it from a website. Some antivirus apps are free; others are paid software.

You install the antivirus software in a similar way to other apps. However, after installing the antivirus software, you may need to restart your MacBook.

Choose Antivirus Software

You can choose from a wide range of antivirus apps to protect your MacBook. Some apps provide only features for scanning files for viruses, whereas other apps are complete security suites. You will likely want protection against malware, which includes viruses; Trojan-horse programs that hide harm in a program that seems helpful; and rootkits, which try to build secret entry points into your computer.

Protection against spyware programs, adware programs, and infected websites is useful, too. Features designed to detect phishing messages may also be helpful, but you may find that Mail's Junk Mail feature and your own evaluation give you more consistent results.

When choosing an antivirus software package, assess your needs and decide whether you need a full-blown security app or simply an antivirus app. Bear in mind that the larger the antivirus or security app, the more likely it is to cause your MacBook to run more slowly, because most antivirus and security apps need to run all the time to keep your MacBook safe.

Download and Install an Antivirus App

The App Store enables you to browse a wide range of antivirus apps. You can examine detailed descriptions of each app's features, see user ratings, and read user reviews.

To download and install an antivirus app from the App Store, first click **App Store** (🅐) on the Dock. If the App Store icon does not appear on the Dock, click **Launchpad** (🚀) on the Dock, and then click **App Store** (🅐) on the Launchpad screen.

Click in the Search box in the upper-left corner of the screen, type **antivirus**, and press Return. The App Store app displays a list of results. You can click a result to display the details screen for the app.

To buy an app, click **Get** for a free app or the price button for a pay app. For either type of item, click **Install**. If the App Store app prompts you to sign in, type your password and click **Sign In**. The App Store app then downloads the app. When the download finishes, macOS installs the app automatically.

You can buy antivirus apps in stores or download them from the websites of antivirus companies. Before downloading any app from a website, verify that the app is genuine and that it gets good reviews on third-party sites — if not, it may be dangerous.

Run Your Antivirus App and Update It If Necessary

After installing your antivirus app, run it by clicking **Launchpad** () on the Dock, and then clicking the app's icon on the Launchpad screen.

When you first run an antivirus app, it may prompt you to update its virus signatures or malware signatures. If this happens, give the command for proceeding with the update. For example, in Bitdefender Virus Scanner, select (✅) **Update threat information before scanning**, and then click **Finish**.

Scan Your MacBook with Your Antivirus App

Many antivirus apps run continuously in the background, automatically monitoring what happens on your MacBook. Other apps you run as needed; for example, if you suspect that your MacBook has contracted malware, you can run a scan to detect and remove it.

Most antivirus apps enable you to choose which areas of your MacBook to scan and how deeply to scan them. For example, in Bitdefender Virus Scanner, you can click **Scan Critical Locations** to scan important locations and folders such as the main Library folder and the main Applications folder; click **Deep System Scan** to scan your MacBook in depth; or click **Scan a Custom Location** to specify the location you want to scan.

What effect running a deep scan has on your MacBook's performance depends on the antivirus app and on your MacBook's configuration. But in general, it is best not to use your MacBook for intensive computing tasks while running a deep scan. Instead, set a deep scan running when you are planning to leave your MacBook for a while.

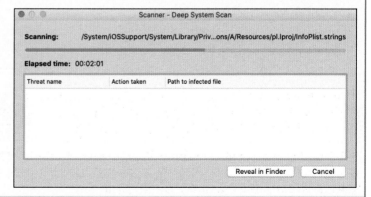

Recognize and Avoid Phishing Attacks

phishing is an attack in which someone tries to make you provide valuable information such as bank account numbers, login names, passwords, or credit card numbers. After acquiring this information, the phisher either uses it directly — for example, withdrawing money from your bank account — or sells it to other criminals.

Mail and Safari help protect you against phishing. Mail scans your incoming messages and marks any that may be phishing. Safari enables you to check a website's digital certificate to make sure it is valid.

Recognize and Avoid Phishing Attacks

Recognize a Phishing E-Mail Message

1 In Mail, open the message.

2 Look for signs of phishing:

Ⓐ Mail has detected suspicious signs in the message.

Ⓑ The message does not show your name as the recipient.

Ⓒ The message has a generic greeting, such as Dear Customer, or no greeting at all.

Ⓓ The message claims you need to take action, such as clearing a security lockout or reenabling your account.

Ⓔ The message contains links it encourages you to click.

3 Position the pointer over a link but do not click.

Ⓕ A ScreenTip appears showing the address to which the link leads.

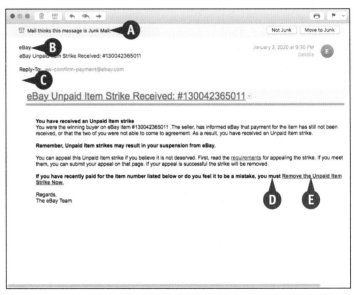

Examine the Digital Certificate for a Website

1 Click **Safari** (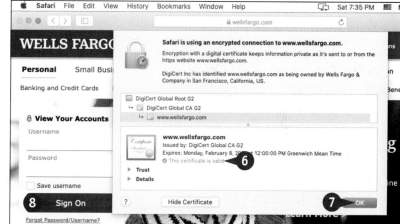) on the Dock.

2 Click the address box.

3 Type the address of the website and press **Return**.

4 Click the **padlock** icon (🔒).

Note: Safari displays the padlock icon when you have connected securely to a website. The address of a secure connection starts with https:// instead of http://. You can view the full address by clicking the address box. A secure connection does not mean that the website is safe.

A dialog opens.

5 Click **Show Certificate**.

The dialog expands, showing the details of the digital certificate that identifies the website.

6 Verify that the certificate is valid.

7 Click **OK**.

The dialog closes.

8 If you are convinced that the website is genuine, log in to it.

TIPS

Is it possible to make a secure connection to a dangerous website?

Yes. The padlock icon means only that the connection between your MacBook and the website server is secure and cannot be read in transmission. The website may be safe or it may be dangerous; it is up to you to establish which.

Is a message definitely genuine if it includes my name?

Even if a message includes your name, be alert for other signs of phishing. Some phishers send customized phishing messages in the hope of ensnaring particular high-value victims. This technique is called *spear-phishing*. Evaluate the message's content for sense and likelihood, and remember that anything too good to be true is usually not true.

CHAPTER 13

Troubleshooting Your MacBook

To keep your MacBook running well, you need to perform basic maintenance, such as emptying the Trash, updating macOS and your apps with the latest fixes, and backing up your files. You may also need to troubleshoot your MacBook, solving problems such as corrupt preference files, disk permission errors, or drive failure.

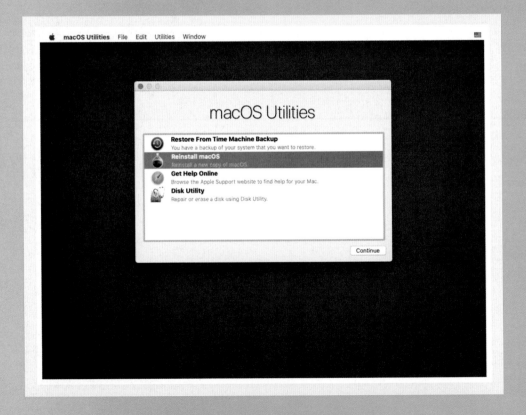

Reclaim Space by Emptying the Trash

In macOS, the Trash is a receptacle for files you delete from your MacBook's drives. Any file you place in the Trash remains there until you empty the Trash, or until the Trash runs out of space for files and automatically deletes the earliest files it contains; until then, you can recover the file from the Trash. You can reclaim drive space by emptying the Trash manually.

Reclaim Space by Emptying the Trash

Empty the Trash

1 Click **Trash** (🗑) on the Dock.

Note: If the Trash icon on the Dock is the empty Trash can (🗑), the Trash is already empty.

2 Look through the files and folders in the Trash to make sure it contains nothing you want to keep.

To quickly view the contents of a file, use Quick Look. Click the file, and then press Spacebar.

Note: You cannot open a file while it is in the Trash. If you want to open a file, you must remove it from the Trash.

3 Click **Empty**.

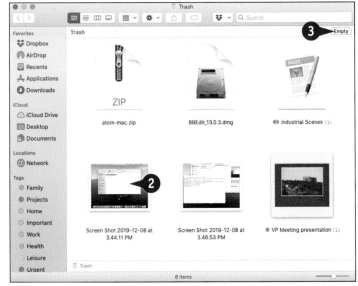

A dialog opens to confirm that you want to permanently erase the items in the Trash.

Note: You can turn off the confirmation of deleting files. Click **Finder** and then click **Preferences**. Click **Advanced** and then click **Show warning before emptying the Trash** (☑ changes to ☐).

④ Click **Empty Trash**.

macOS empties the Trash and then closes the Finder window.

Restore a File or Folder to Its Previous Location

① In the Trash folder, click the file or folder.

② Click **Action** (✱ ✓).

③ Click **Put Back**.

Note: You can also press Control +click an item and click **Put Back** on the contextual menu.

macOS restores the file or folder to its previous location.

Note: To move a file from the Trash to another folder, drag the file to that folder. For example, you can drag a file to the desktop.

TIPS

Is there a quicker way to empty the Trash?

If you are sure that the Trash contains no files or folders you need, press Control +click **Trash** (🗑) on the Dock. The Dock menu opens. Click **Empty Trash**. A confirmation dialog opens. Click **Empty Trash**.

Why does the Put Back command not appear on the Action menu?

If the Put Back command is missing, it means that the folder from which you moved the item to the Trash is no longer there. If the folder is in the Trash, click the folder, click **Action** (✱ ✓), and then click **Put Back**; you can then put back into the folder the file you want to recover. Alternatively, drag the file to another folder.

You can use the App Store app built into macOS to check for updates to your MacBook, its operating system, and your App Store apps. When the App Store app finds updates, you can choose which to install.

Your MacBook must be connected to the Internet when you check for updates and download them. You can install most updates when your MacBook is either online or offline. Some updates require restarting your MacBook.

Keep Your MacBook Current with Updates

Ⓐ macOS may display an Updates Available dialog prompting you to install updates. You can click **Updates Available** to go to the Updates tab in the App Store app, click **Install** to install the updates immediately, or click **Later** to install the updates later.

Ⓑ A badge on the App Store icon indicates the number of updates available.

❶ Click **App Store** (🅰) on the Dock.

Note: You can also open the App Store app by clicking **Apple** (🍎) and then clicking **App Store**.

The App Store app opens.

❷ Click **Updates** (🔄).

The Updates pane appears.

App Store automatically checks for updates.

If updates are available, the Available list shows the details.

Note: If the message No Updates Available appears, go to step **4**.

Ⓒ You can install an individual update by clicking **Update**. If the update requires a restart, click **Restart**.

Ⓓ You can click **more** to display full details of an update.

❸ To install all the updates, click **Update All**.

Note: If installing the updates requires a restart, App Store displays a dialog. Click **Restart** to restart now. Alternatively, click **Later**, and then click **Install in an Hour**, **Install Tonight**, or **Remind Me Tomorrow**.

macOS installs the updates.

🄴 A progress indicator appears for each app.

🄵 The Open button replaces the progress indicator when the app update is complete.

Note: macOS restarts your MacBook if necessary.

④ Click **Close** (⬤).

The App Store app closes.

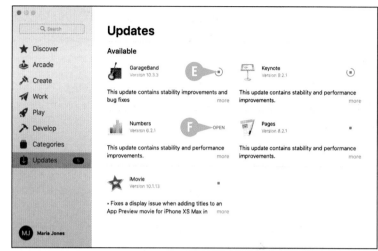

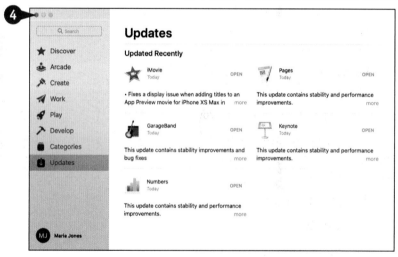

TIPS

Why does the App Store app sometimes prompt me to install updates?

In macOS, App Store comes set to check for updates automatically; when it finds updates, it prompts you to install them. You can change the frequency of these checks, choose whether to download important updates automatically, or turn off automatic checks. See the next section, "Control Checking for Software and App Updates," for instructions.

Which updates should I install?

Normally, it is best to install all available system updates unless you hear that a specific update may cause problems with your MacBook. In that case, wait until Apple fixes the update. For app updates, you may prefer to wait for user feedback, because some updates create incompatibilities for documents created in earlier versions.

Control Checking for Software and App Updates

In macOS, the Software Update feature handles updates for the operating system and built-in apps, while the App Store app handles updates for apps you add via the App Store. To keep your MacBook running smoothly and protect it from both online and offline threats, you should apply system software updates when they become available. You may also want to install app updates soon to take advantage of any bug fixes or improvements they offer.

Control Checking for Software and App Updates

Set Software Update to Update Your MacBook Automatically

1. Press ⌘+click **System Preferences** (⚙️) on the Dock.

   The contextual menu opens.

2. Click **Software Update**.

   System Preferences opens and displays the Software Update pane.

   Ⓐ The status readout tells you whether your MacBook is up to date.

3. To keep your MacBook up to date, click **Automatically keep my Mac up to date**.

   A dialog opens prompting you to authenticate yourself via Touch ID or your password.

4. Touch the Touch ID scanner or click **Use Password** and type your password.

   The dialog closes and the Automatically Keep My Mac Up to Date check box becomes selected (☐ changes to ☑).

5. For more options, click **Advanced**.

   The Advanced dialog opens.

6. Verify that each check box is selected (☑) unless you need to turn off a particular feature.

338

Note: Selecting the Automatically Keep My Mac Up to Date check box in the Software Update pane selects all the check boxes in the Advanced dialog. See the tip for details.

7. Click **OK**.

   The Advanced dialog closes.

8. Click **Close** (⬤).

   The System Preferences window closes.

Set the App Store App to Install Updates Automatically

1 Click **App Store** () on the Dock.

The App Store app opens.

2 Click **App Store**.

The menu opens.

3 Click **Preferences**.

The Preferences window opens.

4 Select **Automatic Updates** (☑) to have App Store download and install app updates automatically.

5 Select **Automatically download apps purchased on other Mac computers** (☑) if you want to automatically install apps you buy or get on your other Macs.

6 Select **Video Autoplay** (☑) if you want App Store to automatically play preview videos with the sound off.

7 Select **In-App Ratings & Reviews** (☑) if you want to allow apps to prompt you for ratings and reviews.

8 Click **Close** (●).

The Preferences window closes.

9 Click **Close** (●).

The App Store app closes.

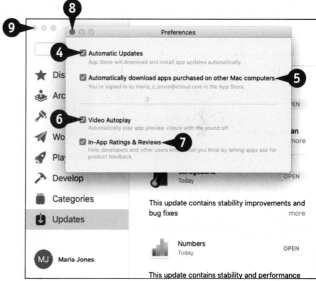

TIP

Should I select the Automatically Keep My Mac Up to Date check box?
This is up to you. But most security professionals recommend installing all updates to keep your MacBook protected against threats and to make sure you have the latest fixes and upgrades for macOS and your apps.

Back Up Your Files

To enable you to keep your valuable files safe, macOS includes an automatic backup application called Time Machine. Time Machine automatically saves copies of your files to an external drive or an AirPort Time Capsule, a wireless router and backup device Apple discontinued in 2018. You can choose what drive to use, how frequently to back up your files, and what folders to include.

To protect your data, you must back up your files. Time Machine is the most convenient choice because it takes only a few minutes to set up and thereafter runs automatically.

Back Up Your Files

1 If you will use an external drive for Time Machine, connect the drive to your MacBook.

2 Press **Control** +click **System Preferences** (⚙) on the Dock.

The contextual menu appears.

3 Click **Time Machine**.

The System Preferences window opens, showing the Time Machine preferences pane.

4 Click **Back Up Automatically** (☐ changes to ☑).

The Select Disk dialog opens.

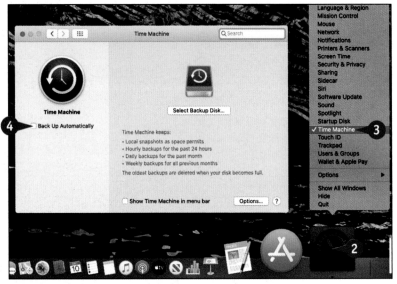

5 Click the drive or AirPort Time Capsule you want to use for backup.

A You can click **Encrypt backups** (☐ changes to ☑) to encrypt your backups.

6 Click **Use Disk**.

The Select Disk dialog closes.

B You can click **Show Time Machine in menu bar** (☐ changes to ☑) to give yourself easy access to Time Machine.

7 Click **Options**.

The Options dialog opens.

8 Click **Back up while on battery power** (☐ changes to ☑) if you want your MacBook to perform backups even when it is running on battery power.

9 Click **Exclude system files and applications** (☐ changes to ☑) to omit system files and apps from backups. Omitting these files keeps your backups smaller. You can recover system files and apps by reinstalling macOS and downloading apps again.

10 Click **Add** (+).

A dialog opens.

11 Select each drive or folder you want to exclude from backup.

12 Click **Exclude**.

The dialog closes, and Time Machine adds the items to the Exclude These Items from Backups dialog.

13 Click **Save**.

The Options dialog closes.

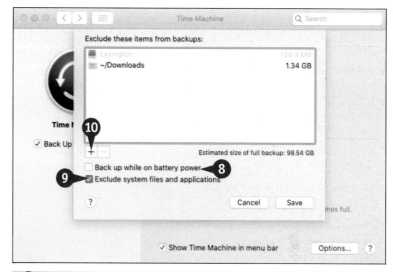

14 Click **Close** (●).

The System Preferences window closes.

TIPS

What kind of drive should I use for Time Machine?
For a recent or current MacBook model, use USB. For an older MacBook that has one or more Thunderbolt ports, you can use Thunderbolt instead; Thunderbolt may be faster than USB, but Thunderbolt drives are usually more expensive. Buy a drive that has at least twice as much storage as your MacBook has, and preferably much more, to ensure that you have plenty of space for backups.

How often does Time Machine back up my files?
Time Machine starts to back up all your files 2 minutes after you set it up. After that, it creates an hourly backup of files that have changed since the last backup. Time Machine consolidates the hourly backups into daily backups, and then consolidates the daily backups into weekly backups.

Recover Files from Backup

The Time Machine feature enables you to easily recover files from your backups. So when you delete a file by accident, or discover that a file has become corrupted, you can recover the file from backup by opening Time Machine. You can recover either the latest copy of the file or an earlier copy.

If you still have the current copy of the file that you recover, you can choose whether to overwrite that copy or keep it. Time Machine refers to this copy as the "original" file.

Recover Files from Backup

Note: This section shows you how to recover files using the Finder. To recover old data within Contacts, Calendar, or Mail, open the appropriate app and make it active before giving the Enter Time Machine command.

1 Click **Time Machine** ( ) on the menu bar.

The Time Machine menu opens.

2 Click **Enter Time Machine**.

Note: If the Time Machine status icon does not appear on the menu bar, click **Launchpad** ( ) on the Dock, and then click **Time Machine** ( ) on the Launchpad screen.

Time Machine opens.

Ⓐ The front window shows your MacBook's drive or drives in their current state.

Ⓑ Backups of the selected drive or folder appear in the windows behind it, newest at the front.

Ⓒ The timeline on the right shows how far back in time the available backups go.

3 Click the date or time from which you want to recover the files or folders.

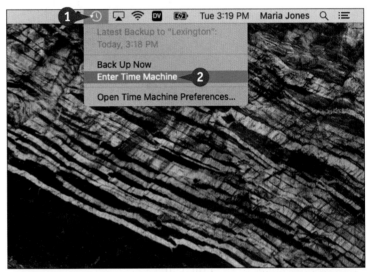

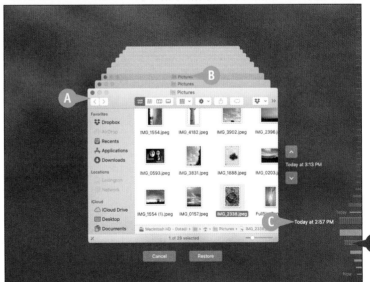

Time Machine brings the backup you chose to the front.

④ Select the item or items you want to restore.

⑤ Click **Restore**.

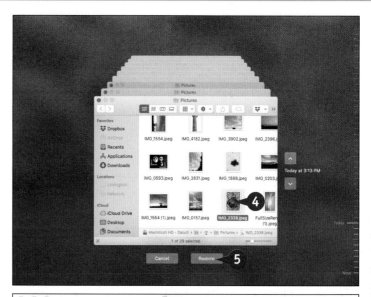

Time Machine disappears.

If restoring a file will overwrite the current version, the Copy dialog opens.

⑥ Choose how to handle the file conflict:

Ⓓ Click **Replace** to replace the current file with the older file.

Ⓔ Click **Keep Original** to keep the current file.

Ⓕ Click **Keep Both** to keep both versions of the file. Time Machine adds "(Original)" to the name of the current version.

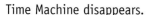

TIPS

What do the arrow buttons to the right of the Finder window in Time Machine do?
The two arrow buttons enable you to navigate among the available backups. Click the upward arrow to move to the previous backup, further in the past. Click the downward arrow to move to the next backup, nearer to the present.

How do I create Time Machine backups manually?
Click **Time Machine** (🕐) on the menu bar and select **Back Up Now**. The menu also enables you to enter Time Machine and open Time Machine preferences.

Recover When macOS Crashes

Normally, macOS runs stably and smoothly, but sometimes the operating system may suffer a crash. Crashes can occur for various reasons, including power fluctuations, bad memory modules, an app that has been corrupted, or problems with disk permissions.

Your MacBook may detect that the crash has occurred and display an informational message, but in other cases the MacBook's screen may simply freeze and continue displaying the same information. Normally, you can recover from a crash by turning off your MacBook's power and then turning it on again.

Recover When macOS Crashes

Recover from the Screen Freezing

1 If the pointer shows the "wait" cursor that looks like a spinning beach ball, wait a couple of minutes to see if macOS can recover from the problem. If the pointer has disappeared, go straight to step **2**.

2 To verify that your MacBook is not responding, press keys on the keyboard or move your fingers on the trackpad.

Note: If possible, connect your MacBook to power when attempting to recover from a freeze or a crash.

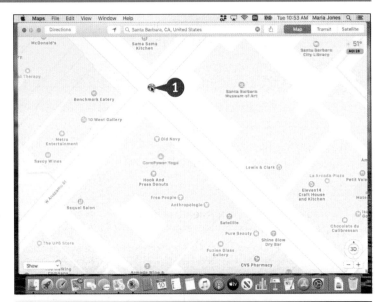

3 Press and hold ⌘ + Control and press the MacBook's power button.

4 If the MacBook does not respond to that key combination, press and hold the MacBook's power button for about 4 seconds.

The MacBook turns off.

5 Wait at least 8 seconds, and then press the power button once to restart the MacBook.

Recover from a Detected Crash

When your MacBook detects a macOS crash, it dims the screen and displays a message in the center.

1 Read the message for information.

2 Press and hold the MacBook's power button for about 4 seconds.

The MacBook turns off.

3 Wait at least 8 seconds, and then press the power button once to restart the MacBook.

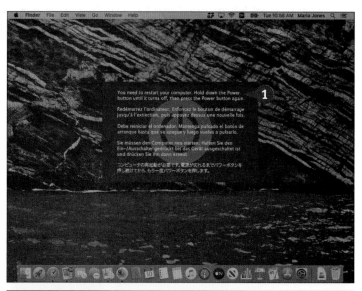

Note: Depending on how your MacBook is configured, macOS may log you in automatically or display the Login dialog.

The login screen appears.

4 Click your username, and then log in to your account as normal.

TIP

How can I avoid crashes?

• Limit the number of apps you run at the same time. When you finish using an app, quit it.

• Keep your MacBook current by installing available updates for system software and apps.

• Keep at least 15 percent of your MacBook's drive free. Click the desktop, click **Go** on the menu bar, and then click **Computer** to open a Finder window showing the Computer folder. Press `Control`+click **Macintosh HD** and click **Get Info**. In the General section, look at the Capacity readout and the Available readout.

• If running a particular app causes your MacBook to crash, uninstall and reinstall that app.

Troubleshoot Corrupt Preference Files

macOS and many apps enable you to set preferences to customize the way they run. Each app stores its configuration in a special file called a *preference file*. Sometimes a preference file becomes corrupted, which may prevent the app from running properly or cause it to crash.

To fix the problem, you delete the preference file. This forces the app to create a new preference file from scratch with default settings. When the app is running properly again, you can choose your custom settings again.

Troubleshoot Corrupt Preference Files

1 Quit the problem app if it is running. Click the app's menu, such as the **TV** menu for the Contacts app, and then click the Quit command, such as **Quit TV**.

Note: If you cannot quit the app by using its Quit command, force quit it. Press (Option)+click the app's Dock icon and click **Force Quit** on the contextual menu.

2 Click an open space on the desktop.

The Finder becomes active.

3 Click **Go**.

The Go menu opens.

4 Press and hold (Option).

The Library item appears on the Go menu.

Note: macOS hides the Library item on the Go menu until you press (Option).

5 Click **Library**.

The contents of the Library folder appear.

6 Click **Preferences**.

The contents of the Preferences folder appear.

7 Click the preference file for the problem application. See the tip for help on identifying the file.

Note: If the application has two or more preference files, move them all to the Trash.

8 Click **Action** (✳ ✓).

The Action menu opens.

9 Click **Move to Trash**.

macOS moves the file to the Trash.

10 Click **Close** (●).

The Finder window closes.

11 Start the application. Continuing the example, click **TV** (📺) on the Dock.

The application creates a new preference file containing default settings.

12 Set preferences in the application. In most applications, click the application's menu and click **Preferences** to open the Preferences window.

The application saves your preferences in the new preference file.

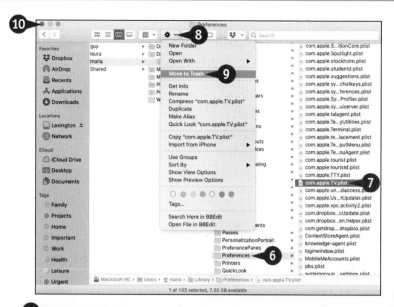

TIP

How do I find the right preference file to delete?
The names of most preference files use the format com.*company*.*application*.plist, where *company* is the manufacturer's name, *application* is the application's name, and .plist is the file extension for a property list file. For example, com.apple.mail.plist is the preference file for the Mail app, and com.microsoft.Excel. plist is the Excel preference file. If you cannot locate the preference file by browsing the Preferences folder, search online to learn the exact name.

Run First Aid from Within macOS

macOS includes automatic tools for fixing minor problems that may occur as your MacBook runs. Normally, the operating system resolves these problems in the background without your involvement.

However, sometimes your MacBook may exhibit disk problems that these automatic tools cannot fix. In such cases, you can run the First Aid tool from within macOS to try to resolve the issue.

Run First Aid from Within macOS

1 Click **Launchpad** (🚀) on the Dock.

The Launchpad screen appears.

2 Press D to type the letter *d*.

Launchpad displays only those items that include a word starting with *D*.

3 Click **Disk Utility**.

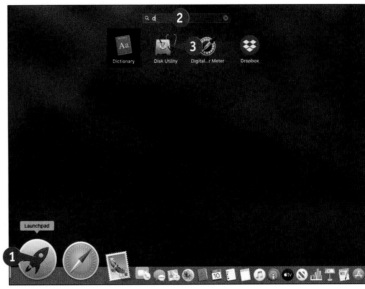

Disk Utility opens.

4 Click your MacBook's drive.

The controls for manipulating the drive appear.

5 Click **First Aid** (🩺).

The Run First Aid? dialog opens.

6 Click **Run**.

7 If the Verifying the Startup Volume Will Cause This Computer to Stop Responding dialog opens, click **Continue**. Your MacBook is likely to become unresponsive temporarily while First Aid runs.

A Disk Utility searches for problems and resolves any that it can resolve. The process may take several minutes. If possible, avoid using your MacBook during the scan.

8 Click **Show Details** if you want to see details of the repairs.

Disk Utility informs you when the First Aid process is complete.

9 Click **Done**.

The dialog closes.

10 Click **Close** (⬤).

Disk Utility closes.

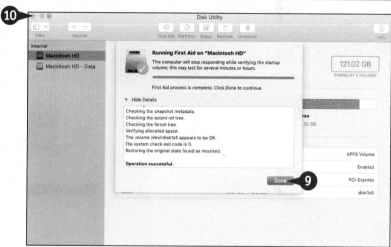

TIPS

For what types of problems would I run First Aid?

Here are three examples. First, your MacBook may not be able to access an external device that worked previously; second, a file you need to open may have become corrupted; and third, you find that apps freeze or quit spontaneously.

What should I do if Disk Utility says my MacBook's disk is about to fail?

Back up all your data immediately using Time Machine, as explained earlier in this chapter. You will then need to replace the disk. Replacing the disk on most MacBook models is a task for trained technicians, but it is worth researching whether your MacBook has a user-replaceable disk.

Run First Aid from macOS Utilities

I f your MacBook will not start, you may be able to fix the problem by running First Aid. To do so, you start your MacBook from the recovery partition, which contains tools called macOS Utilities for recovering from problems. macOS Utilities enables you to launch the Disk Utility tool from outside macOS when the operating system is not working.

Run First Aid from macOS Utilities

1 Start your MacBook by pressing the power button.

Note: If your MacBook is running, restart it by clicking **Apple** (🍎) and then pressing Option+clicking **Restart**.

2 At the startup chime, press and hold ⌘+R until the Apple logo appears.

Your MacBook starts from the recovery partition.

The macOS Utilities screen appears.

3 Click **Disk Utility**.

4 Click **Continue**.

The Disk Utility window opens.

5 Click your MacBook's internal drive.

The controls for manipulating the drive appear.

6 Click **First Aid** (🩺).

The Run First Aid? dialog opens.

7 Click **Run**.

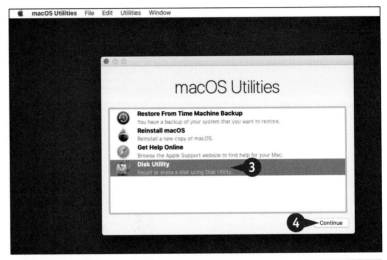

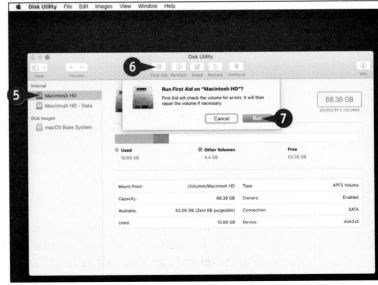

Disk Utility analyzes the drive and repairs problems, displaying its progress as it does so.

Disk Utility informs you when the First Aid process is complete.

⑧ Click **Done**.

The dialog closes.

⑨ Click **Disk Utility**.

The Disk Utility menu opens.

⑩ Click **Quit Disk Utility**.

Disk Utility closes, and the Install macOS dialog opens.

⑪ Click **macOS Utilities**.

The macOS Utilities menu opens.

⑫ Click **Quit macOS Utilities**.

A confirmation dialog opens.

⑬ Click **Restart**.

Your MacBook restarts into macOS from the internal drive.

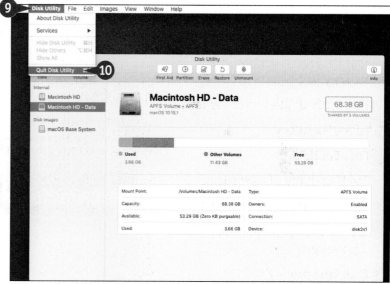

TIP

What do I do if my MacBook cannot start after repairing the drive?

If your MacBook cannot start after repairing the drive, try using a different startup volume. At the startup chime, press and hold ⌘+R. In macOS Utilities, click **Restore From Time Machine Backup**, and then click **Continue**. Click **macOS Installer** and click **Quit macOS Installer**. In the Time Machine System Restore dialog that opens, click **Choose Startup Disk**. In the Choose Startup Disk dialog that opens, click the startup volume, and then click **Restart**. Your MacBook starts from the volume you selected.

Reinstall macOS to Solve Severe Problems

If your MacBook suffers severe software damage, macOS may not be able to run. When this happens, you can fix the problem by reinstalling macOS. You may also need to reinstall macOS if your MacBook runs but crashes frequently and you are not able to restore stability by repairing the permissions or repairing the disk.

macOS normally includes a recovery partition that enables you to begin reinstalling the operating system. Once connected to the Internet, your MacBook can then download the files it needs from Apple's servers and complete the reinstallation.

Reinstall macOS to Solve Severe Problems

1 Press the power button.

2 At the startup chime, press and hold ⌘+R until the Apple logo appears.

Your MacBook starts from the recovery partition.

Note: If your MacBook does not have a recovery partition, you may be able to use the Internet Recovery feature to download the files required for starting recovery. Follow the prompts to connect to a Wi-Fi network and download the files.

The macOS Utilities screen appears.

3 Click **Reinstall macOS**.

4 Click **Continue**.

The Install macOS screen appears.

5 Click **Continue**.

The Software License Agreement screen appears.

6 Click **Agree**.

A confirmation dialog opens.

7 Click **Agree**.

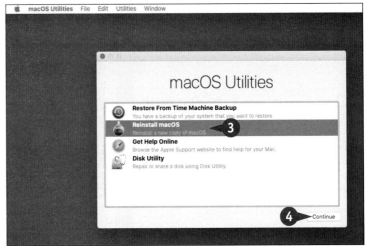

The screen for selecting the installation disk appears.

Ⓐ If a disk is grayed out, you cannot select it.

❽ Click the disk.

❾ Click **Install**.

Note: If the Sign In to Download from the App Store dialog opens, type your Apple ID and your password, and then click **Sign In**.

Install macOS begins downloading the components it needs to install macOS.

❿ After the reinstallation finishes and your MacBook restarts, log in. You can then access your files as before.

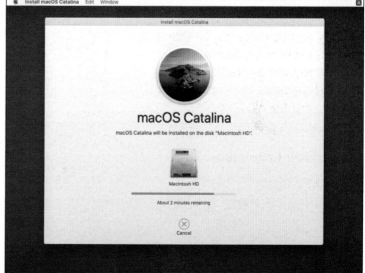

TIP

How do I start the reinstallation if my MacBook is powered on?

If your MacBook is powered on and macOS is responding normally, restart your MacBook by clicking **Apple** (), clicking **Restart**, and then clicking **Restart** in the Are You Sure You Want to Restart Your Computer Now? dialog.

If your MacBook is powered on but macOS is not responding normally, press and hold the power button until the MacBook shuts down. Wait for about 8 seconds, and then press the power button again to start your MacBook.

Index

Numbers and Symbols

A